Contemporary thought
and politics

**

Contemporary thought and politics

**

Ernest Gellner

edited with a preface by I. C. Jarvie
and Joseph Agassi

Routledge & Kegan Paul

London and Boston

First published in 1974
by Routledge & Kegan Paul Ltd
Broadway House, 68–74 Carter Lane,
London EC4V 5EL and
9 Park Street,
Boston, Mass. 02108, U.S.A.
Printed in Great Britain by
Richard Clay (The Chaucer Press) Ltd
Bungay, Suffolk
© Ernest Gellner 1974

ISBN 0 7100 7743 2
Library of Congress Catalog Card No. 73–86571

Contents

Preface

The title of the present collection, *Contemporary thought and politics*, adverts to the unifying idea in it. Heinrich Heine posed the question, 'what is the moral import of this theory?', when dealing with religion, ideology, politics, or metaphysics. Germany, he argued, prepares for war by philosophizing. Gellner seeks the moral and political implications of contemporary climates of opinion. And from the most universalist left-wing rebel to the most parochial nationalist, he feels, they have all succumbed to the attraction of seemingly sophisticated ideas which are facile and easy to master. He centres on the idea shared by far right and far left political ideologists, by some philosophers and by some scientists: you can consider any theory from both within and without; from within it will offer its own justification (i.e. the question will not arise), and from without you may be able to view its limits. With this neat device you can have your cake and eat it too; you may hold any easy theory that looks sophisticated enough. The student who rebels by day and goes to his snug home at night only echoes his professor who pretends to be incompetent to criticize the ideas he expounds. Mock-modesty, mock-neutrality, mock-tolerance, open the way for the doctrine that truth does not matter but commitment does—an irrational and violent corollary. The conclusion Gellner draws (in chapter 13) is both moral and political, both private and public: do not tolerate empty phraseology! Of course, encounter it not with physical violence but with careful, level-headed yet powerful words. We think Gellner's words rise to his own standards.

But Gellner is known to the reading public mainly as a philosopher and a scourge of other philosophers. Whence his interest in politics? The most general answer has to be that in all his work Gellner likes to observe ways of life and systems of thought. Clearly, the views of others and their structures of justification fascinate him because he is struggling to work out his own views and supporting structures. Yet to understand why he has written relatively little about such matters as the universal religions and quite a lot about politics it is not enough to cite personal predilection. Further enlightenment may emerge from setting the author against his background, in his time, and in his philosophical milieu.

To begin with, background. Gellner came to England from Czechoslovakia in 1939 when he was thirteen. At seventeen he went up to Oxford, to Lord Lindsay's Balliol, to read PPE. After a brief period of teaching at Edinburgh he settled down at the London School of Economics of Laski, then Oakeshott, of Popper and other politically conscious academics of various stripes. It would be difficult to have this background and not be interested in politics.

What of timing? Gellner entered academic life in the 1940s, a period of intense political upheaval in Britain and Europe. Mr Attlee's first administration came and went. There was controversy about the future of socialism. Czechoslovakia and other Eastern European countries disappeared behind the Iron Curtain. There was controversy about the relationship between socialism and communism. Gellner also visited America in the early 1950s, when McCarthyism was at its height. There was controversy about controlling the excesses of anti-communist zeal. Khrushchev's speech dethroning Stalin was followed closely by Hungary and by Suez. In Britain, at least, the result was the coming into being of the original New Left, with its journals and coffee houses. As an erstwhile socialist, Gellner seems to have been drawn towards all this, although one's impression is that he was never actually part of it.

But what seems directly to have triggered his first major political piece was the anti-political attitudes of his Oxford philosophy background. Despite having won one of Oxford's highest philosophy awards, the John Locke prize, Gellner always seems to have held himself back from embracing Oxford philosophy. The full range of his reservations was only to be revealed in *Words and Things* (1959). A couple of years before that he took the chance to register some preliminary objections while writing about the collective volume *Philosophy, Politics and Society* (ch. 4, below). Oxford philosophy, or linguistic philosophy, denied both that it was a philosophy and that it endorsed a political philosophy. Gellner begins his career as an academic writer on politics by showing how these two positions add up to a political philosophy badly in need of criticism.

So much for beginnings. In the many subsequent papers, we see Gellner working out his own views. Gellner's political philosophy might be described as an attempt to come to terms with his own profound discontent. Simple discontent with one's surroundings need not lead to an attempt to come to terms—it may instead drive one to idealism, socialism, utopianism. Gellner's discontent is profound because, while he is unhappy with idealism, socialism and utopianism, he is not less unhappy about the possibility of doing without them. Metaphysics, said Kant, is like a mistress to whom we return after a quarrel. For Gellner, the metaphysics of social reform, idealism and socialism, and the prayer for peace and serenity, are at once too desirable to do without and too dangerous to leave un-criticized. The danger is that of fanaticism and other forms of sanc-tioning disregard for the ordinary sufferings of ordinary people which daily surround us. This strong conflict throws Gellner into a reflective mood filled with self-irony, a mood of compassion curiously mixed with detachment. Consequently, one is uncertain as to how close to his own views is the mordant irony of his lay sermon 'Prepare to meet thy doom' (ch. 1, below). In that piece he argues that on all utopian models the future is bleak. One can at least say that his gloomy prophecy did not at all discourage him from thinking that the future is still worth arguing about, fighting for. In 'Myth, ideology and revolution' (ch. 2) and 'The dangers of tolerance' (ch. 13) he distinguishes social pluralism from logical (or epistemological) pluralism, approving the former, not approving the latter. He hints, perhaps, in his 'How to live in anarchy' (ch. 7), that an anarchic balance of forces between the divers bleak possibilities is the best we have thus far!

Gellner's political papers reveal a mind pulled in different direc-tions; this would make it hard to grasp his meaning were it not for the fact that he wears his heart on his sleeve: those papers reprinted here are very obviously expressions of Gellner's concern, rationality, tolerance. He strives to understand the religions of nationalism, communism, democracy; but he returns again and again to the basic values of the liberal: social tolerance, rational criticism, human decency and justice. Dare one deduce from his mourning for the Prague Spring (ch. 12), the depth and extent to which he has become English? The liberal values he so appreciates are very deep-rooted in England: if you add to them the affable excitement of Central European intellectual ferment you practically have the Dubcek syndrome. The Czechs were wonderful when they were allowed to be a little more English. Does Gellner think the English would be more wonderful if they allowed themselves to be a little more Czech?

I. C. J.
J. A.

Acknowledgments

The editors met Ernest Gellner in the 1950s at the London School of Economics when they were students, whom he treated as colleagues. Their appreciation of his work has grown since then, and they were glad to receive permission to edit his work. The editors wish to thank the publishers and editors of the different papers here published. They take joint and equal responsibility for the selection, arrangement, and preface. Most of the technical work in preparing the volume for the press and seeing it through to publication was done by Jarvie, who wishes to thank his research assistant, Mr Michael Burchak. Agassi takes the blame for the flamboyant subject index.

York University, Toronto   I.C.J.
Boston University and *Tel Aviv University*   J.A.

Chapter 1   Prepare to meet thy doom

A sermon on the ambivalences of progress, reason, liberty, equality and fraternity

The belief in progress was the expectation, confident or hopeful as the case may be, of increased human happiness and rationality. It also looked forward to liberty, equality and fraternity. But it can be shown, by juxtaposing the various modern literary anticipations, the nightmarish anti-utopias of Orwell and Huxley, that progress is impossible. *Nothing* would satisfy us. Any future counts as disastrous, in terms of our present visions of the alternatives. Similarly, the various specific values of the progressive creed—liberty, rationality and the rest—seem to be desirable only at a distance, when seen through the dark glass of abstraction. Concretely, they acquire an ambiguity, a capacity to repel by their presence as much as by their absence.

Consider how one could attack that which remains of the faith in progress; how one can positively prove that there can be no justified hope. For there are still people who, though no longer sure, at least think that the world might turn out well. They think progress is at least a possibility. There is still some such sloppy indulgence in hope. But there is no excuse for it.

There is in fact no justification at all for such muddled thinking, for optimism, even if tentative. *Whatever* happens is bound to be no good. This is not just an opinion; this can easily be proved. The simplest rigorous proof is tautology. This consists, essentially, of showing that some statement covers all possibilities. For instance, the assertion that a given horse either will, or will not, win a race is necessarily true. It covers all possibilities. Hence, it is a tautology. Hence, it is proved.

The claim that progress is impossible, the claim that the world *must* go to the dogs, is equally necessary, equally tautological. This may sound surprising. Pessimistic dogmatism looks like a specific prediction rather than a claim covering all possibilities. But it is nothing of the kind.

The belief in progress

Consider, again, the belief in progress. Essentially, it was the conjunction of two ideas: one, man's control over his own fate will increase; two, this increased power will be used benevolently, for good ends. Given these two propositions, we have four possibilities: both propositions might be true. They might both be false. The first might be true and the second false; or, finally, vice versa. And if each and every alternative turns out on examination to be undesirable, then pessimism is proved. *Q.E.D.* Pessimism then covers all possibilities.

One of these four possibilities is of no great interest. The situation in which power is wielded benevolently, but there is not enough power to assure a happy outcome, is really our present condition. In some countries, at least, those who have power are not diabolical: indeed, given the option, they choose the better rather than the worse alternative; yet they lack the power to ensure the effectiveness of their goodwill. And that is not enough. So that takes care of that.

This leaves three further possibilities. The horror of the situation in which both power and benevolence are lacking is obvious. It is well explored in Aldous Huxley's *Ape and Essence*, where we see a broken-down society following on nuclear warfare. It is both malevolent and inefficient. The horror of the situation in which effective power is conjoined with malevolence is even greater. George Orwell effectively explored it in *Nineteen Eighty-Four*. The horror of the situation in which there is both power and benevolence is explored in *Brave New World*.

The fact that each of these three novels is generally considered to be a pessimistic one has led to the mistaken but widespread idea that they have similar themes and that they differ in detail rather than in substance. But, on the contrary, they differ radically in the fundamental features of their predictions. The three novels explore alternative, mutually incompatible, possibilities; and, what is much worse, alternatives which between them exhaust all possibilities. Between them they jointly explore and exhaust all the possible affirmations and denials that one can make with regard to the old optimistic belief in progress. They omit only the admittedly imperfect present. The fact that each of them is held to be pessimistic does not illustrate similarity of content. It shows that *any* possibility which the future may hold counts as a bad one.

'Brave New World'

Brave New World is perhaps the most interesting of the three, for it takes what one would have thought was the most favourable possibility—the situation when human mastery over the fate of man is complete and when it is used benevolently; and it brings out the defects of even so satisfactory a situation. A world is portrayed in which a truly effective technology, manipulating both man and society, ensures general contentment. The novel condemns this situation, but it is remarkable for the fairness with which it states the case. It condemns the cosy, happy, secure Brave New World, and it does so because this world lacks certain things our world still has: a sense of choice and freedom, and the enjoyment—if that is the right word—of intense, dramatic, and unpredictable personal, aesthetic and cognitive experiences.

The case is, however, presented with scrupulous and admirable fairness—for it is conceded that these things are illusory anyway. If conditioning is possible at all, then man is unfree, irrespective of whether conditioning actually occurs: the alternative is only between, on the one hand, planned and deliberate conditioning, which is open and visible and which effectively secures adjustment: and, on the other hand, the unplanned, haphazard and ineffective conditioning left to chance, which, however, gives the illusion of freedom. Similarly, the book frankly concedes that the intense emotional experiences, which have disappeared from the Brave New World, are only the consequences of frustration, of damming up impulses, or of the over-compensations of misery. If so, the Brave New World, undesirable though it may seem to us who have made a virtue of our misery, only deprives us of what we never really wanted.

The novel can be seen as a truly effective critique of Utilitarianism —or rather, perhaps, of the implementation of Utilitarianism in a technological civilization which has the means to do so successfully. But, effective though the critique is on the imaginative plane, it is curiously ineffective on another level: it does not challenge the premises which may lead one to accept such a Utilitarianism. These premises include the denial of the idea that some experiences have value irrespective of the satisfaction they give. This denial is not challenged. Moreover, the argument is carried on within a framework which admits that the evaluation of freedom does not really arise, for there is only the illusion of it anyway. It is also admitted that the non-hedonic valuation of experiences is but another illusion, the fruit of frustration and misery.

The underlying theme of Orwell's *Nineteen Eighty-Four*—the remaining alternative, for what it is worth—is less neat and philosophically unified: or, rather, when a simple theme is isolated it does less than justice to the book, whose impact really springs from its horrifying convincingness as a portrait of the present. Nevertheless, if an underlying theme is isolated, it turns out to be something like the conjunction of these ideas: *one*, nothing is but thinking makes it so; *two*, what we do think has come to be under conscious social control; and, *three*, power is insatiable. The conjunction of these ideas leads to a picture in which, in terms of our initial alternatives, a malevolent, power-seeking and power-indulging Inner Party effectively controls men; when even the inner recesses of secret conviction, the independent certainty of logic, the privacy of personal relations, no longer constitute areas of escape from power.

Orwell's obsession with social control

Of course societies have always had the power to make their members believe things and to indulge the delights of power—that is why Orwell rings so true about so many pre-1984 institutions—but, on the whole, they have in the past had to content themselves with a fairly imperfect and partial subjection, and often with mere outer conformity. (Pharisaism was a possibility: and when deprived of it, we see what a boon it was.) Orwell was obsessed with the consequences of increased social control, with the fact that no restraints will henceforth be imposed by the technical limitations of control and of power. In working out the implications of this, he sketches our remaining alternative. All doors are now closed.

In *Nineteen Eighty-Four*, Orwell—or rather his hero Winston Smith—puts forward a theory of freedom in terms of objective, extra-social or extra-human necessity: freedom is the recognition that 2 plus 2 makes 4: not because there is no escaping such necessity, as in some older theories of freedom, but because only such necessity is a refuge from arbitrary social power. '2 plus 2 makes 4' is an idea which, though true, does not otherwise warm the heart. Yet its objective necessity, *any* kind of objective necessity, is, in *Nineteen Eighty-Four*, a kind of final attempted refuge from social control. (So, in *Nineteen Eighty-Four*, is sex—a satisfaction so strong that it cannot be socially controlled and which thus comes to be an escape from power. This is quite different from *Brave New World*, where, on the contrary, the easy gratification of sex is one of the main ways of binding men to power, and where liberation from control can only be had through the emotional accompaniments of frustration.)

The Orwellian definition of freedom is in terms of clinging—without much hope, success or conviction—to an extra-social objective truth, which accounts for why such fuss should be made of a morally and emotionally rather neutral piece of arithmetic. But the theory of freedom in *Brave New World*—or rather of the illusion of freedom, for that is all that can be had—is, on the contrary, in terms of 2 plus 2 making 5, in terms of the denial of a rational hedonic calculus. Unnecessary, artificial frustration, merely as a means of heightened emotion, is not reasonable: nor is disorder and unpredictability, used as means for providing the *illusion* of liberty, and escaping a rational society. But such irrationality is, it appears, the only way of escaping it.

Huxley did not actually, in so many words, put forward a slogan of the need for 2 plus 2 making 5, the need for irrationality as the only escape from a reasonable, benevolent and effective society; but some of his predecessors, who also feared that the Real would succeed in becoming the Rational and who wanted to opt out of it, did put it this way. They thus provide a neat contrast to Orwell's Winston Smith.

Dostoievsky, in his *Letters from the Underworld* puts a long peroration in the mouth of his hero culminating in the praise of the formula that '2 plus 2 makes 5'. The arguments employed *against* a rational world, in which actual human wants would be satisfied, could all have come straight from chapter 16, the final debate, of *Brave New World*. Dostoievsky foresaw the objections.

Thus we have in Orwell on the one hand and Dostoievsky on the other the literary expressions of two theories of freedom, both of which arise as reactions to increasing power: one, the clinging to rational necessity as the only refuge from socially imposed arbitrariness; the other, the cult of non-rational arbitrariness as the only escape from a reasonable but powerful and all-embracing society. So, once again, it would seem that whichever way things go, we are not satisfied. Freedom is elsewhere, in reason or in unreason, in necessity or in caprice, always according to—and in opposition to—the way things are supposed to be going. So, just as all alternative futures are undesirable, so also, either way, they are unfree.

Meritocracy

The same curious all-exhaustiveness of discontent, the impossibility of specifying a satisfactory alternative, applies to equality and fraternity. Recent sociological studies of social mobility inspired the reflection—later expanded by Mr Michael Young in his book on Meritocracy[1]—that equality of opportunity creates a stratified society in which the lower orders are deprived even of that ultimate consolation, a sense of injustice; and also of the potential leaders who could voice their discontent. Insult is added to injury, and justification to the insult. Whilst the arguments are valid, they do leave one wondering what now happens to the older arguments for equality of opportunity. Those arguments appealed to the feeling of injustice. The elimination of this sense of injustice was the aim of attempts to bring about equality of opportunity. Now that equality of opportunity may be on the horizon, the elimination of a sense of injustice turns out to be an evil rather than a boon. . . . Once again, it is no good either way. Of course, those who point out the evils of mere equality of opportunity perhaps wish for simple equality, without qualification. But it seems plain that if this is possible it would only be so in conjunction with fraternity. A hostile, competing set of equals would soon lose either equality or liberty.

But the ideal of fraternity seems to generate ambivalence no less than the others; just like happiness, rationality, liberty or equality, the whole pantheon of the old belief in progress. In the past, the standard objection to capitalist society was that it destroyed fraternity, that it turned society into a jungle. It now appears that its defects are the very opposite. The most influential recent indictment of modern industrial society is Mr W. H. Whyte's *Organization Man.*[2] His complaint is not that we are all beasts of prey, or preyed upon. On the contrary, Whyte points out that the consequence of modern organization is the most appalling outbreak of fraternity. Everybody loves and is loved with such scientific efficiency that there is no originality or fight left in any of them. Mr Whyte's observations sound true and his revulsion is something one can easily share. Yet again, it seems hard on reality that we never like it, either way. Happiness and control, reason, liberty, equality, fraternity—they all seem sour whichever side you bite them. They offend by their presence as much as by their absence.

Need for a re-examination?

It might be objected that these paradoxes, the rejections which face both ways, arise only through over-simple formulations; or, again, that it is not the same people who reject each of the complementary alternatives. There is something, but not much, in the second objection. For it is the same people, most of us in fact, who can feel revulsion both for *Brave New World* and for *Nineteen Eighty-Four* and for *Ape and Essence*, without yet being satisfied with the present; who can dislike both the jungle and the organization man, inequality and meritocracy. There is probably far more in the other objection— that the ways in which the various dilemmas and alternatives are specified should be re-examined.

That is my final theme—as befits a philosopher, it is rather formal and programmatic. It is often said that political theory is moribund, and it is often supposed that positivism was the culprit. I think that in fact positivism was merely an accessory after the crime. The real cause is that political theory has failed to fulfil its function. It is the archaic formulations of questions in academic political theory, rather than the pseudo- and ultra-modern answers, which are at fault.

Political theory in its lively days was always a kind of general sociology—the drawing of general pictures of society enabling men to assess alternatives and express their choices. It was *not* 'the analysis of political concepts', whatever such a ponderous phrase might mean. And it only came to be narrowly identified with the problem of political obligation because at certain times the issues of loyalty without religious sanction, or of the permissibility of revolution, were of paramount interest.

The problem of loyalty and political obligation is not dead today. Pasternak, the ideological atom spies, or international civil servants have all had cause to ponder it. Nevertheless, it is only one amongst many issues, and it is not seen in isolation from the rest. Above all, no one is interested in having such a problem answered by the 'analysis of political concepts'. What they do want is a general schematic picture which illuminates the real alternatives. This may include 'analyses' but is certainly not exhausted by them. The advance of knowledge simultaneously confers power and indicates powerlessness; it informs us of our limits. But one requires some kind of guidance as to what these alternatives and limits are.

Political theory in the days of its liveliness was the more or less adequate sociology and guide of its time. Though partly a matter of expressing values, it also provided the concepts in terms of which one stated alternatives. But traditional political theory is not adequate sociology today. Its decline is due in part to its failure to be such and in part to the fact that sociology now exists under its own name, or is expected to. People are now less willing to go for their picture of society to an old subject very restricted in its method or field to a mere 'analysis', and of a limited set of notions at that. It is also true that literature has temporarily done some of the work.

It would be interesting to see it continued: for instance, to see the initial pessimistic paradoxes, the social ambivalences of reason, freedom, equality, and fraternity explored by some more thorough and well-informed thinking about society. It does not much matter under what name it is done.

So if the King is dead, long live the King.

1959

Notes

1 *The Rise of the Meritocracy*, London   2   London 1957.
1958.

Chapter 2   Myth, ideology and revolution

The ideology of the protest movement has two marked traits: totality and facility. It stands for 'total commitment'. This it contrasts with the partial, humdrum, moral, and intellectual compromises of ordinary society. Compromise is treason. Any structure, intellectual or social, is likewise treason. When, during the first big sit-in at the LSE, some of the rebellious students organized a 'free' or counter-university, one of its leading spirits announced that it would distinguish itself from the other place in as far as that in it, teachers would be *totally committed* to what they taught, and students *totally committed* to what they learnt.

What could this mean? Presumably, it implies that any tentative exploration of ideas, the entertaining of suppositions for the purpose of exploring their soundness, is *out*. Sexual experimentation is perfectly permissible—but intellectual experimentation, exploration, tentativeness, anything short of 'commitment', are viewed with a neo-Victorian prudery. Propositions at least may only be embraced with total love.

Totality and facility

The implications of this view are interesting. In effect it rejects the division of labour, not merely in production, but also, and above all, in cognition: only that which is known by the 'whole being' is sound and healthy. The hypothetical method, whether in its Socratic form or as practised by experimental science, in which the implications of this view or that are explored for the light they throw on the initial assumption, whilst that initial assumption is only entertained tentatively—all that is rejected. The pure intellect does not play with assumptions and inferences any more than it haggles or bargains. It gives itself wholeheartedly, in careless rapture in which cognition becomes similar to amorous ecstasy. It is ardent rather than lucid.

The origins of this totalist view of knowledge (and social life, of course) are no doubt various. In part, it is the revival of a very old mystical and antinomian tradition, as David Martin has pointed out. More specifically, in America, it is the continuation and inversion of the populist protestant tradition—a protestantism not of the Book but of the heart, of the view that the hearts of pure and simple men are the safe repositories and oracles of truth. Justification by Commitment seems clearly descended from Justification by Faith. They carry a similar epistemology and ethic. One is bearing witness, not exploring the world. An exemption from rational criticism is not merely permissible, but mandatory. The son of the mid-western preacher (spiritually and perhaps sometimes literally speaking), secularized and transported to the more luscious climate of the campuses, articulates a luxuriant variant of the paternal creed. The totalism of the dissident creed is, and is meant to be, in opposition to the sordid horse-dealing, half-measures and compromises of the established order.

But the *facility* of the creed, and of the stance of its holders, is somehow continuous with the doctrineless, pragmatic, non-ideological posture of the official society, as indeed it conceives itself to be. The rebels reach their faith and its articulation, such as it is, without any struggles or labour. Truth, whatever it be, appears to be obvious and easily accessible.

No one fully understands the present protest movement. Perhaps we have here a foretaste of the general problem of social control in an affluent and liberal society. The emergence of man from the realm of necessity, and the first shy steps into the realm of freedom, are accompanied by none of the features which optimistic social philosophers had forecast. The removal of the stick, the carrot, and the faith—the relative absence of sanctions, of effective rewards or of a legitimating set of beliefs, have led not to spontaneous harmony, but to chaotic rebellion amongst those upon whom the greatest amount of physical, social and intellectual freedom is thrust—the students.

Return journey guaranteed

The general features of the protest movement are familiar enough, though they are not really self-explanatory. This *jeunesse dorée* of the affluent and welfare society takes the institutional and economic framework within which they rebel—and which make the rebellion possible, painless and riskless—totally and utterly for granted: their superficial and verbal radicalism is accompanied by a curious absence of social imagination. They reserve their social imagination for nebulous, *carte blanche* alternatives, which are only identified through abstract nouns purporting to name a condition known to be satisfactory but not otherwise specified. Playing with such contentless verbiage gives them the right, they suppose, to look down upon the philistinical lack of vision of those who at least notice concrete differences between social forms that are actually found on earth, and who notice that some achievements and benefits are precarious and cannot altogether be taken for granted. They simply assume that prosperity, security, law and order, free speech, will all still be there whenever the rebel decides to call off, or personally withdraw from, the amateur dramatics of 'revolution'. This tacit, largely unconscious confidence is an important clue. In *Arrival and Departure*, Arthur Koestler makes the police officer observe to the hero, before he has him tortured, that he knows how he feels: he has only just fully realized that this is for real, that he cannot call the game off now. The situation of our rebels is quite other. They can run back to mummy whenever they wish. No one will stop them, and they know it and trade on it.

The techniques and strategy of the movement are also by now very familiar. You pick some morally important and disturbing issue (the bomb, race, a colonial war). The importance of the issue, the fact that it is deep and moral, and hence not suitable for political horse-dealing, clearly warrants the suspension of the ordinary proprieties of political behaviour. When lives and the deepest principles are at stake, etiquette hardly deserves much consideration. To be concerned with it indicates heartlessness at best, and vested interests in camouflage at worst. The systematic violation of formal rules which follows will of course, sooner or later, provoke the authorities into some repressive measures, however mild. The provocation can in any case simply be repeated until it elicits a response. Then one can mobilize further support in the name of liberty and tolerance, which are now enlisted on the side of deep political morality. One has already enlisted vicarious infantilism, the conviction of some academics that somehow they are betraying their deepest values if ever they find themselves not 'on the side of youth'.

It is noteworthy that the *sursis* occasioned by the deep and funda-mental nature of the initial issues suspends not merely the customary proprieties of behaviour, but also of cognition. Methodological carefulness or fastidiousness is as suspect as procedural propriety. On these deep and rousing issues, you must know with your heart. To invoke complex evidence is as repellent morally as it is to haggle and compromise over principles.

In this area, even radical student leaders are liable to find themselves outflanked by their own supporters, and taken further and further into a blind activism by the inherent logic of these ideas. Apparently, during the last and most violent of the LSE 'confrontations', radical student leaders were howled down from their own 'left' when they wished to discuss strategy and tactics: any such calculations of tacti-cal advantage become, in the end, 'opportunism'.

Infant functionalism

The general recipe for revolutionary 'theory' is as simple as that for revolutionary 'practice'. You start from the fact that the institutions of most societies, including this one, can on the whole be expected to favour their own perpetuation. This trite theory is familiar in the social sciences under the name of 'functionalism'. It is not an altogether true theory, but most certainly it is not altogether false, and plenty of plausible instances can be found to illustrate it, in the educational and cultural realms amongst others. But the rebels treat these illustrations as the unmasking of a sinister deception: the general social tendency towards continuity and self-perpetuation is treated as a vicious fraud, which quite invalidates the endorsement which most citizens of liberal affluent pluralist societies tactily accord to them. It places that endorsement, tacit but unconstrained, somehow on the same level as the brutally extorted acquiescence which is found in less liberal political systems. Of course, the rebels do not *call* their theory functionalism-for-infants. They have their own vocabulary, the key term of which is 'alienation'. The effective meaning of this term is, however, simply the obverse of functionalism-for-infants: it designates, generically, the condition of members of all societies which secure a measure of consent from their citizens, without at the same time attaining some total and perfect consummation—in other words, virtually everyone's condition in developed liberal societies. Partial exemption from the condition may be obtained by agreement of the holder of the theory, and is presumably granted to fellow-believers.

These simple devices—made to seem weightier, more complex, by cumbersome terminology—suffice to condemn the present order. But what of the alternative, in the name of which the revolution is supposed to be taking place? Here the rebels are liable to invoke both their supposed intellectual ancestors (Hegel) and their alleged intellectual enemies (Popper) to explain why no specification of the new order need be given. They are not 'historicists', they proudly say—history need not, cannot, should not, be done in advance. So we know nothing whatever about the features of that social order for the sake of which we are to suspend all liberal safeguards, and which would escape infantile functionalism—or, in their language, overcome the estrangement of man from his own generic nature.

But the rebel ideology is not merely in deliberate opposition to the official doctrine: it has also, at the same time, remarkable continuities and similarities with it. The official intellectual climate is marked by three important characteristics: (1) *Constitutionalism*; (2) *Pluralism*; and (3) *Auto-functionalism*. These terms are used in a somewhat special sense.

Constitutionalism

Constitutionalism, in its ordinary and political sense, of course designates a most admirable thing. I am wholly in favour of feelings of respect for a constitution, entrenched in a document or in a set of customs, which enables disagreements to be settled and changes to be made in an orderly and peaceful manner. I am wholly in favour of due process in the conduct of public affairs.

But there is another possible sense of constitutionalism, especially when applied to systems of belief. This other sense is somewhat analogous to constitutional monarchy. A constitutional monarchy develops out of an absolute monarchy by reducing the monarch's powers, but maintaining his symbolic role as an expression of national continuity and unity. A constitutional *faith* is a belief system which has undergone an analogous transformation: it is a belief system which once upon a time was really and near-absolutely *believed*, but whose focus has now shifted to a 'symbolic' role. The assertions contained within it are no longer 'really' believed, they no longer define the effective convictions of the 'believers' concerning the world they live in. Their nominal endorsement in speech, ritual or otherwise, symbolize loyalty, a sense of national continuity, an aspiration towards stability—but their cognitive import has been eroded in a manner analogous to that in which the political role of the constitutional monarch has been diminished.

There is manifestly a very close parallel between the loyalty of a citizen to a constitutional monarch and his loyalty to the organization and doctrine of a 'constitutional' church (in this sense). But, alas, the analogy is not perfect. The analogy is indeed very nearly complete in terms of the attitude and justification of the subject/citizen or the believer/adherent. But there is a crucial difference in the object of the two loyalties.

The monarchy is primarily an institution and only incidentally a theory. It has beliefs and assertions connected with it, but these are not really of its essence. Men were presumably leaders, rulers, kings first, and only then, if at all, elaborated political theories explaining the fact. At any rate, whatever the historic sequence may have been, it is perfectly possible to conceive kingship without any doctrine. The doctrine is logically an accretion: an accretion which may sometimes be of importance, but it is not the central part of the institution.

The case of religion and faith is different. Here the doctrine, the content of the faith, is of the very heart of the matter. So a striking contrast becomes manifest between constitutional monarchy and constitutional religion. In both cases, loyalty is combined with a disbelief in the theory. But in the one case, the doubt is only in conflict with something which is marginal and peripheral to the institution. In the other case, the conflict is between a background of disbelief and something which is absolutely central to the institution.

Pluralism

Next to 'constitutionalism' the other important trait of the intellectual scene is 'pluralism'.

Pluralism in the ordinary sense, the view that a plurality of counter-vailing forces, groups and institutions is the best aid towards the maintenance of both liberty and order, is a view for which I have the warmest regard. Institutional pluralism is an admirable thing: and I have no longing whatsoever for social and political monoliths.

But doctrinal pluralism is somewhat different. It preaches the peaceful co-existence of any and all doctrines, not only within one society or within one person but within, so to speak, one logical universe of discourse. Everything, or very nearly, can apparently be true all at once: to stress and press home difficulties, incompatibilities and so forth is made into a social and moral solecism.

To express doubts about the desirability of pluralism in this sense is to lay oneself open to the suspicion of intolerance and illiberalism. But this is a terrible misunderstanding. For the distinction between social and logical toleration is crucial. Social toleration is admirable. Logical toleration is by no means obviously admirable and it should not be confused with social toleration.

Social toleration requires that no serious *non-logical* pressures—violence, economic blackmail—be used in support or defence of ideas. But it does not exclude argument. The distinction between the two can perhaps best be highlighted by the most common argument in favour of toleration—to the effect that truth is best sought through a natural selection of ideas. This natural selection can only operate if there is, so to speak, free entry into the market.

But equally, no natural selection will take place if all the entrants cohabit peacefully in an unselective, eclectic, unfastidious mishmash. The selection can only operate if the ideas compete, if there is sensitivity to the implications and incompatibilities between them, and if such logical conflicts lead at least to the eventual elimination of one or other of the competing views. If a sloppy and logically un-fastidious syncretism prevails, if ideas live and let live, no advance—at least, no advance by natural selection—will take place. Social tolerance is essential—but so is logical intolerance.

This is the second feature of our intellectual scene: pluralism, in a pejorative sense, the peaceful co-existence of diverse ideas and systems of ideas, logically emasculated and deprived of any rivalry-engendering sense of incompatibility. This kind of pluralism is intimately connected with constitutionalism, which is one of the doctrines invoked for justifying and defending the sloppy logical tolerance. By endowing certain ideas or systems of ideas with 'symbolic' status it exempts them from ordinary scrutiny and criticism, disconnects them from other ideas, preventing any fruitful interaction between them and the rest of our intellectual life and hence, in effect, between them and reality.

In a curious kind of way, intellectual pluralism has become the philosophical orthodoxy, the conventional wisdom of contemporary thinkers. One can find it preached from a variety of viewpoints and premises and in a great variety of idioms. In social theory alone, one can find monism eloquently condemned in Berlin, Oakeshott, Crick, Gallie, Popper and others. It is easy to conclude, whether or not the authors intended it, that pluralism is good. In a variety of styles, we seem to be told that bridges must be crossed when they are reached, that individual cases must be judged on their merits, and so forth. One might be tempted to answer that when one comes to a river it is too late to start building a bridge, and that individual cases have no merits in the light of which they could be judged, unless some general standard or norm is tacitly presupposed.

There is a difference between, on the one hand, desiring that there should be a plurality of power-centres in societies, capable of surveying and checking each other (admirable), or the recognition that the world is an extremely complex and diversified place (true), and, on the other hand, the sloppy pluralism which argues because the world is diversified, therefore our thinking should be untidy, *ad hoc*, use any tool which is to hand, and not even seek any intellectual unification and consistency. The cult of the cognitive or political *débrouillard* or *bricoleur* has no intrinsic merit, and does not follow from the premises which are invoked in its support. It does, however, have a natural affinity with the constitutionalism under discussion. The pluralism in practice enjoins a kind of dissociation—'always disconnect', so to speak—between the intellectual tools or vision we use on one occasion and on another.

Self-validating belief

The third characteristic feature of our intellectual scene is 'auto-functionalism'. This is a special, and currently most popular, manner of validating one's own beliefs and ideas. It appears in a wide variety of superficially diverse forms. It consists of establishing the soundness of one's beliefs not directly, in the ordinary and straightforward way, by showing them to be true, but, on the contrary, of deriving their soundness by showing them to play an essential role, to be 'functional', in the internal economy of one's own personality or society (or tradition, or language, etc.). Of course, the argument needs to be camouflaged and elaborated a little to carry conviction. The first step is to put forward a theory of truth: truth 'really is' the fulfilment of a biological, or social, linguistic, etc., function. Then one indicates that certain beliefs do play some such role. The conclusion—the soundness of those beliefs—is then readily available. Modernist theology is a striking example, and has passed through about four or five different styles of such reasoning (though all employed the same basic principle): religious assertions were reinterpreted in biological, psychological, social, linguistic or existentialist idioms, as fulfilling adaptive, social, psychic, categorical or commitment-expressing functions.

The morally debilitating aspect of auto-functionalism is that it compels its practitioners to indulge in sustained double-think, to live at two different and carefully separated conceptual levels. The major premise, concerning the functionality of this or that belief or idea, is articulated by a neutral and secularized person, who feeds in the belief as a dispassionately, externally observed datum. The conclusion, on the other hand, is received and read 'from the inside' as a belief true in the real, not just the 'functional', sense. But the supplier of the premise and the beneficiary of the conclusion are the same person, albeit wearing different hats; so one can only have some reservations about the intellectual honesty of this conceptual transvestism. But, so be it.

Auto-functionalism also dovetails with the other two traits. It provides pluralist syncretism with a further and omnibus justification, and it does the same for constitutionalism. 'Latent' justification becomes manifest, though in a selective manner. The only thing which remains latent are the rules concerning when and by whom the latent may be manifestly articulated.

Looking-glass rebels

Is our condition a healthy one? It is hard to make up one's mind. The condition described has well-known and well-advertised advantages. The separation of the symbolic from the effective political role has the admirable consequence that a concrete, on-the-ground political mistake does not undermine confidence and loyalty towards the system as a whole *and*, on the other hand, that concrete successes do not make it easy for the holders of political office to absolutize their rule. The strong emotions, positive or negative, are given multiple and distinct objects: the consequence, one hopes, is relative political stability. The same point may (not quite so convincingly) be applied in the field of knowledge: if the serious business of cognitive exploration of the world is kept distinct from the 'symbolic', identity-conferring and loyalty-expressing 'beliefs', the former is freer, and the latter are more stable, and everyone benefits. I wonder. In the sphere of beliefs, this particular kind of division of labour may, in the end, erode respect for truth and sap the vigour of the drive towards it. If almost everything is true in its own fashion, truth cannot matter very much.

But it is not for us to assess our general ideological health. The general intellectual scene was invoked only in order to help us understand the rebels. To a most remarkable extent, they are continuous with it, and exhibit the same traits. They have only inverted the official position at one point, in that they claim to be rebels and critics rather than conservatives. But this inversion is superficial rather than profound. The facile, 'symbolic', disconnected nature of belief, its self-sustaining and circular quality, are the same in both cases. The facility is made possible by the same pluralist, auto-functionalist, symbolic-constitutionalist devices.

Modern liberal society has a two-tier ideological system, a double level of justification. At one level, there are theories which are 'believed' rather than believed. At the other level there are legitimations which are persuasive enough, but which are negative and humdrum. At this level of effective and serious belief, it is idle to pretend that the present social order is a heart-warming ideal. It is not. But it is better than any realistic and known alternative, it is good enough to make the risks of uncharted change unjustifiable, it has some capacity of self-correction, and it is not altogether a fraud. This is cogent, but it does not warm the blood like wine. Its prosaic nature makes it unacceptable to the ardent young as an avowed theory—it cannot be set to music—whilst the fact that it is only half-articulated and not written out in letters of gold on tablets of marble, enables the rebels to go on relying on it in an unavowed manner. At the same time, in their officially proclaimed creed, they take over the facility and the style of the official but non-serious 'belief' system, with its associated self-maintaining devices—only they turn it upside down. Revolutionary verbiage replaces the other kind.

When, for instance, Sartre announces ponderously that his central question is 'how is the myth of the French Revolution at all possible?' he intends his question to be understood as some historicized version of the deep Kantian query. But in a way he is asking the right question, if one takes the term *myth* in its daily, pejorative sense: what is at issue is indeed a myth, not a reality. Just as modern constitutional monarchy is possible without anyone for one moment taking seriously the Divine Right of Kings, so this 'revolutionary' movement and rhetoric is possible without anyone really being at all in earnest. We are in one case, as in the other, dealing with a symbolic re-enactment. Just because there is hysteria, it does not follow that there is any seriousness.

Or take a more contemporary figure, closer to the rebels and more prestigious with them, Althusser. On his own admission, the central question which preoccupied him was not one about the world, but a Narcissistic, second-order one, about the role of Marxist thought—in effect, the Marxist thinker—*in* the world, a world some of whose crucial features are prejudged by such a *Fragestellung*. This kind of formulation and sense of priorities hardly encourages or reflects a genuine inquiry (*Pour Marx*, 1965, 23):

> That passage nonetheless contained *the* crucial question, which our ordeals had irresistibly aroused in us: what of Marxist philosophy? In principle, is it entitled to exist? And if so, what distinguishes it?

This weird formulation presupposes some wider and unquestioned world, in which different styles of thinking, intellectual institutions, etc., have their role, and within which one then sets out to find the specific role of Marxism, or rather, establishes that it does indeed have a specific and distinctive role. (Or does it, on Marxist assumptions, discuss the end of philosophy? Either way it is circular.) Sartre's defence of Marxism also characteristically has this form: the argument assumes, as a semi-tacit, and in any case unquestioned premise, a kind of meta-theory which accords to Cartesianism, Marxism and so on, each its historic role and an epoch in which it alone can fulfil that role. He argues, in effect, not that Marxism is true, but that the Marxist epoch is still with us. What is defended, in the end, is not the truth of a doctrine, but its alleged role. Either a role is found (good), or the search for it is itself the role (just as good), or the role consists of bewailing its own demise, temporary or permanent (just as good). If thou seekest revolutionary theory, thou hast already found it. Modern theology is as happy with the Death of God as it is with God, and likewise the Marxist critic of society wobbles happily between a Marxist critique of society, and a critique of society for its lack of Marxist critique. You certainly cannot lose on this.

Coming closer to the rebels and their intellectual sources, the same underlying logic can be found in the thought of the late Isaac Deutscher. In a lecture brilliantly delivered at the LSE in 1965 (*Listener*, 28 August 1969), his defence of Marxism has exactly the same logic as Sartre's. Neither the poverty of Western Marxist thought, nor the social realities of Eastern Marxist societies, is denied. But Deutscher gives himself a blank cheque on the future, in which the 'real' social structure of the Eastern European societies will assert itself against the present distortions, and in which Marxist thought will flourish again and fulfil its destiny. That it has such a destiny to fulfil is taken for granted. What it will have to say we do not know.

The logical parallel with the auto-functionalist thinkers of the Establishment is perfect.

Or again, consider a remarkable essay by Mr Perry Anderson in which he diagnoses the current cultural condition of England, including the protest movement itself. The poverty of ground-level, first-order revolutionary thought is not denied. (In down-to-earth terms: no one can think of any good general social criticism—as opposed to the 'alienation' gibberish.) But, as in the case of Sartre or Deutscher, he gives himself a *carte blanche* for the future (by tacitly drawing on a meta-theory guaranteeing the availability, in some Platonic heaven, of a 'revolutionary theory', waiting only for a suitable midwife to bring it to earth) (*New Left Review*, **50**, July–August 1968, 57):

> British culture . . . is a deeply . . . stifling force, operating against the growth of any revolutionary Left. It quite literally deprives the Left of any source of concepts and categories. . . . History has tied this knot; only history will ultimately undo it. A revolutionary culture is not for tomorrow. But a revolutionary practice within culture is possible. . . .

The parallel with auto-functionalist logic on the other side is perfect. We have no defensible propositions: only a woolly meta-theory, guaranteeing that some are required and will be available, some time.

The mirror image is not completely faithful at all points. The rebels demand total fulfilment and eschew sordid compromise, and to that extent they do not go in for praise or practice of pluralism. But within their system of belief and action, the cult of spontaneity performs the same role as does pluralism, and the cult of the *ad hoc*, in the Establishment. If the promptings of your ardent, generous and revolutionary heart are sovereign, no pedantic requirements of consistency are likely to inhibit you very much.

On the rebel side, we find facility and totality—but the total picture is empty. A blank cheque is drawn on the future. On the Establishment side, facility and fragmentation. The logical devices which cover up or justify the emptiness on one side, are similar to those which on the other side make the fragmented hotchpotch serviceable and palatable.

In some measure, these affinities of logic are even half-recognized. Various observers have noticed that this revolutionary movement is remarkably free of any anti-religious element. Indeed, there seems to be an instinctive sympathy between modernist, symbolic believers of various kinds, and they are eager to engage in 'dialogue'. The *mot* is *juste*, for they could hardly indulge in *argument*. (I understand that the application by the Communist Party to join the World Council of Churches is at present under consideration.) They also accord each other, and are generally accorded, what might be called Believer's Licence. A certain fashionable art critic sometimes begins his expositions with some such phrase as: 'But, of course, I am a Marxist.' What this means intellectually, no one knows. But socially speaking, the meaning is perfectly clear. One is meant to look solemn and feel too embarrassed to carp. It could be spelt out as follows: 'What I am about to say records my particular deep vision and commitment. Hence to subject it to sharp criticism would be a solecism, like criticizing a funeral oration. Always disconnect.'

Successful careers and reputations can be built on facile spiritual pilgrimages between these various positions—which can also be occupied simultaneously—and all held in an auto-functionalist spirit. The practitioners do not care whether those with whom they indulge in 'dialogue' are believers or not; they can't really tell the difference. There isn't one. All they want and require is that one should take the historic role of their creed solemnly and seriously. Perhaps a Grand International of easy credulity will emerge from the dialogue.

1969

Chapter 3 Democracy and industrialization

We regret any inconvenience to the public
while modernization is in progress.
Notice outside shop in Putney High Street

Looking at the contemporary world, two things are obvious: democracy is doing rather badly, and democracy is doing very well. New states are born free, yet everywhere they are in chains. Democracy is doing very badly in that democratic institutions have fallen by the wayside in very many of the newly independent 'transitional' societies, and they are precarious elsewhere. Democracy, on the other hand, is doing extremely well in as far as it is almost (though not quite) universally accepted as a valid *norm*. It is almost as if its success as a norm of legitimacy were inversely related to its success in concrete implementation.

Its success as a norm should not be taken for granted: nor should it be discounted as mere rhetoric. Democratic theory is very much part of the intellectual climate, and hence there is a certain tendency to take some democratic assumptions as read. But there is nothing self-evident about them. What is so sacred about the will of the people? At other times, many other principles have seemed more compelling, if indeed this one seemed compelling at all. Hence it is an interesting fact that whatever their political practice, most contemporary governments will at least *claim* to be democratic, and very few indeed would openly confess a defiance of the popular will. The fact that they may not practise what they preach is significant, but that they should preach what they do preach is also interesting.

There are of course two, or at least two, theories of democracy. It is customary to distinguish between the 'classical' theory of democracy, and a more modern, sociologically realistic account of 'what democracy really is'.

The key concepts of the classical theory are *people*, *will* and *consent*. Democratic government is, according to this theory, government in which the *will* of the *people* is sovereign. Alternatively, in a democracy, government is by *consent*.

A critic might observe that the idea of government of the people, by the people, and for the people is a conjunction of a pleonasm, a contradiction, and a hopeless ambiguity. Government must, by definition, be *of* the people: what else could it be? Government also means the concentration of power for the purpose of the maintenance of order, and perhaps for other purposes. Hence government *by* the people is self-contradictory. It would mean concentration of power without concentration of power. And finally, the notion of government *for* the people presupposes that the notion of the general good is somehow determinate and unambiguous, which is conspicuously untrue.

Criticisms of this kind, and others, stated at much greater length, have led to the formulation of one of the more modern, realistic theories of democracy. Roughly speaking, this runs as follows: What really characterizes societies known as democratic is the competition for leadership, and the fact that leadership periodically changes in a legal manner. This theory overlaps with the 'classical one' to the extent that it requires that the change-over in leadership should be not merely legal but also, at least in some measure, under 'popular' control. The advantages of this theory are obvious. The notions which it invokes are such as possess concrete, observable meanings.

The relationship of the two theories to each other is complex and subtle. It simply would not do to treat the difference between them as the difference between an old and crude theory on the one hand, and a later and superior theory on the other. For one thing, the 'classical' theory, as presented, may be a simplified travesty of the actual views of the classical political theorists, who were not altogether unaware of the complexities of actual political life. For another thing, the two theories also reflect genuine differences in values and not only differences in sensitivity to social facts. The difference in values is primarily between those for whom the notion of participation and equality is central, and those for whom the notion of pluralism and checks on power is more important.

At the same time, it would also not be adequate to treat the difference between those two theories as one concerning values and nothing else. It would be wrong to say, for instance, that the classical theory presents a normative appeal, whilst the modern theory presents a sociological analysis. The two things cannot be so crudely separated. A normative model, once seen to be a *mere* normative model, one having little correspondence to what is actually feasible, ceases then to be persuasive even as a normative model. It retains an appeal as a norm or standard only in as far as it at the very least highlights the features of *real* social or political structures, features which are relevant to their moral assessment. The norm cannot remain totally in the clouds.

Similarly, the sociological investigation of democracy is not simply a sociological study of a set of societies or states arbitrarily selected by the fact they have a certain label, 'democracy', attached to them either by themselves or by observers. The inquiry is far more interesting than that. Similarly, the oft-invoked fact that the quite different social and political systems, on either side of what used to be the Iron Curtain, both claim to be pre-eminently 'democratic', cannot be explained away simply by saying that two rival systems try to capture for the benefit of their own propaganda the positive emotive loading of one word, whilst endowing it with quite diverse descriptive content.

At the simplest level, the classical theory is related to the modern one as the specification of those elements which when present in the real institutions validate it morally; or the other way round, the modern theory is related to the classical one as a specification of the *nearest* one can get to the classical picture, in this difficult and complicated world. But the matter really is much more involved than this. The modern theory also contains a *moral*, as opposed to merely a sociological, criticism of the classical theory: it highlights the value of plurality and debate, and the institutional safeguards of free debate, as opposed to participation and consensus, even when these are genuinely present.

One of the interesting data of our collective situation is, as indicated, that *democracy* is almost universally accepted as a valid political norm. Sometimes it is conceived as a positive and pre-eminent ideal, the one crucial aspiration of the age. At other times, it is conceived more as a negative or limiting norm: other values matter, but they must be combined with democracy, they must not sin against it. Either way, it receives an almost general recognition as a principle, irrespective of whether it is observed in practice.

Though the modern theory of democracy does have its normative aspects and relevance, it is primarily the classical theory which has to be considered if one is to explain the general popularity of this ideal. Perhaps no general and sociological explanation should be sought: it could be that the popularity of this ideal is an historical accident, without deep roots. Had the Axis and not the Allies been victorious in 1945, would not democracy now be in eclipse?

Despite this element of contingency, it seems to me that something more than an historical accident is involved here—something more than merely the adoption of the slogan of the victors. Perhaps the matter can best be approached through some general considerations about the types of legitimation which are available for social and political orders.

Legitimations or validations of societies can be divided, roughly speaking, into two types: *In* and *Out* justifications. *In* justifications appeal primarily to something accessible and tangible Inside the world or, preferably, inside man, whereas *Out* justifications appeal to something Outside, something beyond us in kind and merit, something superior and transcendent. This distinction of course goes far beyond the field of social and political theories: it applies equally, or even more conspicuously, to theories of knowledge and of morals.

The relative and complementary merits and demerits of the two types of theory are of course well known. The *Out*, or transcendental theories, if true, would solve the problem of validation. By their own rules, the norms they set up are both absolutely reliable and provide adequate motives for action. In their own terms, they provide truly firm guidance, uncorrupted by a worldly origin. Their crucial weakness is that it is difficult to believe in them. When confronted with the question—how do you *know*?—no good reply is forthcoming. And there is a variety of obvious social factors in the modern world, such as the diversity and erosion of transcendental beliefs and the loss of prestige of the groups which are their bearers, which visibly underscore the weakness of the possible replies.

The situation is the very opposite with the immanentist theories. They build with mundane, human materials only. Their theories are not in principle difficult to believe: this or that specific theory may of course be visibly mistaken, but they do not arouse suspicion and incredulity from the very nature of their claims. But, on the other hand, their claims are a little too weak to carry the burden laid upon them. They fail to validate an obligation. Take as an example that paradigm of an *In* theory, Hume's theory of morals. Suppose it were true that we act morally because, or in as far as, we have a certain feeling urging us in that direction. What if the feeling is absent, or if somebody chooses to ignore it? Within the terms of the theory, there is nothing that can be done. Perhaps, indeed, in the nature of things nothing can be done: but if we want a theory to do the job of a social charter, and to persuade people that they are under an obligation irrespective of their transient feelings, this kind of excessively frank theory will not get us very far.

In theories face a kind of philosophical variant of the problem of 'who guards the guardians'. It uses, for purposes of setting up the ultimate yardstick and sanction, some mundane material such as a feeling, sensation or expression of will or consent. But it has to face the possibility that this mundane element may itself on occasions be absent or corrupted. Within the conceptual storehouse of the theory, nothing is available to strengthen the all-too-fragile base which the theory offers.

There is an interesting parallel between the development of the empiricist theory of knowledge and the democratic theory of politics. These two theories are of course old running mates. Both place sovereignty squarely in this world: for one, the ultimate arbiter of knowledge is human sensation, for the other, the ultimate arbiter of politics is the human will. Now the old-fashioned empiricist theory of knowledge places the burden of final decision on questions of fact, on *sensation* conceived as a kind of totally unambiguous, absolutely *given* datum, from which our vision of the world is constructed and which checks its correctness. The trouble with this version of the theory is that the way we perceive and categorize what we call our sensations, is not absolutely given, but depends on our concepts and theories, and that it changes over time, sometimes drastically so. In fact, it changes under the very impact of those very theories which the sensations are intended to check. In other words, the pure and absolute sovereign is not so absolute and pure and unconnected with the realm which he is meant to rule.

So a modern empiricist theory of knowledge has to be modified, so as not to postulate such an absolute, given, unambiguous, fully determinate and external judge. Still, something is saved from the old theory: the requirement that theories, and the worlds which they as it were create, should not control their own sources of validation, but be subject to something external at least to themselves, if not to the world at large. A similar development takes place in the theory of democracy. The will of man or men is no longer conceived of as independent of the social structures over which it is meant to be sovereign. Nevertheless, again something does remain: the requirement that there should be *some* checks, and moreover checks independent of other parts of the social structure of which they are part. The concrete embodiment of this requirement is of course the rightly fashionable ideal of pluralism.

Inside theories concerning knowledge give us theories of knowledge in terms of sensation. *Inside* theories in the field of ethics give us accounts of morals in terms of feelings or pleasure. *Inside* theories in the field of politics give us an account of the legitimacy of the social order or of the power of the state, in terms of *will* and *consent*: in other words, they give us the classical theory of democracy.

This surely is the genesis of the general features of the theory of democracy, and also the explanation, in as far as an intellectual explanation is relevant at all, of the pervasiveness of the democratic assumption in the modern world. The appeal of democracy, specifically in its classical formulation, is a corollary of a general predisposition in favour of *In* justifications.

This way of putting the matter makes the popularity of the democratic ideal a consequence of secularization: the diversity of transcendent beliefs, and the decline of all transcendent beliefs, make it necessary to justify political arrangements from Within rather than from Without, and democratic theory and its appeal are the consequence. And where shall we find a justification within society and man, if not in the will and consent of men, in *people*? Thus, for instance, the Populism noted amongst thinkers and leaders of the Third World may perhaps in part be no more than a consequence of a general intellectual situation, in which Outside appeals are impermissible, and of a specific political situation which makes the pluralist version of democratic theory unattractive, and without much other significance.

The whole point can be put in a social rather than an intellectual way. In a period of rapid social change and absence of intellectual or other stability, thinkers and leaders must phrase their appeals in a 'to whom it may concern' form, rather than addressing specifically people assumed to have this or that identity, this or that transcendent conviction, this or that value-loyalty, this or that moral standard or authority. Minimizing the as it were receptivity-diminishing specificity of their appeal, they naturally in effect say something like this: my acts, or my doctrine, are validated by *your* consent, *whoever* you may be or become and *whoever* your gods may be! Thus a populist formulation becomes a consequence of a situation of rapid change, mobility, fluid identities and eroded previous belief.

Of course, this picture is much too simple. If this were all there was to it, democratic enthusiasm should go hand in hand with transcendent *dis*belief. In fact, as Tocqueville pointed out in a famous passage, democracy in America worked in conjunction with firm religious *belief.* Or again, even the more extreme democrat theorists do not necessarily abstain from *Out* beliefs, though they may camouflage them. In a famous 'thesis' on Feuerbach, Marx draws attention to this 'Who guards the guardians' regress implicit in ordinary reformist thought and appears to hint that he at any rate can avoid it. Perhaps it can be avoided, within some systems, though only at the price of endowing a certain direction of development with an absolute, and hence in effect a transcendent status. Perhaps there was a good deal in Tawney's gibe to the effect that Marx was the last of the scholastics.

The present argument is concerned to relate the concept of democracy to transitional societies. In the main, it sets out to show that transitional societies illuminate the problem of democracy, rather than vice versa.

What is a transitional or underdeveloped society? A variety of definitions exist, in terms of social features such as low productivity, low consumption, low level of administrative or economic skill, absence of general education or literacy, and so forth. These characteristics and the definitions based on them are of course of very great importance, yet for our purpose a different definition is relevant.

A transitional society is one in which legitimacy is based on the promise of a future achievement, where this achievement requires a very radical transformation, but one to be attained in this world by this-worldly means. This definition excludes, as it is intended to, religious messianic societies which also legitimate themselves in terms of an expected transformation, but which expect the transformation to be suffused by the supernatural.

This definition incidentally becomes equivalent to the other definitions (in terms of poverty, etc.) under certain conditions, and these conditions in fact hold: namely, that poverty, low levels of technical skill, etc., should be seen to be avoidable, and to be incompatible with human dignity and the basic rights of man. It is not poverty, or even the partial presence of advanced technology and a population explosion as such, which turns a traditional society into a transitional one; nor is it the erosion of traditional institutions, which has not taken place everywhere. What does turn society into a transitional one is that the poverty and the other features are no longer considered tolerable, so much so that legitimacy comes to hinge on a credible promise that they will be abrogated. This is the essence of the social 'transition'.

In terms of the modern, sociologically realistic theory, the defects of democracy as a generally valid norm are well known. Contrary to the naïve supposition that democracy is somehow the binding norm for all men and all conditions, the new picture makes it plain that it is only likely to work under certain specific conditions. As it is most commonly put—democracy presupposes consensus. When the members of a society are in agreement on a basic range of fundamentals, it is easy, it is agreeable, it is desirable for them to settle the remaining marginal disagreements by 'democratic' methods, by putting them to the vote, by having a rotating leadership dependent on popular suffrage and so forth.

The conditions of consensus in turn can be spelt out in further detail (though there is no general agreement on just what those conditions are): it is desirable probably that there be a strong middle section of the population sufficiently well-off to have a vested interest in the preservation of order. It is desirable that politics, violence and corruption should not offer the greatest available rewards in the society, but that, on the contrary, politics should be only one, and preferably not at all a privileged, way to power and wealth. The conditions of consensus can also be elaborated in a quasi-tautological manner: it is desirable that members of a society should be agreed on fundamental values and in basic outlook, or if they are not, that they should hold their divergent views in a lukewarm and tolerant manner.

This theory of democracy has had a considerable vogue of late. It is associated with the 'end of ideology' theme. Roughly, the argument is that a healthy society does not seek its basis in ideology, or seek the fulfilment of some ideology, but conducts its affairs from a kind of pragmatic consensus.

From the viewpoint of a supposedly universally valid ideal, this theory highlights a manifest weakness in democracy. Where the consensus is lacking, can it be *brought about* by democratic means? Sir Karl Popper once called the 'paradox of democracy' the fact that democracy can democratically reject itself, and opt for dictatorship. In the period between the two world wars, this was for obvious reasons the relevant paradox. But in our present condition, the more poignant paradox is one highlighted by transitional societies: are the preconditions of democracy such that they themselves can be attained democratically?

The modern theory of democracy does not give us much of a validation of it. It gives us primarily a recipe for attaining it, and rather a weak and a negative one at that: if conditions are favourable, *then* democracy is . . . possible, perhaps even likely.

Note incidentally how, in the contemporary consciousness, the democratic and the communist ideals have changed place. Time was, when the communist ideal had the locus of its appeal somewhere in the future, when the pains of achieving industrial society had already been suffered, in the main, under a different and less desirable social order. Nowadays such appeal as communism has is as a recipe for overcoming those ardours, not as a blueprint or promise of a future order. Democracy, on the other hand, once claimed to be a political recipe for the here-and-now: nowadays it is more often seen as the reward to be enjoyed after the attainment of more essential economic preconditions.

Note also the very amusing fact that the Prior Consensus theory of democracy is merely the old Fraud theory of democracy, associated with Marxism, read backwards and transformed from a reproach into a song of praise. The old Marxist critique of democracy ran, in simple terms, as follows: the elections, the show of consultation and consent, in the so-called liberal democracies, are but a fraud. The electors are only allowed to express their will, and see it implemented, as long as that will remains within certain limits. The whole cultural machinery is geared to obscuring from the voters the fact that more fundamental, more basic choices could be available, that they could change the fundamental features of the society in which they live. *If* they came to perceive the real alternatives, then force would have to be employed to restrain their democratic choice, and the façade of democracy would be destroyed. But generally, it is not necessary to destroy this façade, for the cultural befuddlement works only too well. (Consider the importance of the 'Tory working man' in recent accounts of the stability of British politics.)

But let us not be deceived! This free choice is only tolerated if it is not used. (Note incidentally that this critique is so constructed as to ensure that nothing would count as true democracy, unless the electorate chose to do that which the critic wants it to choose. The popular will is, operationally, equated with *his* will. Any other choice is, by definition, a case of alienated will. This is an important point, showing that the radical leftist is generally a crypto-objectivist in ethics.)

What the modern consensus theory has done, in effect, is simply to transform the reproach into a merit. Democracy is only tolerated as long as it does not upset the applecart; it is not allowed to go beyond certain limits—so said the old critic. The modern theory runs: democracy only works on the foundation of a substantial consensus. The points are absolutely identical. Only the language and the assessment contained in it are different.

The normative potential of the modern theory, at least in its verbal formulation, is relatively restricted. The model that can be drawn up, of a plural society in which the multiplicity of forces and institutions prevent any one of their number dominating the rest, and which function on the basis of a broad and non-doctrinaire consensus— this picture does not warm the blood like wine. To appreciate and savour its appeal, one needs to have a rather sophisticated taste, perhaps. Those of us whose values do lie in this direction nevertheless can only hope that this taste will become general through the prior diffusion of the suitable conditions, notably of affluence, and hope that such other conditions as it may also need will also come about somehow or other. We are back in the circle—the conditions which favour these values do indeed favour them, but the values themselves do not seem to have any internal power to impose their moral authority irrespective of all conditions.

The old classical model, on the other hand, does have a much more powerful, immediate, less refined and more universally accessible appeal. It seems to follow, almost immediately, from a determination to justify political arrangements by human considerations alone. If only human considerations are allowed, what else, other than consent, could justify authority and government? And what justification could be invoked for any asymmetry? If justification is to be by consent, and is to be symmetrical as between various people, does not something like *general* consent follow as the only possible basis of politics?

Democratic political theory of this kind stands at the middle point between non-normative theories, concerned with politics simply as the expression of force or custom or something of the kind, on the one hand, and on the other hand political theories invoking some externally imposed, objective, absolute norms. They are, as it were, at the point at which the minimum amount of normativeness is allowed to enter and disturb the purity of an empirical, positive account of politics.

It would no doubt be wrong to say that democratic political theory simply follows from the determination to apply an *In*, non-transcendent approach to politics, that it is the only possible *In* theory. For instance, the political theories of Fascism and Nazism were probably of the Inside kind (though the lack of high-powered intellectual elaboration makes it difficult to document this), yet clearly they were not democratic. They lacked the logical symmetry, or, in human terms, the egalitarianism. But given this symmetry as an additional premise—and it too is favoured by modern circumstances —the theory probably does follow in something like a unique manner.

But it too, despite its luminous appeal, has its defects. Interestingly, its logical defects spring from the same sources as its appeal—from its this-worldly purity.

A pure democratic theory appeals to will and consent only, and not to *any* extraneously introduced norms. So far so good. But suppose the majority wishes to exterminate a minority? An intolerable and repugnant ambition, you say: and so it is. But why should it be excluded? The enforcement of the minority's right to survive means, *ex hypothesi*, the thwarting of the will of the majority. And in the name of what? Not, evidently, will and consent, for just these are being, in this imaginary case, violated.

It would be agreeable to be able to say that the example is far-fetched. Twentieth-century history has made it not at all far-fetched. But if we were living in a better world and could happily say that it is far-fetched, we should still have to go on to admit that many other less far-fetched examples can be invoked.

My point is this: a 'democratic' society, governed by the will of the people, interpreted as the will of the majority or in any other way, can only be acceptable when it respects certain limits, certain *entrenched* principles. It is a matter of logic that these additional and entrenched principles themselves cannot in turn be based on will and consent, for they *limit* that consent. It is a matter of fact that these entrenched principles are not stable and permanent, though there must always be some in operation, and generally a large number, and they are not themselves determined by any simple and self-evident logical premise. One might suppose that they could be delimited in some simple and orderly way, so as to include survival, and the opportunity to reverse the majority verdict (if majority is to be the criterion of the popular will) by persuasion and legal means, and so forth. But for various reasons no such orderly delimitation will do.

There are some other neat formulae which are popular in this context: for instance, one often hears a claim that everyone is constrained to observe the current rules, irrespective of whether they are considered just, as long as legal and orderly procedures exist for getting them changed. But this presupposes a clear notion of what is or is not a 'current rule'. Codified law is ever ambiguous, and only operates in the context of tacit and half-formulated rules of operation. These in turn are pliable and depend on context. In brief, a community 'wills' things at two levels: the basic and tacit, but not total or rigid and stable consensus concerning the entrenched rules; and *within these* there is a more superficial level at which greater disagreement is tolerable. When nowadays it is said that democracy presupposes consensus, these levels are generally not distinguished. It is probably true that democratic institutions require a fair amount of consensus even at the superficial level, but it is far more essential for them to possess it at the fundamental level concerning the entrenched, often tacit, rules. It is also important however to note that in a complex and changing world, the levels cannot be rigidly separated.

The really important point which follows is that a society cannot be based on will and consent alone. The entrenched rules *limit* will and consent, or cannot without vicious circularity invoke them. Why has this not been generally noticed? The answer is of course that in relatively stable conditions, the 'entrenched clauses' may be so much part of the intellectual atmosphere that they are absolutely taken for granted. A given social structure, and the central normative ideas which would express it if it were made explicit, may be so much part of the social atmosphere that, like the air we breathe, we simply do not notice them. It is then possible to formulate a seemingly viable theory of democracy, which appeals to will and consent *only*: for, in practice, the will and consent will only need to exercise themselves on marginal decisions *within* that tacitly assumed structure and set of limiting norms.

There is a profound irony about this. The 'pure' democratic theory (and I do not think this theory, though I have simplified it, is a travesty of the underlying inspiration of democrats) is inherently incomplete. It is workable only because it presupposes some norms as externally given. The American democrats observed by Tocqueville in his account managed to make democracy work because they shared a certain firm religious faith. Yet the persuasive appeal of the democratic ideal springs precisely from the fact that it seems not to invoke anything. It makes us sovereign. It seems to say: we men come together, either without a faith at all or with many divergent faiths (and in any case we tolerate our divergencies), and we shall base our worldly political arrangements on agreement, and not on any attempt to impose our respective doctrines on each other. This abstention from as it were extra-social dogmatism only works if it is spurious, if covertly it presupposes a consensus after all, a consensus beyond the reach of 'will'.

Note that this present argument has invoked only very abstract premises, and has demonstrated the incompleteness and circularity of the model on the basis of very abstract reasoning. Yet it reaches the same conclusion as has been reached by more concrete observation of actual societies: democracy works on the basis of a fair amount of consensus, but not without it. We have here a truth (if such it is) which has both a logical and a sociological basis. Logically, *will* is an inadequate basis, for simply appealing to 'will' does not prejudge the content of that which is willed, and what is willed might well be destructive of a social order, and incompatible with its perpetuation. Sociologically, it is absurd to speak of will, or consent, apart from a concrete social structure which provides the alternatives between which choice can take place, which gives content and objects to 'will'. Once such a structure is presupposed however, it cannot in turn be validated by the same kind of consent as are the choices within it. Tacit consensus or social structure provide the frameworks for 'will', but cannot in turn be based on it.

This would not raise a practical problem if indeed the societies took their own basic structures for granted, ignored them like the air they breathe, and could quietly presuppose them in their theorizing and understanding of themselves. But this, most conspicuously, is no longer true of the world we live in, and above all, it is not true of *transitional* societies. The point of our definition of 'transitional societies' was precisely to highlight the fact that their own basic structures are *sub judice*. That is what makes them transitional. Their basic structures *are* objects of deliberation and choice, of 'will' and 'consent'.

Thus transitional societies illuminate the notion of democracy (as they do much else). It is not so much that they have a great deal to learn from the older accounts of democracy and its preconditions: it is our understanding of democracy which is enhanced by *their* predicament. Past understanding of the idea was hampered by the fact that some of the crucial conditions were taken for granted. Transitional societies are so lacking in social oxygen, that no one inhaling their atmosphere is tempted to take it for granted.

The trouble with the old theories, formulated in simple terms such as 'will' and so forth, was that they assumed certain simple models in terms of which these terms were interpreted. We 'will' something: this simple sentence presupposes an identifiable ego which does the willing, and a range of objects or of possible situations which are willed, desired, brought about. In order to be identifiable, an ego must have a reasonable degree of permanence. We can identify a cloud or a wave at sea, but only for a brief time and if conditions are not too turbulent. To what extent is this condition satisfied in conditions of 'transition'? Objects of desire, preference and aspiration also only exist in the context of what may be called the rules of the game. The choices and desires open to a chess player are different from those open in golf or in football. Perhaps some very basic biological needs generate objects which transcend all optional games, but happily most of our life is not so crude or so penurious as to be dominated by the satisfaction of these crude needs, in an undifferentiated state. But what if the games themselves are rapidly changing? The stability of the object-generating games is something which, most patently, cannot be assumed in developing societies. It is thus that transitional societies demonstrate, in a very forceful and concrete manner, something which previously was manifest only to those endowed with philosophical subtlety or social imagination.

The philosophy of will tacitly assumed by much unsophisticated democratic theory is rather like those naïve theories of knowledge which tacitly (or even overtly) take for granted the world which is to be known. If you only know one world and are so unimaginative that you cannot think of any other, then such simple-mindedness is easy: you can give an account of how that one world is known, by describing some supposed processes within that same world which lead to the happy end-result of the world being correctly perceived. If, on the other hand, you are endowed with some philosophic imagination, or if conditions of rapid and turbulent and disturbing change bring home to you the availability and questionable status of given total outlooks, then you are faced with the painful awareness that any attempts to assess rival merits, or to move from one to the other, presupposes, whether you like it or not, some attempts at standing outside. Conditions of what may be called social creation are just of this kind: it is not possible, in setting up the criteria of what and how is to be created, to rely upon the given assumptions of some one and given social world, for all is in flux. The politics of transition are the politics of social creation.

The philosophical significance of this point is of course that Inside validations are almost as mythical as Outside ones. It is not merely untrue that we possess private lines to the Transcendent for purposes of validating our values. It is equally untrue that we can conjure up that validation from our own consciousness, will, consent, etc. We have no such given Ego. It is curious that this myth can be found in apparently hard-headed, this-worldly doctrines such as Marxism. The idea of non-alienated man, freed in his choices and values from social constraint, is about as realistic as the idea of a quintessential onion, left when all the leaves have been stripped. Our romantic neo-Marxists may be right in claiming that an *ethical* theory can be extracted from the young Marx, and that it lies under the historicist formulations of later Marxism. But this theory, though endowed with existence, is not endowed with merit.

Consider the logic of what may be called the Creation-situation. A traditional deity, creating the world, can act in a manner analogous to the conduct credited to man by classical democratic theory. Such a deity is assumed to possess a pre-existing will and plan, and it can design and erect a world in accordance with it. But a traditional deity is not much of a model for our current social situation. A Hegelian deity, which creates itself along with its creation, is more apposite (though still not quite right). The design, plan, norm, emerge with the creation which embody them.

When social (or, for that matter, any other kind of) creation is at issue, the democratic model has no clear relevance unless there is a reasonably articulate pre-existing 'will' which can at least 'consent' to that which is being created. It was sometimes supposed that the paradigm of a democratic situation was that of the Pilgrim Fathers, setting up a society, freely consenting to a social contract. Nowadays, we are inclined to stand this observation on its head. Where there is a pre-existing social order (or a consensus such as tacitly or overtly existed amongst the Fathers), democratic procedures are feasible and desirable; but where a social order is being brought into being, democratic procedures may be difficult, perilous or self-defeating, and democratic criteria have no clear meaning.

To place the problem of democratic theory in the context of social *creation*, to stress the distinction between marginal decisions within accepted structures, where no great burden is placed on either theory or institutions, and 'creation' in which an enormous burden is placed on both, is not to say that in our time, political inventiveness has no limits. On the contrary, it has very definite limits. The significance of the notion of 'industrialization' is that it indicates what those limits are. The utilization of technology and effective administration for purposes of achieving affluent living happens to be the imperative imposed on contemporary governments. This datum enables us to escape a relativism which otherwise, in the abstract, might perhaps be inescapable.

If industrialization is our big datum (which I think it is), an alternative formulation of the question would of course be to ask

what is entailed by it, what is excluded by it, and what is left optional.
What *must be* and what *cannot be*, always assuming we get it right,
does not perhaps concern us. As Aristotle observed, no man de-
liberates about what cannot be otherwise. As a piece of psychology
this is false, but it is good advice. I suspect that the middle range of
that which is neither entailed nor excluded is in fact rather large.

Classical political theory was of course born of the preoccupation
with quite a different hump: the hump of power and order. The
question was: how is social order as opposed to moral anarchy
possible at all?

Relating this question to the problem of liberty, there were three
famous answers to it. One runs: the attainment of order is so important that all else, including liberty, is secondary. The other answer
is: the attainment of order is indeed very important, but it is valuable
only if combined with liberty. The third answer is: the right order is
important but it must constitute a moral fulfilment. The right
social order is not a precondition but the good life itself.

Our own preoccupation with society does not spring from the
concern with political order as such, which does not seem unduly
precarious in our time, but with the achievement of industrial
affluence, i.e. a mode of organization enabling man to enjoy that
which scientific technology has made possible. But the answers
concerning how this new hump is to be overcome, and how its overcoming ties up with legitimacy, tend to fall into the same pattern.
We too have those who consider the overcoming of the hump the
supreme and sufficient principle; those who supplement it with a
concern for liberty; and those who wish it to be a way to some total
fulfilment. (My own sympathies, it happens, are with the middle
group.)

Thus the problem of democracy must in our time be considered
within the limits of (A) the heightened sophistication concerning
what 'will', 'consent', etc., can possibly mean, in either social creation
or stable contexts, and (B) of what we know or need to find out
about the one big datum, the drive to industrialization. Each of these
conditions must be considered in turn.

(A) Men do not perpetually re-create their societies by acts of
will of the power-holders ratified by the consent of the rest. Neither
will nor force is the basis of the state. The state, and other institutions, are parts of a social structure which perpetuates itself,
among other ways, by moulding the consent of the participants,
and also by providing the alternatives to which they can give or
withhold consent, and the concepts in terms of which they isolate
and evaluate alternatives facing them. Hobbes was wrong: it is not
a sovereign but a social structure which enables us to escape and

avoid anarchy. The recognition of this modifies what we can mean by 'democracy' and the reasons we can have for valuing it.

All this is perhaps obvious. But, ironically, it required the prevalence of societies whose structures are disintegrating, or grossly inadequate for their tasks, or in need of fundamental reorganization, in other words of 'transitional' societies, to bring it home. Where social structures are adequate, they can be ignored. It was the rarity of social oxygen in the Third World which made us all atmosphere-conscious.

There are a number of further ironies in this. At the very moment when we fully perceive that total social creation is impossible, that societies are not made by acts of will of pre-social men, we also see that social creation is mandatory, owing to the fundamentally unviable and unacceptable nature of a large number of societies. In a sense, the Third World must act as if social creation were possible, after all. Who are to be their *ersatz* pre-social designers and ratifiers of the Social Contract? Those who have stepped outside the existing and unacceptable order, by means of a 'Western' education, or an 'Eastern' training, acting as caretakers on behalf of their fellow-citizens in a social chrysalis stage, whose consent, if required, must be taken as, once again, 'tacit'? In fact, this looks like the solution which imposes itself.

It is a consequence of this situation that the notion of democracy can be applied to transitional societies in at least three quite distinct senses.

(1) Popular consultation or determination of the basic question— what kind of society, fundamentally speaking, is to be forged during the transition, when all is in flux. This is the deepest sense in which this kind of society could be 'democratic'. Ironically, this kind of very profound democracy may be in conflict with other more humdrum kinds: because, before a population can be consulted on this deep issue, it must be roused into a conscious awareness of it. But this kind of heightening of consciousness, this kind of sense of general participation, can perhaps only be achieved through that kind of mass mobilization and enlistment which, for one thing, may prejudge the issues, and, for another, may be incompatible with political pluralism and checks on power. This sense of democracy really amounts to deciding democratically where, in the basic sense, the society is to go.

(2) There is the quite different issue as to whether this society, once approaching stability in a new form, is to have democratic institutions, in the sense of competition for leadership and popular participation in the choice of leaders. This is an important characteristic, but it is in no way identical with the preceding one. The democratic procedures, in this sense, could come into operation, or

for that matter remain in operation, when the basic structural features of the society have been decided and cannot any longer be affected by a political decision. Democratic political decisions can indeed work all the more smoothly when they no longer need to deal with such basic issues, and need only concern themselves with marginal ones. This sense of democracy amounts to the presence of democratic institutions and practices in the mix, established as the society emerges *from* a transitional state. In this sense, democracy is something *chosen* during the transition, but not the method of choosing it.

(3) The presence of democratic or at any rate the pluralistic institutions *during* the period of transition. As this early period is characterized by enormous cultural and educational gaps between the élite and the mass, by bad communications, poverty and a host of other factors which inhibit either the crystallization or the expression of the popular will, the presence of the appropriate institutions can only with difficulty be in any way assimilated to the classical model of 'democracy'. Nevertheless, in various other ways, democracy in this sense may still be extremely important and desirable. For one thing, it may be conducive to efficiency in economic and social development by providing some measure of check on rulers during this period. For another, the continuous presence of some kind of pluralistic institutions may, perhaps, be a precondition of their effective presence and functioning during the post-transition stage. This sense of democracy really amounts to a degree of institutional liberalism and pluralism during transition, which may be symbolized, rather than effectively implemented, by democratic rituals such as elections and universal suffrage.

(B) If we return to the issue of social 'creation', that fundamental, conscious and partly directed transformation most conveniently described as 'industrialization', the question arises of how in fact the direction and criteria of this transformation are determined. The answer to this question—and of course we do not know the answer —will delimit the ways in which the aims or criteria could be chosen 'democratically', if such ways exist.

To begin with, possible answers can be classified into (1) horizontal, (2) vertical and (3) diagonal types.

(1) Horizontal theories are those which put forward a one–one correlation between type of society and degree of economic development (conceived as industrialization or *proximity* to mass affluence). Raymond Aron has castigated[1] this view as the new orthodoxy and pointed out that it is a kind of inverted Marxism. Given that the richest society is at present both democratic and liberal, it is of course an optimistic doctrine—for it follows that it is sufficient to enrich a society to ensure that it is also liberal and democratic. Para-

phrasing Dr Nkrumah's paraphrase of the New Testament (which used to adorn his statue outside Ghana's Parliament, prior to its recent demolition), one might say: seek ye first the Kingdom of Affluence, and all else will be added on to you. The doctrine has the possible merit of underwriting and encouraging economic aid. It has both liberal and illiberal implications for transitional societies: it tells them that they do not need to seek or suffer authoritarian developers, for they are not essential, but it also makes them, and, more significantly, the suppliers of aid, rather too tolerant of traditional or other non-left authoritarians. (It won't make any difference in the end, either way, is the tacit argument.) A version of the doctrine can be credited to influential Americans both in economics and in political sociology (e.g. Rostow, Lipset). But all that the evidence really allows us to assert is that industrial ('affluent', diffused) wealth tends to stabilize the social order. If this is so, it means of course that a democratic liberal society which enters the period of mass consumption with its democratic institutions intact, may be unlikely to lose them thereafter. It does not mean, alas, that one which enters this stage without them, will thereafter acquire some variant of them.

(2) Vertical theories are those which credit each post-industrial society with the same crucial characteristics as those which were possessed by its pre-industrial ancestor. On this view, the characteristics of industrial society are merely shot through the pre-existing pattern, without modifying it drastically.

In a pure form, this type of theory is even more unacceptable than the horizontal species. For one thing, many societies simply do not re-emerge on the other side of the Niagara at all: the biological descendants of their members do, but not the societies themselves. This is plainly true of many small-scale tribal societies. Nevertheless, it may well contain a fair amount of truth concerning the major pre-industrial civilizations, which enter the Niagara with a bulk and a structure which makes the survival of many significant traits conceivable or even likely. One crucial question in this area is precisely: just how *much* truth is there in the vertical view?

An important variant of the vertical view would be one which correlated the features of the post-hump society not with its own social ancestor, but with the features of the society under whose aegis the society in question overcame the hump. (This theory is only applicable, of course, to those societies which made the transition under foreign leadership or at least inspiration. But, if such leadership or inspiration *at some stage* at least is counted, these societies make up a global majority.)

Within this variant, an interesting sub-group would be one which insisted that the relationship is an *inverse* one. There is an oft-quoted remark of M. Houphouet-Boigny's, to the effect that if you wish your son to be a Communist, you should send him to be educated in Paris, but if you wish him to be pro-Western, you should send him to Moscow. This observation clearly makes some sense not only for sons, but also for societies as a whole. It is amusing to reflect on the fate of the British and Soviet decolonizations. The British left behind, throughout Africa, carefully designed democratic constitutions. Those to whom they bequeathed them could hardly wait to turn them into one-party states or military regimes. The diminution of Soviet authority in Eastern Europe, on the other hand, left the decolonized satellites at least visibly striving for more liberal forms. It is of course possible that this should be explained not so much in terms of Houphouet-Boigny's dictum as 'horizontally' (Eastern Europe being richer than Africa) or 'vertically' (in terms of the previous local traditions).

This inverse relationship, in as far as it exists, is of course connected with one crucial difference which seems to obtain between the Western and Soviet models of the drive to industrialization. The Soviet structure seems to be like some kind of crystal which can reproduce itself in the suitable material, with both its merits and its demerits, but in some measure faithfully. The lateral reproduction of liberal society, on the other hand, seems to generate a parody of the original model. Perhaps the conscious following of the liberal path across the hump requires too much patience, too much willingness to put up both with political risks and, less laudably, with temporary misery, dislocation and inequality. Should one allow the shanty-towns to suffer in squalor, one's enemies to organize within them, and the economic sharks to enrich themselves, just because, in the long run, this may mean both affluence and liberty? The run is too long and too risky. In practice, all too often, it only means that whilst the shanty towns cannot but be allowed to suffer in squalor, one's enemies are *not* allowed to organize, and the sharks are only allowed to get rich on condition that they pay up—in other words, under the liberal constitutional form, there is both a secret police and corruption and in the end there is progress neither towards affluence nor liberty.

(3) Diagonal theories are those which make the post-industrial social form depend on the *relative* point in the temporal series, at which the society in question overcomes the hump. For instance, a possible version of this type would be a theory claiming that the first industrializers (therefore) become liberal, for the first industrialization had to be both unconscious and individualistic; that the subsequent emulators tend to be authoritarian; but (perhaps) that at the end of the series, there will be another group of liberal ones, thanks to (let us say) the easy availability of aid and know-how

at that stage, which would make such a late transition less painful than its predecessor, or to the fact that, in this period, maximum aid can be obtained by playing off both sides and by not congealing the internal structure and ideological commitment.

It seems fairly obvious that no one of the three types of theory, in pure form, can be adequate. To be realistic, each needs to allow both for elements drawn from the others and for sheer historical accidents (e.g. consequences of wars, etc.). Nevertheless, these are the elements from which, it seems to me, an adequate theory may be built. But this cannot be done by reasoning and classification. We need to find out what actually happens.

What remains of the notion of democracy on this account? In the main, of course, unanswered questions; and a stress on the difference in *meaning* (quite apart from differences in difficulty of implementation) of democracy in 'creation' situations and in situations of marginal management. Perhaps one relevant observation would be to say that even developed societies do not approximate closely to this 'marginal' model. One might also ask to what extent, in the developed societies, concern for democracy really boils down to concern with liberalism plus the symbolism of general participation, of universal incorporation in the moral community. The argument would run: the significant thing about elections is not that the electorate supposedly exercises choice, but that the life of governments is limited, and that their conduct is determined by the awareness of this. The socially relevant effects could be achieved just as well by deciding elections by lot, except, of course, for the symbolic expression of equal citizenship, etc. This is an exaggeration, in as far as genuine elections, where they occur, also exclude some policies and leaders who are strongly distasteful to the voters. But it is true that most issues are unintelligible, technical, parts of long series of related decisions, and come in enormous package deals with other issues, so that not much meaning can be attributed to the notion of electoral choice and consent.

The analogous point of course also holds for transitional societies. Concern with democracy can simply boil down to concern with liberty. Political pluralism and competition can be seen not as a means for basing social creation on the general will, but as a means of preventing over-concentration of power, an end desired either for itself or as a means to greater efficiency.

The shift from a concern with the merits and demerits of 'capitalism', to a concern with industrial society, corresponds roughly to the shift from a concern with 'democracy' to a concern with pluralism. Up to and including the time of the Second World War, people still thought in terms of both democracy and capitalism. Both terms have a slightly old-fashioned ring now. The division of societies into industrial and non-industrial ones, and into pluralistic and non-pluralistic ones, is far more significant than the older dichotomies.

To say this is not to deny that something of importance is retained by the older ideas. Within a society which is pluralistic, it is of some importance whether the competition between various groups and institutions within it is decided in a manner which involves popular consultation and which ensures that, on the whole, decisions are not reached which are deeply unpalatable to the majority. In other words, it is of interest and importance whether a pluralistic society is also specifically democratic. But it is far more important, first of all, to know whether it is pluralistic. If it is not, the democratic ritual of mass participation in 'elections' is of far smaller importance.

Similarly, within an advanced industrial society with its inevitable concentration of power in the state, and with its consultation between the state and industry, it is still of some interest to know where the society is also 'capitalist': whether, in other words, people can inherit wealth (as opposed to merely inheriting educational advantage), whether the legal form and conceptual folklore of the society is capitalist or anti-capitalist and so forth. The question of the relative advantage on either side of this alternative is interesting: a so-called 'capitalist' advanced industrial society may have the disadvantages of public squalor, or pointless consumption, of restricted social mobility, of an economic as opposed to a political interest in an arms programme and perhaps others. It has the possible advantage that the concentrations of economic power in hands other than those of the state can aid and support pluralism in the social and political sphere. It might even be true that social and political pluralism cannot survive without economic pluralism, and it might even be true that economic pluralism cannot be genuine without the legal institution of private property.

In other words—and this is what is important for the present argument—some genuine importance remains to the older questions about 'democracy' and about 'capitalism', but they are submerged under and reformulated in the light of other questions, now seen to be more profoundly important and more sociologically realistic.

To sum up: the old crucial political problem of 'who guards the guardians?' arises for modern transitional societies in a novel form: who manipulates the manipulators? The question has been transformed. It is no longer simply the question of what can prevent the corruption of the power holders, a question that Plato answered by trying to give a recipe for training an incorruptible, or nearly so, set of rulers, and which pluralistic political theory tries to answer by having a multiplicity of power holders checking on each other. This question of course survives, but added to it there is a much more profound question: given that politics is no longer in general a matter of attending to marginal adjustments in a social system which is, in the main, taken for granted, but on the contrary the inescapable total transformation of the whole system, what are the criteria which are to guide the transformation, and what checks can there be on their validity? Or, if you prefer to formulate it in a personal way, *who* is to guide the transformation and *who* is to check on this guidance? In the past, society itself provided these ultimate standards, from the fund of its own tacit assumptions, and presented them to itself externalized, as a set of independently given absolutes. It can no longer do so, for two reasons: first, society itself is in flux, its own assumptions are *sub judice*, and it cannot in this situation present itself with any certainties.

Second, the appeal of the democratic ideal springs precisely from the denial of external norms, and the shift of sovereignty to us, to our will. But we now have no fixed identity or will, and if we had, this theory prevents us from presenting it as an external norm. External norms are ruled out.

There is a profound irony about all this. Democratic society arises in a period of transition when, amongst other things, scepticism erodes belief in external norms. But the transitional conditions also make the need for external norms particularly acute, for there is no inner stability which could justify them either.

The longing for self-government was all very well, as long as we tacitly assumed the given identity of that self which was to do the governing. We could wish to be free, not having the imagination to conceive of alternatives to that identity, or to wish the choice between them also to be free. The tacitly assumed identity was outside the range of the decisions which were to make up government. This is where the important consensus took place; it concerned the framework within which decisions were to be taken. But the framework was not subject to that democratic will which was being enthroned as sovereign. It was taken for granted.

But the idea of self-determination becomes more awkward when the very self is *en jeu*. Who chooses the choosers? As a piece of social technology, democracy looks more effective for taking marginal decisions, than for fundamental ones. As a form of validation, as a theory of political legitimacy, it suffers from an analogous weakness. It makes sense as the ultimate arbiter of marginal decisions, but becomes circular when basic issues are at stake.[2]

1967

Notes

1   R. Aron, *Essai sur les libertés*, Paris 1965.

2   The first draft of this paper was prepared for a conference on 'The idea of democracy in transitional societies', held at the Villa Falconieri at Frascati in April 1966, under the auspices of the Social Science Research Council (of the United States of America). I should like to express my gratitude both to the Council and to all the participants. I am particularly indebted to conversations with Professors R. P. Wolff, R. P. Dore, P. H. Partridge, John Plamenatz, Giovanni Sartori and the Honourable Charles Frankel. Needless to say, the responsibility for the views expressed is mine alone.

Philosophy, Politics and Society, edited by Peter Laslett (Oxford 1956) attempts to give a picture of contemporary academic political thought by collecting ten papers by different authors. This task is made somewhat difficult by the fact that, as the editor puts it, 'political philosophy is dead'. I shall not for the moment consider whether this means that these studies are funeral orations, commemoration ceremonies, inaugurations of a succession regime or just plain hauntings by guilty souls. The editor says that the murderer has been the movement known to the general public as logical positivism. There is evidence for this view, and I shall try to reconstruct the crime, if such it is.

Let it be said at the start that this is a useful book if one wishes to teach social philosophy without changing one's normal philosophical terminology. For good or for ill, it is philosophically contemporary, despite the fact (or rather, and obviously, *because*) little or nothing could be inferred from it about important contemporary general issues.

The ten essays fall into three groups, one of them residual. First, there are those which, under one title or pretext or another, really discuss the general issue of the possibility of political thought, of the status of valuation and of political assessments, of the place of politics on the map of possible knowledge. These essays are best discussed in the context of the nature and implications of the positivist *Weltanschauung.* Second, there is a group of essays which applies the principles and axioms of that *Weltanschauung* to specific issues. And finally there is a group of three essays, Professor Oakeshott's, Professor Gallie's and Mr Laslett's, which are either by authors who do not belong to the tradition shared by the first two groups, or are tackling a problem without making use of that tradition. Professor Oakeshott's, which as an inaugural lecture has made its impact prior to the publication of this book, is more profitably discussed in the context of his other articles, and in any case deserves fuller treatment which I hope to give it soon and separately. For the moment suffice it to say that there are interesting parallels between his conclusions and those of the majority party in this collection, and even that there are parallels in their respective ways of reaching those conclusions. The crucial premise in his case, as much as in that of the latter-day positivists, is the stress on the hard facts of actual human doings, the refusal to endow abstractions with existence or power, which incidentally in both cases deprives philosophy of its critical social function. Linguistic philosophy goes one step further back in its premises. Its insistence on concrete activity is not a postulate, but is itself deduced from a theory of meaning.

As indicated, the majority of the contributors are profoundly influenced by the current linguistic movement, when indeed they aren't members of its Inner Party. Now the central preoccupations, ideas, symbols and war cries of that movement are not social or political, but belong to logic, semantics and epistemology, with ethics and politics on the whole treated only in an extremely formal way inspired by logical doctrines, not by moral preoccupations. It follows that to assess the movement from its efforts in the field of political theory is to observe the small visible part of the iceberg and to disregard the much larger and crucial part that remains submerged. Happily we know about the submerged part from sources other than the volume under review. I shall treat the theme of *politics and linguistic philosophers* twice, once deductively and once inductively; once by sketching the submerged parts and seeing what one should expect the visible, political part to be, and once by observing the visible part as presented in this book and comparing it with the former.

Herewith a crude sketch of the submerged part. Linguistic philosophy has passed through two stages. First came logical positivism proper, an admirably clear and simple doctrine to the effect that two, *and two only*, kinds of meaningful discourse were possible. One was the eliciting of the consequences of a conventional code (e.g. chess, mathematics), though the conventions may never have been explicitly drawn up but only exist implicit in practice. The other was the matching of linguistic units (empirical sentences) with extra-linguistic reality, again in accordance with a usually tacit set of conventions. Actual language was a *mélange* of utterances functioning in either of these ways, plus the intrusion of elements functioning in neither way and hence meaningless. The philosopher's job, by separating the two types of grain from each other and from the chaff, was to show us what we were doing and to eliminate the nonsensical part which was sometimes noxious and led both ordinary men and scientists to be worried by unreal questions. Note the immense force and appeal of the model on which this doctrine is based: given that language *is* visual and auditory tokens of certain kinds, what non-arbitrary ways of using them other than the two indicated are possible? The positivist model, if true, makes knowledge unmysterious in principle. If mysteries other than empirical ignorance exist, they must be due either to mere complexity, destined to evaporate as soon as the necessarily unmysterious and simple elements are located, or to plain muddle.

The well-known implications of this for ethics, for any kind of evaluation including of course the political, was that its assertions were technically nonsense, even if not of the noxious kind. And this led to a violent polemic in which both sides to some extent missed the point. Critics such as Professor Collingwood or Dr Joad (or indeed those who still echo their strictures today) did not seem to appreciate adequately the point that if this doctrine is true, it is irrelevant to argue that it is harmful. Defenders of the view such as Professor Ayer tended to reply that giving a formal analysis of a kind of utterance, saying that no member of that kind is anchored either to fact or to calculation (and hence is anchored to nothing at all), is not to make pronouncements about the merits of individual and rival members of that logical type: and hence that the alleged *immoraliste* implications of logical positivism did not hold. Altering a famous aphorism of Marx's, he might have said that the philosopher's job was only to understand language, not to change it. (Or anything else, for that matter. Their own impotence, the lack of implications of their own formal analyses, later became something of a dogma with some linguistic philosophers, if not a masochistic indulgence. Reacting against the wide claims of some traditional philosophers, their linguistic descendants are happy to boast of their own insignificance, of the modesty and minuteness of their labours.) Now for a reply along the line that 'analysis does not alter what is analysed, nor affect its merits' to be adequate, would have required this dogma to be better justified than it is. It would require the following premise to be *absent* from our minds: 'Indeterminate topics, assertions from fields in which there are no objective, impersonal ways of choosing between a proposition and its negation, are not worthy of attention, obedience or respect.' Now it so happens that this statement, or something like it, is believed or acted upon by many if not most people: and this statement in conjunction with the 'formal analysis' does have the implications with which critics had credited logical positivism. In the collection under discussion, Mr Weldon, the late Miss Macdonald and Mr Bambrough return to this theme.

We have seen that logical positivists disclaimed substantive ethical implications for their doctrine, and in some formal, technical sense they were right. It is indeed true that from a general analysis of ethical statements as such no formal deduction of specific moral judgment or their denials is possible.[1] But they were right in this formal sense only. In effect logical positivism was a radical, destructive doctrine, even if the direction of its radicalism outside technical philosophy was necessarily unspecific. It undermined a variety of metaphysical, religious *and* common-sense ideologies and thus weakened the moral valuations associated with them. However much the positivist might protest that *qua* philosopher he is concerned with formal or 'second-order' analyses, his doctrines inevitably made him a rebel or at least a radical, for they *entailed* the rejection of most traditional ideologies. If he accepted institutions which these ideologies defended, he did so for reasons other than the official ones. If the radicalism of logical positivism wasn't always particularly extreme, this may have been due to the political background of the time when logical positivism flourished. In the world of the 1930s, more powerful and immediate considerations may have submerged epistemological ones.

The dispute is rather reminiscent of J. S. Mill's defence against the charge that utilitarianism would undermine morals and weaken the sense of obligation. Mill's reply was to bring in Hume's doctrine that feelings not propositions motivate, and that consequently the appropriate motivating feelings could be brought in to sanction Utilitarian morality as much as any other. Technically this is correct, but yet it is obvious that by withdrawing transcendental status from an obligation its psychological impact is often weakened. This can be incorporated within Hume's schema of conduct which Mill took over; one can say that there is an independent emotional preference for non-contingent aims, or aims believed to be non-contingent, and that empiricism merely informs us that certain aims do not satisfy this condition. J. S. Mill's insistence that assertions of obligation do not have a transcendental meaning, and the positivist insistence that assertions of it have no objective meaning at all, have a very similar impact and logic. In both cases it can be argued that the discovery makes no practical difference; in both cases in fact it does, and in both cases this can be explained by assuming that certain other premises about what is and is not worth while are operative.

But logical positivism proper, with its radical, destructive if unspecific implications, is with us no longer, as indeed linguistic philosophers like to remind us. The change in linguistic philosophy has not on the whole percolated through to the general public; but it is also true that the profundity of this change is widely overestimated by the philosophers themselves. Later linguistic philosophy no longer operates with the simple clear model sketched above. Instead of allowing but two kinds of meaning it is imbued with a deep sense of the variety of ways in which language is used and in which consequently words 'have meaning'. All these ways share, however, the very general feature of being *uses* of language—doings, attitudes, etc., of concrete people. The little word 'use' employed in a very broad sense and occupying the key position of the new outlook, contains all the anti-transcendental and anti-normative implications which had been previously more openly displayed in the exclusive insistence on verifiability. But this is no longer a philosophy of elimination or *épuration*, but of acceptance. The philosopher is not a critic but an observer of usages. Now the starting-point of this new philosophy, of the rejection of logical positivism proper, is, oddly enough, something that the logical positivists had been perfectly aware of, namely, that their model does not fit language as actually used. For them, however, this only indicated that *in as far as* really meaningful, actual language had 'ultimately' to be reducible to the model; if in some case it was not so reducible, so much the worse for ordinary language. The latter-day linguistic philosophers drew the opposite moral from the fact that the model never seems to fit: so much the worse for the model.

Now these contemporary philosophers falsely exaggerate the difference between themselves and logical positivism proper,[2] in as far as they have taken over a certain basic outlook and set of tacit premises, of which the crucial one, that no transcendental knowledge is possible, is only demonstrable by means of the rejected model. (The model has been abandoned but what the model had been used to show is still in use.) They always forget to tell us and themselves how profoundly their own practice is indebted to logical positivism, how much the conclusions of logical positivism are required to make linguistic philosophy, as now practised, at all *relevant*. Roughly speaking: certainly they understand actual language better than the positivists did; but if it were not for the continued, probably justified but *unacknowledged* central thesis of the positivists, who would dream of treating language, ordinary or other, as crucial for philosophic issues?

Now the acceptance of what is commonly said is, in the case of these linguistic philosophers, quite genuine. The doctrine isn't—it is important not to misunderstand them here—that anything that is commonly said is true, but that the kind or type of thing that is said is *ipso facto* meaningful. For instance, not that common beliefs about material objects are therefore true, but that, because material objects are commonly spoken about, statements about them are meaningful and do not need legitimation by translation into conjunctions of basic propositions or what not. The distinction between what is said and the type or kind of thing that is said works well enough for material–object statements, and perhaps for some of the other kinds. It works far less well for statements such as religious ones and in general for statements about the viability of which *as a class* or type there can be genuine disagreement; and this is probably one of the fatal weaknesses of this outlook.

What concerns us here are the ethical and political implications of the outlook. Logically, they are conservative. This does not mean that a person subscribing to this outlook cannot consistently be in favour of specific innovations, but it does mean that he cannot subscribe to any fundamental innovation on ideological grounds. He cannot call for the abolition of religion because it is superstition, or for a re-ordering of political life because some past ideological premise has been found mistaken, or because some new premise has been discovered. The practical implications of this outlook are similar to those of the views of Professor Oakeshott.

It is a conservatism of abdication, at least of the abdication of any systematic critical function. Philosophers have not in the past, by definition, been concerned with specific application; but linguistic philosophy having told them that with regard to general issues no innovation or criticism is necessary or possible, that the general procedural rules embodied in 'rules of actual language' are in order, it follows that there is nothing left to be done, except list and explain the procedures and correct errors made by those past thinkers who were less given to abdication and acceptance. When Kant once removed reason to make room for faith he merely did so in a limited sphere in which reason seemed to him to have no application. These philosophers do so with a vengeance throughout the field of human thought to make room for established but philosophically baseless actual practice, be it 'faith' or anything else. The reaction to a procrusteanism which had tried to force all thought into one easily intelligible mould (i.e. to logical positivism) is the abandonment not only of moulds but also of any philosophically inspired standards of criticism. One of the contributors to this collection has in another and highly revealing discussion[3] made explicit the state of mind underlying this outlook. Characteristically he describes, in that same discusson, rationalism in the sense of trying to apply rational criticism to religious and other doctrines, as 'comic'. The difference between past and contemporary philosophizing which makes the former often of greater importance, and the latter often of unspeakable triviality, is expressed by describing the former as ridiculous! Only the inbred atmosphere of certain philosophical discussions, or a failure to understand what goes on accompanied by the assumption that this intellectually nude Emperor must have some Higher Clothing, can prevent one from seeing *them* as comic. Still, Mr Quinton deserves much credit for having expressed this widely assumed view with admirable vigour, honesty and clarity. I hope I may be forgiven for this heavy barrage of critical comments on what, after all, is only a discussion in a non-technical journal; but my justification is that Mr Quinton has in that place expressed so well what otherwise is half tacitly assumed.

This outlook faces the difficulty of accounting for the fact that traditional philosophers did *not* conceive of themselves in so passive a way, and indeed in many cases seem to have been highly influential—and *not* merely, as Quinton tries to insist, through aspects of their thought logically irrelevant to their philosophizing proper. As the current philosophers, unlike the logical positivists, are no longer keen to dissociate themselves from the philosophical past, this is indeed something of a difficulty. They have recently attempted to surmount it by means of a grotesque distinction between what they pejoratively call *Weltanschauung* and philosophy proper.[4] It is a pretty picture: on the one hand, hard, technical but emotionally unexciting problems, distinguished from scientific ones mainly by their second-order nature; by working at them a modest man can make a sober contribution to human knowledge. On the other hand, florid and wild *Weltanschauung* (rather un-English and non-U, really). Only by an unfortunate historical accident the two pursuits have come to be associated with each other. But we have finished with all that. We concentrate on logical problems and the understanding of how various kinds of usage work, and we leave *Weltanschauungen* to those willing to soil their hands with them. These philosophers are quite willing to bequeath *Weltanschauung* to the intellectual *demi-monde* of 'literary criticism'.

What is suggested is a kind of complete, more than Marxist epiphenomenalism with regard to thought. All ideological wars, revolutions, reforms and experiments must for Mr Quinton and those like-minded be either self-delusion or grotesquely absurd conduct. (Some of it is, but not all and above all not necessarily.) The origin of this very odd view of Quinton's is something like this: from the theory that sentences must be seen in context of their verification, it was natural to proceed to the discovery that many sentences had contexts other than verification. From this again it is natural to make the further step that these varied contexts are what give sentences their meaning, and hence that it would be absurd to judge sentences, and hence convictions, by criteria that ignore those contexts, or indeed by any criteria other than those already contained in those contexts. It then seems to follow that thought and human activities are never open to rational, general, abstractly-based criticism; that thought in the sense in which rationalists recommend it is never called for. This plausible idea that practices can only be understood in their contexts (with the less plausible and only half-avowed insinuation that they are always perfectly adapted to those contexts) is one which anthropologists have held under the name of Functionalism in a more open and explicit way. It is interesting to see philosophers approach it in an indirect way.

But whilst there is an important truth in this insistence that convictions must be seen in the context of their decision-procedures, and that these are extremely varied in type, sometimes vague, and built into the practices of daily life, it simply does not follow that thought does not have a dynamic of its own, that non-contextual logic is never called for, or that practice can never be criticized by thought. In most or all human activities some abstract beliefs are involved, and an alteration in these beliefs rightly produces an alteration in the activities; and sometimes philosophic reflection can rightly produce those alterations. This truism would be too platitudinous to assert were not Quinton and his fellows given to denying it by implication. His and their epiphenomenalism is based on no empirical evidence but on the misapplication of a theory of meaning (and on unjustified extrapolation from what happens in philosophy when someone tries to deny from abstract premises that we can see tables, that time is real and so on).

Linguistic philosophy claims to have unmasked and terminated the fallacious philosophic habit of inferring from language to the structure of the world. The boot is on the other foot. Linguistic philosophy consists of inferring from a muddled theory of meaning[5] to a dreary view of the world: from the view that 'meaning is use' to the theory that the world is substantially what it seems. (I.e. that no surprising philosophical theory, claiming that the world is substantially different from what we naïvely think, *can* possibly be true. This falls foul, amongst other things, of the truth that what is naïvely obvious isn't the same at all times and places. As Pascal might have said, what is naïve is not the same on both sides of the Pyrenees.) It consists *only* of this in as far as it sees itself as providing solutions for philosophical questions. Otherwise it also consists of a very impressionistic attempt at a sociology of linguistic behaviour.

The *appeal* of this doctrine lies in the image it gives the philosopher of himself. He can see himself as a man modestly and competently doing a solid, limited piece of work, quite unlike the nebulous, melodramatic, world- or outlook-changing and over-pretentious claims of his non-linguistic predecessor. A fine picture this, a kind of philosophical cross of the bluff, straight-from-the-shoulder man and of the stereotype of the natural scientist who does one manageable job at a time, and it is well done when completed. All this must appeal to those whose upbringing contained good doses of warning against *flashiness* of dress or manner.

Unfortunately this picture is utter nonsense, for philosophy is essentially about *Weltanschauung*. In general, the so-called technical, specific problems are easily soluble, and not worth solving, given the acceptance of a general outlook, or they depend for their interest on the existence of such an outlook. An *ad hominem* argument is that linguistic philosophy is itself a *Weltanschauung*, however much its protagonists may naïvely hold themselves to be beyond all *Weltanschauungen*: and it is quite an interesting one, with its tacit presupposition that there is no mystery or fundamental problem in the world, that mysteries which are not empirical ignorance can all be solved by clearing up our thought or language, that the world is substantially what it seems, that language is used in a wide variety of ways and that both the genesis and solution of so-called philosophical problems is to be sought in this variety and the fact that this variety has been disregarded; with its assumption that the meaning of any verbal pronouncement is to be sought in the context of real activities that surround it and that these justify it, that these should not be criticized from the viewpoint of *a priori* theories of meaning, and so on. Moreover it is this interesting and coherent *Weltanschauung* which gives linguistic philosophy its interest, not the alleged minor advances which out of their context would be both unintelligible and utterly dull. (The question about the class of all classes not members of themselves is, out of context, at least as silly as the one about the angels and the pin; it is also probably a little less difficult. And note that many questions earnestly discussed of late hardly bear comparison in intrinsic or indeed other interest with that famous and, in its context, immensely important problem.) The fact that the founders of this outlook, unlike other great innovators in philosophy, try to abstain from explicitly asserting the overall view and preferred to *suggest* it by devious means, for reasons which are themselves a part of that outlook, doesn't alter the fact that it is essentially a coherent and overall view of things.

Finally, the argument against ruling out *Weltanschauung* is this: linguistic philosophers do not say that there are *no* rules or criteria in the discussions men have about ethical, aesthetic, world-outlook, etc., issues, they merely say that philosophy is not to establish or judge their criteria. But if that kind of talk is governed by some criteria, i.e. is not arbitrary and random—why then the specification of the ways in which it is non-arbitrary *is* philosophy. By what right could one rule out one non-arbitrary and highly interesting kind of discourse in favour of an admittedly also non-arbitrary, but rather dull subject of the so-called 'technical philosophy proper'? (Note that the old pure logical positivist could have—and did—rule out ethical and world-outlook talk without being in any way inconsistent, for he maintained that it was arbitrary talk, discourse in which no rules existed or could exist. But the linguistic philosophers of today do not say that. They say, nebulously, that such talk has its own rules of procedure. Mind you, they either leave it at that without specifying what those standards are, or if they do, the account of such talk turns out in the end to be that it is a mixture of the old verification-by-fact and appeal-to-emotion themes, with minor variants that introduce nothing new in principle.)

To sum up: old 'straight' logical positivism was in its logical consequences radical in that it undermined most if not all ideologies that are associated with moral values—which of course does not preclude individual logical positivists from holding moral convictions with vigour and firmness. The 'linguistic philosophy' which developed from it is logically conservative, without again this precluding individual adherents from being psychologically non-conservative. In either case, both the radicalism and conservatism are so to speak non-specific and formal; it is not possible to deduce from these outlooks any statements as to the direction in which we should be radical, or about what in particular we should conserve. It is merely that logical positivism undermines most ideologies (admittedly revolutionary ones as well), but to do that *is* to be, negatively, revolutionary; whilst linguistic philosophy undermines primarily the possibility of criticism on principle or by philosophical theory, and even if it also undermines the possibility of validation, it is through this, in an unspecific way, conservative.[6]

The last point can be illustrated by the curious fact that linguistic philosophy is not merely held to be compatible with religious belief, but that the ranks of its practitioners now contain a considerable number of religious believers, and amongst these the most uncompromising and dogmatic of religious traditions is well represented. Of course, if you like, and as Quinton insists,[7] examining usages and solving 'logical problems' as such, is compatible with *anything* (though not because as Quinton thinks, it is separated by a logical iron curtain from general issues, but because it has been made trivial): but if one thinks of the presuppositions which make usages and 'logical problems' of interest and of exclusive philosophic interest—the profound nominalism and anti-transcendentalism for instance—one cannot but wonder. But I fear we cannot hope for a new St Thomas who will square Wittgenstein with the Church as Aristotle had been squared, for what these philosophers seem to see in linguistic philosophy is not so much an opportunity for a synthesis but a reason why none is required.

It is amusing to reflect on how right, and yet how wrong, Lenin was about all this. His instinct told him quite rightly that empirio-criticism would lead to reaction, to denial of the outlook that required philosophers to help change the world as well as understand it. But his philosophical incompetence, his preoccupation with the Berkeleian analogy, and his lack of prophetic powers—shared by all of us—led him to a completely wrong analysis of how reaction would find its rationale in empiricism. In fact, hardly anyone uses the argument from empiricism via phenomenalism to either theism or mysticism which Lenin feared. Only pathetically loyal Marxists, totally oblivious to fact, persist in seeing it despite the virtually complete lack of all evidence. (They find shreds of it in some of the particularly obscure aphorisms of Wittgenstein.) In reality the connection *has* been established but along altogether different and new lines. From the premise that words are words and mean what they mean (which is roughly true) it is inferred that things are just what they are (and, by and large, what they seem), irrespective of how we choose to describe them (a dangerously misleading near-tautology, which is usually invoked just in the cases when it does not apply), and that in consequence we cannot ask whether in general some broad basic category is applicable, but only in particular whether in concrete cases it actually applies, from which it is inferred that there is no call for a philosophical, general, systematic, abstractly based criticism of our customs and beliefs (which may even be true but is certainly reactionary).

The three essays which in effect discuss these general issues of the status of valuation, etc., are Mr Weldon's, the late Miss Macdonald's and Mr Bambrough's. Mr Weldon's is a cheerful essay (impressively so to one of my melancholy disposition), clearly unperturbed by any of the issues it raises. One is tempted to wonder a little why, when cheerfulness not merely keeps breaking through but appears to be in undisputed possession, one should bother to go on philosophizing. This paper is not really about politics, it is about the status of philosophy in general, with particular reference to why it cannot have any substantive implications in politics. The premise is that philosophy is essentially a 'second-order' study, and this premise is neither substantiated nor consistent.

The argument intended to show that philosophy must be a second-order study is what may be called the argument from incompetence; 'What qualifications have philosophers . . . for . . . such a task?' (i.e. first-order work) (p. 22). The answer is meant to be an obvious *none*, and the rest is intended to follow. But this argument has plausibility only in empirical fields, in as far as philosophers, by definition, do not go in for empirical testing of their pronouncements. In a normative or evaluational field his *ex officio* commitment to the armchair does not automatically confine the philosopher to 'second-order' work, for in such a field the 'first-order' work does not necessarily take place outside the armchair either. And historically, if we must use this terminology and deal in these rough approximations, philosophers were people who did second-order work in factual fields, and first-order work in normative ones.

The inconsistency of Weldon's view emerges when he makes clear that there are some criteria by which political principles may be judged, some rules in the game of political discussion. 'Any particular set of [political principles] may be [and should be] criticized on non-philosophic grounds' (p. 33). Does it not occur to Weldon that what is called political philosophy does and should consist in the main of this substantive exercise and not of the allegedly neutral second-order study which would fit into his simple and preconceived *schema* of what philosophy may be? Now what is this activity, the practice of which Weldon admits and commends, if not philosophy? Or rather, how on earth can he justify his arbitrary *ukase* of withdrawing the appellation philosophy from that activity? (He could only justify it if, like the earlier positivists, he believed that activity to be essentially arbitrary and devoid of any rules; but he implies the contrary.)

In as far as Weldon tells us anything about politics, he tells us that political principles are essentially rules of conduct that are intended to be exempt from any questioning by those who subscribe to them. This will be news to debating societies, and as a piece of 'second-order' study is quite inaccurate; it simply is not true that (p. 32) 'it is pointless in this country to ask whether freedom is a good thing'. Weldon's account of political principles describes the attitude of some citizens of Alabama or the Transvaal to the question whether their sisters are to marry Negroes. It does *not* fit the complex and in large part reasoned political attitudes such as are discussed, for instance, in Professor Gallie's paper in the same volume. How is Weldon to account for the difference between the real 'discussion-stoppers' and sophisticated, rational ideologies? He might, it seems, want to admit this difference but make it extra-philosophical, by a ruling about the use of the word 'philosophy' which is as arbitrary as it is inconvenient. Or he might deny some of the difference by maintaining that the logical complexity, the apparent openness-to-argument of some ideologies is in fact spurious. But that simply is not always so. Even in a communist country the principle that means of production should not be privately owned is not an axiom but the conclusion of a long chain of reasoning to which some men have subscribed without being under pressure. The fact that in such countries a serious questioner of this principle might find himself in prison is a fact about the social structure of those countries, but not a part of the analysis of 'political principle'.

What leads Mr Weldon into this error is a curious confusion between *arguing* and *bargaining*. There is some case to be made out for the view that 'political principles' can be defined in terms of what one will not bargain about. If one's *principles* forbid some course of conduct, it follows that one should not be prepared to consider it even if the promised reward is raised.[8] But it simply does not follow that because we are not prepared to bargain, we are also not prepared to argue. On the contrary, if there is any relation between reasoning and haggling, it is an inverse one. The very fact that something can be bargained about makes it less susceptible to argument, for the subtle and subjective evaluations of barter cannot be conveyed by the crudities and sharpness of entailment and contradiction. Supply and demand curves do not express syllogistic reasoning. But when we firmly take our stand, *on principle*, then the proof of inconsistency, the discovery of an implicit consequence, become of the utmost importance. And it is no use objecting that argument would be pointless when we had already annunciated our principles: for we can take a stand on principle so as to inform the world that it is useless to try to raise the price, but not necessarily that it is useless to argue. Those of us, for instance, who object to racial segregation *on principle* mean by this that we consider the possible advantages that particular cases of segregation may bring irrelevant even if true. It does not mean that we are not prepared to argue, and argue in good faith, about why they are irrelevant, about why the principle seems to us important and valid. Only repressive societies employ the discussion-stoppers which Mr Weldon claims to see in all principles as such. Intellectually lively and free ones may know topics about which some or all members refuse to haggle, but they know none about which they will never reason (assuming that they are brought into the open by being made explicit); and this is *not* affected by the truism that you cannot discuss everything at the same time, that you must make assumptions in order to act and share some of those assumptions with your fellow-citizens, and that time for discussion is limited.

Weldon oddly enough is perfectly aware of one of the main ways in which analysis does have substantive implications, i.e. by destroying the epistemological props of political ideologies, doctrines about means of arriving at warranted principles; but he considers this to be a minor concession instead of giving it the weight it deserves. The interesting part of Weldon's essay lies where he attempts a diagnosis of why his second-order analysis is mistaken for first-order pronouncements. The reason is, he thinks, a misleading similarity between his second-order doctrine that principles are discussion-stoppers and the first-order statement in political sociology, associated with Marxism, that principles are devices by which ruling classes help to maintain themselves in power. Of course, Weldon wants to say that despite the appearance of similarity the two statements are about totally different things, but the only reason for thinking so is his dogma of the quite impassable iron curtain between first- and second-order talk (a dogma which does indeed seem to be a 'political principle', a discussion-stopper, in Weldon's sense, in Weldon's universe of discourse). Of course, there are indeed some differences. Marxism goes further in that its relativism about political doctrines specifies a mechanism which determines the emergence and decline of various principles: but in as far as Marxism says that political principles are *exhaustively* described in this way, it needs something like Weldon's positivism as a premise. Marxist relativism presupposes positivism.[9] So, far from being neutral, the kind of view that Weldon advocates is a necessary premise of a certain kind of first-order political outlook, even if it does not by itself entail it.

Mr Weldon says that the sin of the nineteenth-century philosophy was preaching, and he seems clear in his own mind that he and his fellows are not guilty of this. There is something comic about the missionary zeal with which Oxford, only belatedly weaned from seeing itself as the underwriter of right values, now preaches through Messrs Weldon, Quinton and others what one might call the doctrine of logically necessary non-commitment, the meta-ivory tower. Of course, they would say that they are preaching not non-commitment, but the irrelevance of philosophy to the substance of commitment. But it comes to the same. Philosophy *must* always be either a theory of the criteria of correct commitment, or the doctrine that its direction is arbitrary. Logical positivism said the latter: linguistic philosophers are too muddled about this for one to be able to say which alternative they adopt.

Mr Weldon's diagnosis of what is wrong with most old political theories (apart from preaching) is that they irresponsibly 'upgrade' the epistemological status of political principles. He seems to have *necessity* and *certainty* in mind, but fails to distinguish between two or three quite distinct further things that are involved: (1) The upgrading of non-cognitive or arbitrary things to cognitive or uniquely determined ones; (2) the exaggeration of the logical openness or generality of some principle, of replacing here/now by always/everyone; and (3) the exaggeration of the extent of diffusion of a principle or the number of people who accept it. For instance, a very high grade under (2) and a very low one under (1) is the essence of Mr Hare's ethical theory. Certainty, which Weldon chiefly has in mind, arises only if (1) has been answered affirmatively, and is almost totally independent of (3) which he also seems to be thinking of. Whom is Mr Weldon justified in castigating? The question of (3) must be left to comparative sociology. If high grades with respect of (2) are to be condemned, Weldon will first have to refute all the neo-Kantians amongst us; and with regard to (1) it is the common man rather than the philosopher who is generally responsible for erroneous, unjustified ascription of objective validity to moral judgments.

Of course, the general movement of which Mr Weldon is the ambassador to the *partes infidelium* of political theory is given to ruling out of court the idea that the common man might ever be *ex officio* speaking through his hat, that on some topic his very notions, *en gros* and irrespective of the individual use of them, should be absurd. (I am now going beyond anything said by Mr Weldon himself.) This view of the inherent rightness of the prejudices embodied in ordinary usages is not *quite* as absurd as it may seem to those unconditioned by recent philosophy, for it is a simple corollary of the interesting and plausible theory that meaning resides in use. Roughly speaking, if meaning 'is' use, then use cannot, naturally, be meaningless. Just as a generation ago philosophers sought the safe bedrock of meaningful discourse in sentences directly anchored to a piece of experience and not going beyond it, so today or yesterday they seek it in the locution whose undisputed use by ordinary speakers guarantees its meaningfulness (it all follows, you see). The view of philosophic procedure which follows from this is that you must either stick to these usage-authenticated locutions and be bound by their common rules, or, if you must depart from them, be conscious of, fully describe, and justify each such departure.[10] If you do not, you are either saying nothing when you think you are saying much, or at best there is no telling what it is that you *are* saying. This plausible-sounding and widely accepted account of how we should talk and think, based on a tacit model of meaningful discourse built up from safe watertight bricks supplied by established use, is in fact grotesque, and completely misrepresents the way in which any original ideas are reached, or (if the genetic question seems to you irrelevant) the way in which an original idea is of value. To think that ideas, philosophical or other, are built up, Meccano-wise, from prefabricated bits is as complete a fallacy as the older notion that science is built up from the safe little bits of unquestionable direct experience.

The history of these views really goes back to the healthy reaction of common sense to Bradley, to the kind of philosophy which held it possible to discover by abstract thought that everything we normally take for granted is fundamentally mistaken. The reaction that Bradleian paradoxes provoked would have been hard to formulate other than 'linguistically'; to say 'we all normally think so, so it must be true' sounds feeble.[11] But to say 'we all normally use this term in this way, so that this is, until we choose to change it, what it means', sounds quite all right, and within limits which have not been observed, it *is* all right.

But the fallacy which it suggests, or which has been inferred from it, apart from the prejudging of normative questions, is that meaning is manifest, that it is fairly easy for a competent, honest, unpretentious mind to tell what is sense and what is nonsense by simply looking carefully at how we normally use words. Professor Popper has rightly drawn our attention to the fact that the error of Cartesianism resides in the assumption that *truth* is manifest, and the same holds of *meaningfulness*. Much modern philosophy is Cartesianism with regard to meaning, Cartesianism with regard to truth having been abandoned and truth itself consigned to the scientist (cf. Mr Weldon's remarks about first- and second-order studies). We are no longer concerned with the attempts to make the boundaries and typologies of meaning manifest by means of an explicit criterion —that was logical positivism proper; we are concerned with the idea that meaninglessness, absurdity, can be safely and manifestly avoided by sticking to an established use and only departing from it, if at all, in explicitly announced ways.

But common usage is not a safe way of avoiding absurdity, and there is *no* safe way. Above all, even unexplained departures from it are not safe indices of absurdity. Linguistic philosophy disclaims having a general recipe: but in its *practice* if not in avowed doctrine, in what it counts as a problem and as a solution, it uses something like this. The inadequate and self-defeating nature of that way is beautifully if quite unintentionally illustrated by Mr Quinton in the discussion quoted, when from the plausible use-meaning tie-up he arrives at the absurdities he then has to defend, such as the total irrelevance of philosophy to life and even to religious belief; he in fact performs the logical miracle of deducing from a formal theory of meaning the substantive doctrine of epiphenomenalism of thought. (He notices this and by an uneasy qualification avoids committing himself to this outright.)[12] The possession of such remarkable logical powers should make him beware and re-examine his own premises.

The truth of the matter is that just as in science many counter-intuitive theories may be valid,[13] so in the necessarily oblique, un-formalized, often second-order, unhomogeneous pursuit that is philosophy, in exploring what has meaning and what has not and how that which has meaning comes to have it, there is no simple general test for arriving at our conclusions. Neither verification nor actual speech habits are master-keys for all problems, infallible criteria of a manifest meaningfulness. The only thing to do is to explore the consequences of our assumptions and see what happens. (As indeed Quinton does. I do not mind the fact that the consequences which he has deduced are absurd. It is that which makes his experiment useful in showing the limitations of the 'use' theory of meaning.

What I do mind is his obvious devotion to the actual practices of mankind—linguistic *and* other, such as going to church—as something that *cannot* be criticized by philosophical criteria. This devotion seems too firm to be shaken by the oddity of the inferences he has drawn from it.) I am not recommending a return to oracular mysteries such as 'Time is unreal', though I am pointing out that the so-called Ordinary Language School has its own inverted versions of them; and I am not denying that some absurdities are manifest, only that absurdity as such is, or that it has a manifest criterion.

The relevance of all this to the up-grading of moral and political principles is that this is a matter in which the common man, ordinary usage, may well be and probably is basically mistaken. I do not suppose that the philosopher can sensibly correct the common man in his assumption that material objects exist or that time is real, but he *can* set him right on the subject of the objectivity of morals. For in this matter it is the common man or ordinary usage, aided by some but not all philosophers, that is guilty of up-grading, irresponsible or not, if up-grading has occurred.

The late Miss Macdonald's essay about 'Natural rights' succeeds in really being about that subject to a greater extent than Weldon's essay succeeds in being about political principles, but still, it is essentially an exercise along the following lines: given that all meaningful discourse is either factual, or logical, or evaluative, what kind of meaning can be ascribed to assertions of 'natural rights'? The answer is what you might expect—that claims of natural rights 'really' fall into the third category and that it is misleading and even dangerous to misinterpret them as falling into either of the former two. That the argument is actually carried on within these terms of reference is a little odd in view of the fact that these are not the limits that Miss Macdonald had set herself: on page 37 she says 'there are an indefinite number of different types of proposition and other forms of human utterance'. In other words, she pays lip-service to what I have called the later stage of linguistic philosophy, the nebulous polymorphism-of-language tradition which tries to seek out the variety of actual linguistic activities, but the real logic of her thought follows the more clean-cut rules of earlier logical positivism. The real brass tacks of her argument come in the final part of the paper when the logic of evaluation in general is discussed. Making less use than Weldon of the first/second-order distinction, she nevertheless tries to steer some middle course between saying that rational criteria exist and admitting that the moves in this game are arbitrary. But can one really have it both ways, or rather, neither way? *Qua* observer, perhaps one can, perhaps one can be content with saying that both elements are present: arguments in politics, aesthetics, etc.,

are indeed a mixture of rational presentation of evidence and of trying, causally, to produce an effect. As Miss Macdonald says, 'the
lawyer . . . uses voice, gesture, facial expression . . . in order to
influence . . .'. But when we think of ourselves, in the first person,
when we are interested in the rights of the case, then there are no two
ways about it: to discover a mere causal influence is to *unmask* and
neutralize it.[14]

The third of the essays which is in effect about valuation in general
is Mr Bambrough's discussion of 'Plato's political analogies'. It is
to my mind by far the most interesting of the three. It is in effect
about one particular, crucial analogy, namely the one between
political and ethical expertise on the one hand, and knowledge in
more indisputably cognitive fields on the other. Mr Bambrough
neatly opposes the Platonic error—because value problems can be
rationally discussed, therefore answers to them are cognitive—and
the anti-Platonic error—because answers to value-problems are not
uniquely determined and do not embody knowledge, therefore they
are beyond the pale of reason. Of course Mr Bambrough cannot,
any more than the other two authors, show us concretely how the
latter error can be avoided once we have rejected the former, apart
from repeating the old suggestion, best expressed by Hume but here
attributed to Mrs Barbara Wootton, that it is a good thing if we get
our facts right first. Still Mr Bambrough's point is a neat one and I
should use it to bring out something that has been neglected of late,
namely that dubious entities have in traditional philosophy had the
important role of explaining how indeterminate or semi-determinate
fields could be determinate, in plainer language of being guarantors
of values. The current diagnosis of Platonic mythologies over-
stresses the fact that such entities are would-be nominees or words
that aren't really names, and tends to omit that they were also
meant to function as arbiters, as judges or decision-procedures.

Of the essays which really deal with specific political points, Mr
W. J. Rees neatly analyses the theory of sovereignty. This is indeed
a careful, painstaking, workmanlike job which does the kind of thing
which modern philosophy claims it can do. It leaves us with a set of
clear distinctions and answerable specific questions where before
there was an embarrassing muddle and nebulous questions which did
not seem to allow of any answer, nor yet of being disregarded. Mr
Rees's analysis is too detailed for it to be possible to reproduce it
here, but, very roughly speaking, it makes clear that the notion of
sovereignty was meant to do a variety of jobs that are in fact independent: mainly, to provide a final decision-procedure for legal issues
and yet also a guarantee that right will prevail; to embody morality
in law and law in force, and endow the result with a permanence,

with an aura of trustworthiness. In this would-be fusion of *de jure* and *de facto* infallibility it is meant to do for society what God does for the universe, provide a reassurance that ultimately the management is sound. The appeal of the doctrine must be rather like that of the kind of belief in God which is an unwillingness to be seen in an improperly run universe, like the unwillingness of respectable people to be seen in questionable establishments.[15] Reading Mr Rees one feels that one has the logical mechanics of the idea of sovereignty plain before one; it is not clear that one will want to use the notion again. But the fact that it is a post-mortem is not a criticism of the analysis.

Mr Quinton's brief essay on punishment is at first sight rather exciting in that it seems actually to get somewhere with a live problem. On second thoughts I do not think the argument gets so far after all. Mr Quinton claims to have resolved the antinomy between retributivism and utilitarianism with regard to punishment by pointing out that retribution is what punishment *means*—a logical theory— whilst utilitarianism is about the conditions under which *in general* we should punish—an ethical theory, and never the twain shall meet. This is a nice point, and certainly the air is clearer once it is made; but unfortunately logic and ethics are not so easily separable. The reason why 'punishment' means what it does to people is in part that they subscribe to a certain ethical theory, and the fact that the word means what it does to them helps to keep them supporters of that ethical theory. Similarly, whilst Utilitarianism is primarily an ethical theory about the proper role of punishment in general, it is also a kind of normative–logical doctrine about what the word sensibly should mean. (All this would have to be worked out in more detail with reference to the indisputably useful distinction borrowed by Quinton from Sir David Ross between asking what *kind* of action should be punished and asking on what *particular* occasion one should punish.) We really have been here before, a century ago. J. S. Mill drew the distinction underlying this article, *nur mit ein bischen anderen Worten*, when he distinguished between the sentiment (roughly equals *meaning*, in modern parlance) underlying punishment, which he admitted to be retributivist, and that which is truly moral in it.[16] And if the utilitarian does not need the distinction or is already using it, the retributivist does not either. A defender of capital punishment would, I imagine, tell Mr Quinton not merely that punishment *means* inflicting something on the guilty, but that it *rightly* means this, or, if you like, that what is meant by this is a good thing.[17] So, alas, the advance-by-clarification claimed by Quinton turns out to be illusory. It is interesting to note that the premise used, the separability of ethical and descriptive discourse, is one which members of this school are otherwise at present keen to criticize. Terms can have meanings in ways calculated to support certain valuations; and, in turn, revaluations can call for changes in connotations.

Mr Mayo's essay, 'Is there a case for the general will?' is less an application of modern philosophical method than an attempt to go against its current and say some kind words about the General Will whilst remaining intelligible to members of that tradition. The claim that Mr Mayo is making is that there is a kind of pragmatic justification for using the term *will* with regard to societies, as there is for using it with regard to people. What he appears to have in mind is the fact that social situations, climates of opinions, etc., do seem sometimes to call for things which none of the individuals composing them necessarily or explicitly want. Indeed, social historians and anthropologists might find it hard to abstain from this manner of speaking. I think we may agree with this claim.

The last of the essays in this group, Dr Glanville Williams's spirited discussion of 'The controversy concerning the word "law" ' was first published in 1945, but in its spirit and analytical tools belongs to what may be called the Stone Age of logical positivism. It is, however, great fun, in that the author is obviously greatly thrilled with his ideas, passionately committed to them, and derives great pleasure from eliminating the heresies which he is castigating. There is about this essay none of that air of indifference, of knowing-it-all in philosophy but turning to the lower spheres of social thought from professional obligation, which hangs around some of the other papers.

When I say that the spirit of this article belongs to the first enthusiastic dawn of positivism, I mean that Dr Williams is overjoyed by the discovery that words are—words. This is perfectly true. The rest of the argument can be easily inferred; that the word 'law' means whatever we care to define it as meaning, and that in consequence the famous controversy about 'the nature of law' is spurious. The fact that this magnificently clear and simple argument is made to last for about twenty pages does not mean that they are dull ones— far from it—for the author illustrates his point, or rather the (to him) surprising failure of others to see it, in a lively manner from all over the range of the controversy with which he is intimately familiar. The essence of Dr Williams's attitude is conveyed by the quotation he uses from *Alice Through the Looking-Glass*:[18] 'The question is which is to be master—that's all.' Dr Williams has no doubts at all about this. He means to be master and tell words what they will do, and he will not have *them* telling *him*.

This is all very jolly, rather like a little boy driving a steam-roller and drawing our attention to who is master. Unfortunately it is not quite as easy to be master as he thinks: and not merely because the word 'law' already has a deeply engrained meaning which will not be psychologically eradicated by a new definition. If a new word, 'haw', were used and then incorporated in the traditional contexts of the word 'law', the difficulty would persist. Above all, the sharp separation between definition and synthetic, contingent characterization simply does not hold of language as actually used. It is at best a very illuminating model which separates what in actual use is fused, and thus brings out the elements that go into that normal use. As we actually use language, a definition *can*, however para-doxical this may seem to Dr Williams, be contradicted by facts. For instance, if the factual evidence brought to bear against Austin by Lawrence and quoted on page 145 is valid, if municipal law would break down if every rule had to be enforced, then it may indeed follow that Austin's definition of law is invalid. It may do so by showing that Austin's definition would then cover nothing or virtually nothing, and as Austin presumably thought that he was defining a far from empty concept, this shows his definition to be mistaken.

Immensely important moral issues hinge on how we define 'law'. To take the extreme but plausible cases, it depends on this definition whether the violation of recognized but unenforced rules of inter-national morality is 'illegal', and whether the carrying out of an admittedly inhuman act commanded by a *de facto* authority is 'legal'. What view we take on ('merely'?) terminological desirability in these cases depends in part on our moral outlook, but also in part on our possibly implicit sociological or historical views, on our assessment of the context and consequences of either 'terminological' alternative. This shows that how we choose to define 'law' depends directly on our moral views and indirectly on our convictions about matters of fact—and the latter may be mistaken, and the former are open to correction. Hence to say that we can define the word 'law' as we please is to misapply grossly the truth that in the end words derive their meaning from human use and that we can change it by our decision. To paraphrase Schopenhauer's admirable aphorism about human freedom, *we can make words mean whatever we will, but we cannot will what we will.*

Of course, there is an important kernel of truth in Dr Williams's thesis. It may be that lawyers are professionally inclined to be un-perceptive of the truth of nominalism, and I even suspect that logical realism may be a fiction necessary for jurisprudence. (If so, no wonder Dr Williams gets excited by the discovery of nominalism.) But I cannot resist pointing out to Dr Williams how easy it is to refute him by the very argument he himself employs over and over again. For Dr Williams is entitled to use the word *definition* itself just as he pleases—for he will be master in his own verbal house—but what right has he to prescribe to others, who also like being masters, how they should use it? Note that, not being professional philosophers but lawyers, they are not obliged to be familiar with the classification of kinds of definition, nor to make their choice amongst these explicit. What they mean by 'definition' and what, being masters too, they are perfectly well entitled to mean by it, is *not* 'prescriptive definition' of the logical kind which clearly separates what analytically belongs to the concept from what does not, but on the contrary *definition* as that term is normally understood. In that sense 'definition' means, roughly, the specification of characteristics which must be present if the defined word is to apply, *provided that* the range of application so determined corresponds more or less with the range determined by an intuitive appeal to what things are covered by the word in question (unless there are very strong reasons for disregarding that range); and with the proviso that no one of the set of characteristics is by itself absolutely essential but can be shown to be 'false'. In this sense, a definition can be corrected or refuted, *even if* it was introduced by the person using it with the phrase 'what *I* shall mean by X is . . .'. It is still usually understood that if '. . .' is shown to determine a range quite unlike the one which the speaker had intuitively supposed X to be covering, then his definition can be said to be erroneous.

In fact Dr Williams is better aware than I am of the issues that hinge on the definition of 'law', but he persists in his conviction that a definition can do no wrong. If, *per impossibile*, everyone were fully aware of what his definitions entailed, Dr Williams might be right in the sense in which he intends. But we do not know what our definitions entail, and they *are* mistaken (or 'mistaken', if you wish) when they turn out to have unacceptable implications. The notion of a pure definition, unassailable by any fact, is a logician's phantasy. It is a device usable for short-term purposes only and not for long-term definition of crucial concepts.

Which sense of 'definition' the legal theorists criticized by Dr Williams were using can only be decided by looking at the logic of their argument, rather than pre-judged by the assumption that there is only one rightful sense, and the very fact that Dr Williams can criticize them along the lines he does shows that what they tacitly had in mind was definition in a sense other than his preferred one. But by what right is he implicitly suggesting that 'definition' *must* in the nature of things have just the rather inconvenient meaning *he* attributes to it? It looks as if at least one word had been a bit of a master with him after all.

There remains the heterogenous essays not fitting in the above groups. Professor Gallie's 'Liberal morality and socialist morality' is the most genuinely political of all the papers. Of the essays discussed it is almost alone in being about politics and morals in a sense that would be understood by people reaching the subject from an interest in politics and not in logic or epistemology, and it is such without in any way abandoning academic standards. Professor Gallie hopes to endow contemporary academic moral philosophy with a little flesh and blood by posing the question *one morality or many*?

He distinguishes between the 'monarchic' and the 'polyarchic' view of morals, between the view that there is but one correct answer to moral questions and the view that there are many equally valid moral systems. I wonder whether he does not overestimate the unpopularity, even in the past, of the polyarchic view? Is it not a new name for relativism, or perhaps for what one might call non-pejorative relativism? Both Hume and the kind of moral philosophy most closely associated with contemporary philosophy are monarchic only at the formal level, holding that all moral valuations necessarily share certain logical characteristics. With regard to the normative *content* these moral systems are polyarchic and (*vide supra*) they have been much criticized for this. But Professor Gallie is almost alone in this collection in that he actually analyses current political outlooks —socialism and liberalism—as well as discussing abstractly the logic of such analysis, and he does this in a very interesting way. His paper does *not* call for the comment that the book should have been re-named 'Philosophy and its lack of implications for politics and society'.

Finally, there is Mr Peter Laslett's article on 'The face to face society'. Two souls seem to dwell within Cambridge University, one committed to idolatry of clarity, the other not. Mr Laslett belongs to the latter. The world of thought in which he moves is certainly not that of the linguistic philosophers, nor is it one with which I am familiar. I have to try to reconstruct for myself why some things are obviously true or obviously problematical to Mr Laslett, and I do not always succeed.

At one point, Mr Laslett speaks of 'us', 'dating our arrival with the Renaissance'. If he had pondered the total difference in language between himself and some of the contemporaneous authors he is editing he might have been less inclined rashly to imply community of outlook to the intellectuals of four centuries. For instance, whilst not sharing to the full Dr Williams's enthusiasm for a nominalistic outlook on definitions, I really cannot make much sense of the longish passage in which Mr Laslett bewails the lack of a definition of the individual and seems to be implying that this lack bodes ill not merely for thought but even, in some circumstances, for societies. I really don't see what it is that he is missing. But I do wonder whether Mr Laslett simply did not see the point of some of the essays he is editing (especially Dr Williams's), or whether he saw it but is in total disagreement—in which case one cannot but take off one's hat to his editorial impartiality.

Mr Laslett's central distinction is between 'face to face society', in which 'all activities either are, or can be, carried on by means of conversation', and territorial society in which this is not possible. This seems to me somewhat to overstress the role of *conversation*, and Mr Laslett does not attempt to specify the inner mechanics of this process over and above reminding us that it is largely alogical and that reacting with the whole personality is involved. This might be called the *mystique of Mrs Dale's Diary*.

Britain is a territorial society consisting of a large number of fellow-listeners to *Mrs Dale*, and Mr Laslett's point is (not quite in these words) that the relationship of these numerous fellow-listeners to each other and to their leaders is different from the kind of relationship obtaining within Mrs Dale's family, and that we are not sufficiently aware of this difference. He points out that any collectively active society that is too large to be a face to face society *must* find within itself a subgroup that can be face to face and that will act for it. The contention that only face to face societies are capable of interacting and reaching decisions, of 'mutual response in terms of whole personalities' seems to me to verge on the tautology that only those who can interact can interact, though there may be no harm in that. The doctrine of the need for a small intimately interacting group within a larger one may be the Iron Law of Oligarchy under a new name, and Mr Laslett may well have provided us with an interesting clue to the latter. Mr Laslett seems to be suggesting that political theory in the past suffered through failing to consider the territorial un-Dalesque nature of modern society,[19] and he makes some general suggestions towards understanding the working of such society. But to say that they are 'religious' (because they involve the 'internalization of norms') does not seem to me to throw any more light on territorial society than 'interaction of total personalities' does on small intimate groups. Also, I am rather doubtful about the suggestion that territorial society is less rational than intimate society. Its reactions may be less familiar, but the very fact that, being large and diffuse, it has to make use of formal methods of communications, causes a diminution of what has been aptly called 'the centuple-think of rural life', which, however cosy to those at home in it, seems to me the quintessence of the non-rational. But just what Mr Laslett wishes to do with his distinctions, just where his central conclusion lies, I have not altogether understood.

1957

Notes

1 Logical positivism may even formally
have implications of a first order kind.
Take a system of thought S which
contains a number of metaphysical
propositions m_1, m_2, . . ., etc., and a
number of valuations e_1, e_2, . . ., etc.,
and proposition n asserting that all
constituent propositions of S are equally
valid. The assessment which logical
positivism necessarily makes of m_1,
m_2, . . ., etc., in conjunction with n,
has obvious implications for e_1, e_2, . . .,
etc. There is no reason why we should
abandon n. Many systems of thought
are in fact complicated versions of the
schema S.
2 Cf. A letter by Mrs Mary Warnock
in *Encounter*, 4, January 1955, 63–4,
rebutting criticisms of contemporary
philosophy by Mr Philip Toynbee in
the previous number of the same
journal. Mr Toynbee was technically
quite wrong, and substantially right in
equating contemporary philosophy with
logical positivism. From the viewpoint
of what the general educated public
wants to know, the differences are not
great. The critic of linguistic philosophy
faces the dilemma: *either* he will be
accused of being out of date, *or* of not
having substantiated his charges, for the
latest and most typical representative of
the movement doesn't publish much.
3 Cf. Mr Quinton's contribution to
'Philosophy and belief' in the
Twentieth Century, 157, June 1955,
495–521.
4 Ibid.
5 As for example in Professor J. L.
Austin's 'Other minds', in *Logic and
Language*, A. Flew, ed. (second series),
Oxford 1953, 123–58; see especially the
summary on 158. For expansion of
my argument, see 'Use and meaning',
Cambridge Journal, 4, 1951, 753–61.
6 I need hardly say that in either case,
and especially with regard to the latter, i.e.
linguistic philosophy, my diagnosis of
what it ethically and politically entails
or fails to entail is based on a
simplified model which doesn't perhaps
quite correspond to any individual
thinker. With this qualification, I should
claim to have captured by means of that
simplified model the essence of a
common way of thought.
7 'Philosophy and belief.'
8 Though even this analysis may be
questioned, for we have the opinion of
no less an authority on first-order moral
language than Lord Halifax that there
are times in the lives of nations when
expediency takes precedence over
principles. Cf. Chaim Weizmann, *Trial
and Error*, London 1949, 496.
9 Cf. H. B. Acton, *The Illusion of an
Epoch*, London 1955, 109.

10 For a striking example of this kind
of reasoning, see Professor H. L. Hart,
'Is there knowledge by acquaintance?',
Proceedings of the Aristotelian Society,
suppl. vol. 23, 1949, 69–90; see
especially 79 f. It is interesting to
observe Professor Hart's obviously
sincere conviction that the limpid
clarities of Bertrand Russell's thought
can be shown by this method to be in
some deeper sense inadequately
endowed with meaning. This type of
linguistic philosopher finds depths of
unsuspected lack of meaning, just as his
metaphysical predecessor found most
unsuspected significances. The common
man on whose behalf these doubly-
sophisticated philosophers defend
pristine usage would be even more
surprised by their discoveries than he
had been by those of the
metaphysicians.
11 Even if, according to Mr T. S.
Eliot, it is a sound principle of classical
Indian logic.
12 'Philosophy and belief', 519.
13 Cf. J. O. Wisdom, 'Psycho-analytic
technology', *British Journal for the
Philosophy of Science*, 7, 1956–7, 13–28;
see especially 16.
14 To avoid misunderstanding, I
should perhaps state quite explicitly
that I am not criticizing Miss Macdonald's and Mr Weldon's crucial
premise about valuations not being
testable as factual assertions are. What I
am criticizing is a certain evasiveness in
facing the consequences of this position,
and certain inconsistencies that arise
when this piece of positivism is
incorporated in the broader linguistic
philosophy of today. The unwillingness
to face this issue, often disguised as an
impatient and almost irritable
unwillingness to admit that there is a
problem that is being evaded, is
characteristic of the movement's position
on this question. It is found in the
otherwise much subtler analysis of Mr
Hare. Cf. R. Hare, *The Language of
Morals*, London 1952, 195, and
'Universalisability', *Proceedings of the
Aristotelian Society*, n.s. 55, 1954–5,
295–312; see especially 302–4.
15 Fewer people believe in sovereignty
nowadays than believe in God. I
imagine this is because the necessary
combination of *de facto* and *de jure*
characteristics can only be located with
plausibility in a transcendental realm,
and for some reason people are at
present more disinclined to be
transcendentalists about society than
about the universe at large.
16 J. S. Mill, *Utilitarianism*, ch. V.
17 Actually, Mr Quinton strengthens
his case by reducing retributivism to the

doctrine that guilt is the necessary but not sufficient condition of punishment, which he defends by pointing out the discretionary element in penal systems. Though technically correct, this misrepresents the spirit of retributivism, for 'guilt' also entails the desirability of punishment, even if it does so with certain limiting conditions that may be vague. But in any case, even for this weak form of retributivism, my general point holds. Even this meaning of 'punishment' embodies an ethical theory, and the meaning may be altered if the theory is abandoned. Consider the *hilfsbegriff* of 'objective guilt' in Arthur Koestler's *Darkness at Noon* (tr. Daphne Hardy), London 1940, where a radically utilitarian attitude of punishment is squared with the old Quintonian meaning of the term by inventing a new sense of 'guilt'. As far as logic goes the trick could have been brought off as well by a new sense of 'punishment'.

18 The defects of philosophy may have something to do with the fact that there are too many philosophers whose favourite reading is Jane Austen, just as defects of economics may be connected with excessive dependence on Lewis Carroll. But the occasional quotations from *Alice* in philosophy show healthy cross-disciplinary stimulation.

19 This might be a fair comment on Professor Oakeshott, as Laslett seems to be implying at one place, but seems to me inapplicable to a great deal of political theory. But Laslett discounts this by declaring, flatly, that the key notion of such philosophy as avoids this criticism, namely *representation*, is a 'typical muddle'. Why?

Chapter 5   Behind the barricades at LSE

> Legal authority still rested with the governors, and might need
> to be exercised by them in an emergency, but they came more
> and more to lack the intimate knowledge of the school necessary
> to enable them to decide wisely, and they lacked legitimacy
> in the sense . . . [of being] recognized by those over whom it
> is exercised.
> . . . The governors . . . and this was true even of the Standing
> Committee . . . were left with less and less to do, uncertain
> of their role and uncomfortable; cold-shouldered collectively
> by the academics, and pushed out of touch with the life of the
> school, yet still . . . possessed of the final authority, *especially
> in a crisis* (italics mine).

This devastating comment on the internal government of the
London School of Economics comes not from some bolshie-minded
academic, but from page 6 of Mr Harry Kidd's book *The Trouble at
L.S.E.* (O.U.P.). Harry Kidd was, under the director, the senior
administrator of the LSE at the time of the first wave of troubles. He
was manifestly an efficient, humane and devoted university civil ser-
vant. Almost by accident, the role of prosecutor was thrust upon him.

Subsequently, his position became such that he chose to resign
from the school. Self-deprecatingly, he called himself 'expendable'.
In fact, his life and career suffered at least as violent an upheaval as
did the recently dismissed lecturers, and after a far longer period of
dedication to the LSE. It is remarkable that the book shows no trace
of bitterness.

Nevertheless, one may suppose that the wound was deep, and
that the book had to be written so that, as the saying goes, he could
get it out of his system. He does it, as one might expect from an
administrator, with quiet decorum and attention to fact and orderly
presentation, rather than with panache. (A sense of theatre might
have been a greater asset during the crises, but none of our administrators, so far, has displayed this flair.)

He tells us that the policy of Sir Sydney Caine—the director to whom Kidd was visibly devoted—was to transfer more and more power from the governors and their standing committee, to the academic staff, because 'a university must approach to being a self-governing community of scholars'. I suspect that we academics feel little gratitude for this transfer to us of day-to-day administrative decisions and chores. We noticed that it was happening, and cursed, loudly or quietly, according to temperament.

We never saw it as a transfer of *power*. Most of us are only too happy to leave such power in the hands of correct and dedicated administrators, if only to keep it away from pseudo-academics, whose idle hands and minds tempt them in this direction.

The power we do want, however, is to have our voices heard and heeded, as of right and not intermittently and selectively, when really important moral and political decisions are taken. The dismissal of a colleague—apparently the first such dismissal since Bertrand Russell's case during the First World War—in a political, and legally ambiguous case, is just such a crisis. It is one in which the moral tone of the institution may be decided for decades. But at this juncture, real power returns—*where*?

In law, as Harry Kidd tells us, to the board of governors, a body of some eighty members. In fact, to its standing committee, a body of about a dozen, of whom *three* were, in Kidd's day, elected by the academic staff. (This number has since been raised.)

How about the nine or so others? Apparently they emerge from the wider body of governors by some process of spontaneous generation. Their elections are not, it appears, contested. I am not quite sure about this, for it is perfectly possible to teach at LSE for two decades, and achieve senior rank, without having any such information easily available.

If power is nominally vested in eighty people, who are distinguished and busy, who meet intermittently without any assurance of continuity, who can hardly organize parties to articulate given viewpoints and press for the election of spokesmen in contested elections; and if in these conditions power is delegated to a small subgroup, what are the effective consequences?

Harry Kidd does not spell out the answer, though he provides us with all the premises. Ironically, he does spell out, a few pages later (10 and 11), the parallel reasons for why it is that the Students' Union is so very unrepresentative. A minority controls it because the average student is 'apathetic', laudably so: as Kidd puts it, the average student 'might be someone who found things in life more interesting than the affairs of a union . . .'. These other things might even include his studies.

Kidd quotes, with approval, the union's own newspaper: 'At

weekly union meetings we watch small boys playing games . . . behind this democratic façade there lurks, the old dog of rumour tells us, a process of self-generating nepotism.'

The average governor must also be 'apathetic', in the sense that he can hardly have the time, energy, or presumption to organize pressure groups which could actually affect decisions. In fact, it appears that some governors have recently resigned in protest against their own impotence.

The difference between power in the union and among the governors seems to be that in the latter case there is no façade, democratic or other, but secrecy instead. Without relying on the old dog of rumour, who in any case did not waste much of his time whispering to me, but turning instead to the younger dog of structural analysis, I cannot but entertain the following supposition: when power is nominally vested in a group so constituted that it cannot possibly exercise it, it must in fact be held by some other and smaller group.

This smaller group need not be stable or identical with the standing committee, though it must presumably have an important voice in its composition. It need not, and perhaps does not, interfere much at normal times. In a crisis, however, it becomes the locus of decision, if decisions in any coherent sense are taken at all.

Kidd's comments on the profound separation of the governors from the daily life of the school must also apply to this informal inner party, if it exists. Of course, if the school had a viable, acceptable and effective formal constitution one would not need to speculate about its informal power structure.

It might then also be capable of dealing with the admittedly difficult consequences of the present situation. (I would not wish to be over-confident here.) It might then devise a way of dealing with the implications of the following facts: this is a school of social studies, the most important one in the country.

Within the social sciences, one important tradition is inspired by the idea that radical change (i.e. revolution) is possible and desirable. One could hardly give an adequate account of the scientific study of society without taking this viewpoint into consideration. In a teaching staff of nearly 300 members, representatives of this viewpoint could only be excluded by some deliberate political test.

At a time when, as their opponents gleefully remind them, the workers are quite un-revolutionary, and the only glimmerings of revolutionary activism are found among ethnic minorities and among students, the adherents of that viewpoint face a painful dilemma, between hypocrisy and the endorsement of student violence.

Their views may indeed be absurd: but that does not distinguish them from many other views widely held and academically tolerated. What does distinguish them, just at present, is that these views must

lead them to flirt, or worse, with university disruption (partly for
lack of better causes with realistic prospects).

Keeping violence out of the university must of course be our
first priority. But whenever possible this should be done by discreetly
encouraging hypocrisy rather than by dismissals. Expulsion should
not be multiplied beyond necessity. An authority with political
flair might have contented itself with applying it only to the case
in which incitement to violence was proved in a straightforward
sense, rather than in a strained, metaphysical one.

Before expelling a colleague, ought we not to be concerned with
whether or not he is basically a man of academic values, which,
however, are in conflict, in his heart and in reality, with the requirements of a Che Quixote conscience? Our far-away politbureau
clearly could not possess such intimate knowledge when it had to
decide in the case of Mr Robin Blackburn.

But did its members solicit such information from, say, Blackburn's immediate superior? Not a bit of it. Blackburn's superior at
the time happened to be the impeccably pluralist, mid-Atlantic
Professor Robert McKenzie, a man hardly open to the suspicion
that he views Blackburn through some rosy Castroist spectacles. But
his considered opinion was not solicited by the committee which had
come to a fateful decision. He had to beg to be allowed to have his
views considered.

A distant authority, vacillating between the posture of Charles
Laughton on the bridge of the *Bounty*, and a frightened legal for-
malism which is alas far from convincing, even on its own terms, does
not seem ideally equipped for handling this difficult situation. Those
of us who think about these issues, or are forced by their own
position to do so, will find much valuable material in Harry Kidd's
book.

1969

Chapter 6   The panther and the dove

Reflections on rebelliousness and its milieux

An American professor, a man in no way lacking in sympathy for the Protest Movement, a man with a fine record of active social commitment, one of the main organizers of the national Teach-Ins, was describing to me the state of mind of some 'activist' students he had been addressing. He did not mind in the least that they were ignorant. He did not mind that they could not tell a coherent argument from an expression of attitude. All this could be remedied. What he did mind, he regretfully admitted, was that they did not seem in the very least interested in such a distinction.

Yet this is a movement of intellectuals, and it passionately wills itself to be a doctrinal one. The specific grievances it feels and the injustices it champions are meant to be united by some common thread of doctrine. Others have wished to be open-minded and were in fact doctrinaire: this movement wills itself to be doctrinal, but is in fact doctrinally invertebrate. Such doctrines or rather slogans as it possesses ('alienation' and so on) could endow no one with an intellectual backbone. Perhaps the best way to approach the movement is through an attempt to understand this paradox.

The movement is international, and its deepest roots are not geographically specific. Nevertheless, it may be best to begin with local sources. Two intertwined strands lead up to the present: one can be traced from the 1930s, the other from 1956.

The term *intelligentsia* is hardly used in England to describe any local phenomenon, and the term intellectual, as a noun, only with a feeling of awkwardness. It sounds pejorative and foreign. 'Are we workers, peasants, or intellectuals, Fotheringay?' asks one clubman of another, in an Osbert Lancaster cartoon. A don is a don and not an intellectual. All this is significant. An *intelligentsia* is by definition a class dissociated from the beliefs and values of its own society, by virtue of a superior education. In this sense, England has not had an intelligentsia for a very long time. At some periods, it looked as if it might acquire one—but, in the end, social conscience and criticism found channels for expression and action within the existing structure. Intelligent awareness did not face a stalemate and did not need to face the alternative of either rebellion or inner emigration. In all this, the situation differed markedly from that of other, less fortunate lands. Even the secularized nonconformist conscience learnt to speak Hegelian, and used this idiom to draft the foundations of something as constructive and unrevolutionary as the liberal welfare state.[1]

The real significance of the 1930s is that they constitute an exception to this happy state. In the 1930s, intellect felt both outraged and helpless. In retrospect, the remarkable thing is not that some intelligent people became Marxists, but that some did not. The depression had unmasked the economic reality behind liberal society. The fascist regimes, and the ambiguous attitude towards them of liberal states, had unmasked its political reality. The façade was down, and what seemed to be behind it was not pretty to behold. Admittedly, neither the very existence of the Soviet Union, nor the political realities within it, fitted the Marxist analysis: but these two solitary discordant facts could hardly outweigh the others.

Facing a terrible and in fact insoluble situation, the generation of the 1930s really did rather well. Looked at in detail, the antics of some of its members may look comic; and some of them did not know clearly whether they were opposed to fascism or to fagging in Public Schools, and had some difficulty in distinguishing the two. But all this hardly matters. There was *no* solution. Fascism could only be and was stopped by force, and the force was in the end applied by those members of their own societies who did not share their anti-military values, and by Stalin. The only thing the intellectuals as such could do was to register a protest, and this they did with lasting effect. Their protest left a deep mark, and affected the collective conscience for good.

The real failure of this generation came not before the war, but after it. Before the war, they had faced an impossible situation which had no peaceful solution, and events moved faster than they could think. But after the war, things were different and, on the whole, much better. Now there was time enough, and a situation which, even if not satisfactory in all respects, at least offered a basis from which to work. It was in this situation that the real failure occurred. The interesting case is not that of the Philbys who never extricated themselves from the 1930s, but of that majority which sank back, exhausted evidently by their earlier exertions, into an uncritical and indiscriminate complacency. The real work of demolishing Stalinism intellectually had been done by others (Koestler and Orwell in literature, Popper in philosophy, Aron in sociology): if this lot joined in, they did not add anything, other than a kind of routinization.

The post-war rejection of left extremism was not, in England, marred by any McCarthyism. They came quietly and no one harassed them or called them to account. On the contrary: the movement was only eased along and gently lubricated by an organization financed, as we are now told, with the help of the intelligence services of the United States.

This second historic incarnation of the generation of the 1930s, in the post-war period, is deeply significant. As I do not wish to be misunderstood, perhaps I may say that I consider freedom to be a supreme value; and that, in the modern world of massive organizations, I can conceive that it may need to be organizationally defended, and that its defenders may sometimes be forced by their opponents to be less than fastidious in their methods. The case against the Aparatchiks for Freedom Inc. and their clients is not what they did but how they mismanaged it. They were told to sell cultural freedom (admirable) and in so doing they sugar-coated it. Actually, the quality of the coating was remarkable: for instance, their intellectual journalism, though not *sympathique*, was of a very high order. What it did not do was to sell the idea of freedom. The case against the Aparatchiks for Freedom is that they did for *liberty* what the communists were doing for *peace*. They gave it a slanted image and a bad name. The sugaring was excellent but it only hampered the product.

The social reasons for this failure are mildly amusing. The days of the Anglo-American marriage (in a literal sense), in which a fortune weds a title, are probably gone and belong to the world of P. G. Wodehouse. Today, an American fortune is more plausibly incarnated in a Foundation than in an heiress, and the cachet is embodied not in a groom but in some person occupying a key position in that socially prestigious set of institutions and ambiance which can surround intellectual life in England. Nowadays, organization is everything, after all: it is not a case of boy meets girl, but a person with access to institutional resources, above board or not, meets another with access to institutional prestige. The Aparatchiks for Freedom, who had the former, appeared to be recruited from some tough Budd Schulberg world, and in England they were liable to the same weakness as the English once displayed in the Middle East— they simply adored the Sheikhs. Here they could indulge in fantasies of social grace for which they quite lacked the preconditions at home. This intoxication rather showed up in the sugar-coating they offered for liberty, and for this reason, one rather doubts whether any real waverer in the cause of freedom was ever seduced or fortified in his faith by them. Rather the reverse, one fears.

What of the outlook that was being sold under that coating? If any one slogan can sum it up, it is the 'End of Ideology' theme, the view that societies are best run on the basis of a pragmatic consensus and, above all, the negative view that the greatest enemy of liberty is general doctrine. The curious thing is that at that time, this kind of view did not need to be imported or encouraged: well before the official announcement of the End of Ideology, under that name, there had been local and spontaneous ends of ideology, springing unprompted from local and quite diverse roots, ranging from a local Hegelianism to radical empiricism. Views such as that social theories have no injunctive force, that theorizing must be separate from action and can only follow it, that theorizing must be quite distinct from social and other belief, that general theories and synoptic ideals are the very devil, were locally current and fashionable anyway. The various groups propounding such views rated their own originality, style and premises so highly that they did not always at once recognize the similarity of their own views to each other: nevertheless, the atmosphere generated by such ideas fused easily with the conservative-liberalism encouraged by the Aparatchiks for Freedom.

The trouble with this kind of conservative-liberalism was that the conservatism was quite unselective, whilst the liberalism was only too selective. Most sensitive to the danger to liberty from social doctrine, especially Marxist doctrine, it did not puzzle too hard about the conditions in which liberty must labour in the mid-twentieth century, or worry about other dangers to it. Its unselective conservatism was as regretable as its selective liberalism. The point about our world is that a great deal about liberal affluent society is very much worth preserving—but omnibus, abstract, indiscriminate conservatism is absurd. Yet the social doctrines in question were quite unequipped to make subtle or probing or indeed any distinctions in their endorsements.

So much for the conservative liberalism, which the young rebel will encounter—if he deigns to notice it—as he charges against the Establishment. Neither the force or subtlety of its formulations, nor the stature or record of its carriers, seem likely to awe him or make him falter in his steps.

1956 is of course a crucial year in the history of contemporary protest and rebellion. One member of the editorial board of *Universities and Left Review* put on record, in a letter to *The Times*, the as it were official view of what happened in that traumatic year: apparently, the twin shocks of Hungary and Suez awakened a generation, hitherto somnolent under the influence of the beginnings of prosperity, and brought home to it the need for political action. At the time, I asked the author of this letter to give me some names of young people who had been political vegetables prior to 1956 but were galvanized into consciousness by it. He could not recall any names just then, but promised to think of some. I still see him from time to time, but at the time of writing (1968), somehow no name has yet come back to him.

What really happened, from the viewpoint of the ideological evolution which concerns us, is somewhat more complex. Not Hungary alone, but Hungary preceded by Khrushchev's speech, had liberated, on the far left, a reservoir of political and intellectual talent, hitherto frozen in the Stalinist ice age. One doubts whether Hungary alone would have freed any who had lasted that long: the self-maintaining circle of ideas would have absorbed this shock as it had so many others. But since Khrushchev's speech, a charter for dissent existed *within* that circle, and once this was the case, the shock was able to make its impact. Thus, a talented political leadership was liberated.

It could meet, lead and enlist a new followership of a kind that had not been foreseen and which could *never* have been forced into the doctrinal or organizational strait-jacket of an old-fashioned extreme left-wing party: the marching-fodder of the new protest, the generous, free-floating, doctrinally amorphous young of the relatively affluent society. The leaders were now freed from the inept and restrictive discipline and directives of their erstwhile party, and this new liberty affected even those who had been enlisted in rival organizations. With the old restrictions, they could never had led the new social potential, not for revolution but for protest. The leadership looked like a kind of disembodied party, and in its disembodied way it floated freely, breathing in the free air with commendable joy.

Here the story must be related to the other one (the progression from the 1930s to conservative liberalism). The leadership of the new left also had some roots in the 1930s, even if many of the leaders were too young to have been active then. Not all the leftists of the 1930s had, after all, trodden the primrose path to anti-doctrinaire liberal caution. Some had stayed on the far left, no doubt with increasing discomfort—and now they were free at last.

They remained faithful to their leftism in considering doctrine to be important. Unlike their opposite numbers on the other side, they were not going to turn against doctrine as such. But which doctrine? One thing was close to hand: the woollier, more philosophical views of Marx's Hegelian youth, recently rediscovered, fed by other continental streams, suitable for fusion with existentialist and psychiatric themes, hallowed by the courage of East European liberalizers, and above all, loose enough to be usable with the new followers, who would never have put up with the rigid, scholastic Marxism of the dark ages. The result is well known: alienation is now as familiar as the Oedipus complex. (I find it amazing to think that until quite an advanced age I had never heard of it and yet managed to keep up a fairly active intellectual life, and that in my youth

I supposed Marxism to be about historical materialism and the Labour Theory of Value.)

All the same, this kind of philosophizing did not absorb all their theoretical energies.

They must also turn to the real world, and here too, many at least remained faithful to the key concept of the radical left—revolution. But they could not and on the whole did not deny that revolution, in any ordinary and real sense, was unlikely. Leaving aside the device of exporting one's revolutionary ardour overseas ('Thou shalt not covet thy neighbour's revolution,' as a French technical assistant observed in Algeria), this only leads to metaphysics and circumlocution: revolution *is* conceivable, but in some new and special sense; revolutionary potential *does* exist, but in some very new sense, and so on.

In fact, they know that the Revolution is dead, just as God is dead, and in similar fashion. (Some even took part in both.) The decease is in both cases accompanied by much publicity and is by some curious twist of logic made the occasion for a revival of faith. Just as the death of God is somehow turned into His latest manifestation, warranting increased theological activity and zeal, so the death of Revolution is made into one further complaint against society, justifying revolutionary protest. The machine, the cultural apparatus, affluence, consensus—these have deprived us of a dimension of choice, and thus call for one further denunciation.[2]

The tacit or other recognition that revolution in any normal sense is out has curious consequences for the kind of reward a revolutionary can expect. No doubt I may be misunderstood on this point, so I would like to stress that I do not know, or believe, these revolutionaries (either lot) to be particularly self-interested. I imagine their motives to be humanly mixed, like everyone else's, and the distribution of ambitious and selfless individuals among them not to differ too drastically from that found in other groups. My point concerns not the existence of ambition, if any, but the nature of the objective prospects facing it, if and in so far as it exists. Here again there is a parallel with the Death of God situation: the old believer could expect his fulfilment to come in another world, but his modern sophisticated successor must seek the meaning of religious fulfilment here and now. The same goes for 'Revolution'. A revolutionary of the 1930s, if he was ambitious, could look forward to power *after* the Revolution. (This only came to pass for those who were East Europeans, who could be rewarded with positions in the new communist regimes. Some paid for it with their lives or liberty during the anti-intellectual witch hunts of Stalin's last years.) But if ambitious men exist among the leadership of the present protesting left, they cannot and do not expect rewards of this kind. But they can expect some rewards in this, pre-revolutionary world whether they want them or not.

For the ironic fact is that the World of Protest is *not* alienated, whatever it says. Not only does it have its rich culture and shared norms which many of us, yearning for human warmth, may well envy: but also, it is a world continuous and overlapping with many other worlds, in that series of overlapping circles which make up British society. (America is different in this respect.) The worlds of pot, pop and protest adjoin the world of culture, education, entertainment and the mass media; and prominence in any one can easily lead to, simply, prominence. I repeat that I am not attributing motives, but only noting objective situations and opportunities.

Here there is a certain contrast with the earlier wave. The revolutionary of the 1930s could only look to a reward after the revolution, if he looked to a reward at all, but he was, unexpectedly, rewarded by the pre- and non-revolutionary society when he returned to the fold after the war. The returning prodigal was welcomed back, and resources were made available to ensure his comfort. Not all those earlier revolutionaries had started off well-connected, but those who were and those who were not moulded into a network, which may compare or surpass in importance some more familiar old-boy networks. There is an excellent thesis subject here for some young sociologist. This very important social function can still be performed by the organizationally disembodied left leadership of today, but it can no longer be quite so innocent: the this-worldly reward, whether desired or not, cannot any longer come as a total surprise, for they do not expect any other world to make its appearance. In some ways, the new protesters can retrace the steps of the old, but with far greater speed: the transition from the journal of protest, to regular contributions to the CIA-sponsored journal of consensus, can be achieved not in a matter of decades, but in a mere year or so.

In one of the earliest manifestos of the new protest, one of its spokesmen claimed that English intellectuals are haunted by the thought of the fates of Keynes and Trotsky. As a statement of fact, this is quite untrue: few English intellectuals, even economists, are obsessed by the fate of Keynes, and fewer still by Trotsky. But as a confession of the Walter Mitty inner life of such a thinker, mirroring the vistas as they appear to *him*, this was accurate. As he takes a little time off from a perfectly satisfactory and smooth academic career in the rotten society so as to try to foment strikes, and as he lifts the receiver, hears a click and fancies that his telephone is tapped, is it fear or is it hope that tells him that the end-point will be, not an ice-pick in the skull, but perfectly comfortable success? Without quite endorsing the comparison with Keynes, one supposes that these fears of martyrdom-deprivation will prove entirely justified.

These, then, are the ideological leaders, who offer *encadrement* and doctrine to the young rebel, as he goes charging against the Establishment.

What of the followers, the erstwhile marching-fodder, now sitting-in-fodder? They are, after all, the most interesting, important, least understood element in the situation.

Perhaps the mystery is not so very great. Perhaps these rebels simply offer a foretaste, like those almost symbolic harbingers, the Swedish delinquents, of the problems of social control in affluent, liberal, welfare and doctrineless society. When the new non-ideological consensus was being celebrated and the embourgeoisement of the proletariat commenced, certain inconveniences were ignored. After all, a part at least of the old bourgeois youth regularly went Bohemian, in one form or another, and loudly repudiated the values of their fathers, whilst generally keeping open a line back to dad and society, the repudiation being verbally violent but neither total nor final. If the bourgeoisie and middle-class life styles spread through so much larger a part of society, this type of ambivalent rebellion can also be expected to grow in proportion.

Of course, not all the rebels come from such comfortable backgrounds. Here again, something had escaped earlier notice. When people wrote of meritocracy, they generally expressed regret that the process of upward selection by education would deprive the discontented classes of potential leaders. It was too easily assumed (on the basis of premature extrapolation from the first post-war wave of entrants who seemed willing to swallow *anything* the universities dished up) that all these would be digested with ease, that none of them would rebel during the very process of upward suction.

Social control in liberal, affluent, non-ideological society works under very special and restrictive conditions. It lacks a doctrine which would justify anything. It has deprived itself of the economic stick. If Marx were living in this hour—he would have no need to sponge on Engels. He could, like other authors of books on Marxism, obtain a subsidy from the Congress for Cultural Freedom, and if he refused to do this, it is quite easy to keep body and soul together in Kentish Town by, say, giving extra-mural lectures on economics and social philosophy for the University of London.

Whilst largely deprived of the economic stick, liberal affluent society is extremely inept in its use of the prestige carrot. It possesses an educational system whose nominal function is preparation for the full life, but whose latent function (which is perfectly manifest to everyone) is preparation for a privileged life and position. Those skills of lucid expression and essay-writing would be somewhat irrelevant for people to whom no one will listen and whom no one will read. At the same time, the society drastically expands the educational system: even allowing for changes in occupational structure, this means that for many who pass through the educational machine, it must appear that they are being prepared for something which they will not be allowed to enjoy. The fact that the biggest or initial rebellions took place at Berkeley and LSE may be significant. In universities which are socially more prestigious, the majority of the students know that they can expect positions commensurate with their training. In intellectually less glamorous centres, appetites and expectations may be less titivated. But it is the middle area which is most explosive: here the students know that some, but some only, will make it, and they suppose that many of their teachers already have access to the perks of modern society, to power, the mass media and so on. When the sweet smell of success constantly wafts through the overcrowded and anomic corridors, but it is known that some only will be allowed a bite, the irritation may become intolerable.

In America, it is customary to distinguish two types of rebel— the hippy and the activist. These are indeed good 'ideal types', and represent the classical alternatives facing groups which reject the values of the world and the dominant society: either to attempt to change the world forcibly, or to opt out into a haven of quietist withdrawal. (This dilemma faced the English nonconformists, and as David Martin has pointed out, they tended to choose quietism *after* their Revolution had failed. In America, the time-order seems curiously reversed: Beat quietism preceded the revival of activism.) The interesting thing is that, on the whole, these *are* only ideal types: most of the rebels are clustered not at the two ends of the Hippy/Activist spectrum but somewhere along the ambiguous middle. A real activist, who fully believed his own rhetoric about the rottenness and ruthlessness of the society he is opposing, would train, organize and brace himself for the merciless struggle which is to come, and not waste his time on elaborating an absorbing sub-culture, which in its lack of discipline seems ill suited for a social Armageddon. He would not solicit the support of the hippy, and a consistent hippy, withdrawing into his private world of sanity and freedom, would not be available for recruitment.

The interesting thing is how very few people are located at either of these logically consistent poles: the culture of rebellion is clustered in the middle, fusing both attitudes. This inner contradiction no doubt contributes to the doctrinally invertebrate condition of the rebellion.

Though not endowed with much of a theory, the movement does

possess some nebulous outlines of an epistemology. The elements of this are somewhat different on either side of the Atlantic. In America, it possesses a theory of knowledge, and above all an associated style of expression, which goes back to populism and beyond it, presumably, to some form of popular protestantism. Its basic idea is that *sincerity* is the key to truth, and above all that any kind of order or structure is a betrayal. The view of truth manifests itself above all in the manner of its communication—that terribly *sincere*, carefully unstructured, conspicuously groping, free-associative style of speech, which has received so much confirmation from literature and some additional reinforcement, one imagines, from psycho-analytic theory and practice.

Despite the fact that the cis-Atlantic protest movement learnt a vast amount from the trans-Atlantic pioneers, especially in matters of tactics, it never quite took over this epistemology of sincerity. Another theory of knowledge can be discerned here. It runs in terms of 'theory and practice': the validity of thought hinges on being rooted in *practice*. In reality, this theory turns out to be a camouflaged version of an argument from authority. Everyone alive is involved in *some* practice: to make 'practice' into the legitimator of ideas is, covertly, to single out the practice of *some*, and to make their ideas sovereign. If those whom one likes, and wishes to enlist, turn out, despite their privileged practice, not to have the right ideas—if, to be specific, the workers are not revolutionary, and are racialist into the bargain—well then this is known as the 'problem of consciousness', and can be discussed with much learned reference to Lukács and Gramsci. The 'problem of consciousness' arises from the fact that the workers are known to have the right ideas, really, underneath, only sometimes these ideas remain latent and quite unperceived by their very owners, and then one has to wait for their awakening.

This rather simple-minded circle of definitions and escape-clauses could of course easily be manipulated to justify anything. In its defence be it said that it does not differ significantly from an epistemology fashionable on the philosophic right, which also values 'practical knowledge' above all else, and also defines valid social or political knowledge in terms of the practice, and hence the identity, of its bearers. The privileged bearers and the type of practice are of course a somewhat different lot, and the nature of the ideas is specified so little that the problem of consciousness hardly arises for this version. English philosophical conservatism of recent decades is remarkable in that it has worked out a populism-for-upper-classes: it reveres the inarticulate folk wisdom of a ruling class and seeks to defend it against the parvenu intellectualism of theorists—an amusing inversion of the usual pattern. Epistemology is only one of the areas where the protesters and conservatives mirror each other fairly faithfully.

The price of the doctrinal looseness of the movement, combined with the rhetoric of angry rejection, is of course a deep ambivalence. If you draw no fine distinctions, if the dissent is indiscriminate and vehement, it lashes out against society as a whole. But this total rejection, whilst it could be sustained by a tough, ruthless, determined, long-range revolutionary, is difficult to sustain for people who are nothing of the kind. If you draw no distinctions in isolating the *objects* of your emotions (and you cannot in fact have the same strong emotions towards everything), the inevitable consequence is that the emotions themselves become ambivalent: the distinctions which are not allowed to enter at the level of concepts, make their surreptitious but uncontrolled entry at the level of feeling.

This is true even of the extreme wing of the Negro Protest movement, whose members really would have good cause for genuine total rejection of society. Yet even their rhetoric is not accompanied by any corresponding consistency of attitude and feeling. The society which is declared rotten is also solicited for support, and failure to receive it, or enough of it, is bitterly resented rather than tough-mindedly expected. Some consistency can be introduced into this attitude by bringing in a time-scale: we are giving you one more chance to help us peacefully, and 'the fire next time'. But one feels that the inner ambivalence is there right now.

What is worrying about the student part of the movement is its occasional illiberalism. However libertarian its members may be about legalizing marijuana, they do sometimes put forward proposals such as the student control of 'what is taught and how'. It does not seem to occur to them that the implementation of this proposal would involve not the *transfer* of power from one set of people to them, but the *institution* of control where none exists at present. I do not wish to idealize the present situation: there may be junior teachers, without tenure, who believe that their careers hinge on pleasing their seniors. But at least in British universities, teachers obtain tenure very soon, and thereafter, though their promotion could depend on conformity, their security does not. They are safe and free to teach what and how they wish, and the students, who also complain, not without justification, of the quality of teaching, know that there is very little control of teachers. Those who demand control by themselves over 'what' is taught do not seem to realize the enormity, not of giving *them* control, but of instituting control *at all*: nor do they seem to have pondered the institutional implications of their proposals. What is to happen to teachers who disobey their instructions? One can only wonder whether they *do* know what they are saying, and are profoundly illiberal and totalitarian, or whether they do *not* know what they say, and the proposal is merely part of this generally invertebrate thinking.

These then are the rebels and protesters. Their economic base is the almost accidental discovery of the Beat generation of how easy it is to opt out and survive. Their social base is at least partly the uneven distribution of other goods. The movement generously concerns itself with real and specific ills, such as racialism, but, whatever its rhetoric, has quite failed to fuse its specific angers into a general, theoretical critique. It wills itself doctrinal and total: in fact, it is doctrineless and ambivalent.[3]

Perhaps a society gets the rebels it deserves. It is amusing to reflect in how many ways the protest movement is a fulfilment of the indiscriminate, doctrineless or rather anti-doctrine attitudes of the End-of-Ideology period.

That period preached the politics of pragmatic consensus, as against ideology. This had an element of novelty: past political philosophers had striven to give reasons why we should subscribe to this or that consensus. They said—the nature of things, or our interests, are such and such, and *therefore* we should all subscribe to a certain view or loyalty. The End-of-Ideology boys made consensus a premise rather than a conclusion, and preached it in a *l'art pour l'art* spirit. Consensus was self-justifying: not based on reasons, but a substitute for reasons.[4] Very well: but two can play this game. If consensus can dispense with reasons, so can dissent. And here it is.

Why should the devil have all the good tunes? Why should the conservatives have a near-monopoly of un-reasons? For centuries now, the left has, on the whole, been the intelligent party, kept on its intellectual toes both by its own super-ego (the left believes in reason), and by internal competition. The conservatives could on the whole make do without reasons, treating the status quo as self-justifying, and only offer indiscriminate, omnibus reasons for preservation or caution. But if, for instance, *intimations* are good enough for the conservative goose, they are now also good enough for the radical gander. The rebels, short on theory, are rich in intimations. One indisputable achievement of the protest movement has been to rectify this old injustice, and deprive the right of its monopoly of loose thought.

Yet in most ways, the rebels are a fulfilment of the End-of-Ideology prophecy, if not exactly in the manner foreseen. In their doctrinelessness and ambivalence, they have paid liberal affluent society a far greater—because involuntary—compliment than the conservatives ever managed. Consider doctrine: when the Church faced the Reformation, when Absolute Monarchy faced democracy and constitutionalism, when feudalism faced egalitarianism, when capitalism faced socialism—in each case, there was a real contrast, and the old order had cause to tremble. But when alienated society faces the shining image of non-alienated society, one can only laugh. If this is the best (or worst) you can think up, the old order cannot be in any grave danger.

Nor is it. Society will not crumble under the impact of these rebels, not only because it is probably too rich, too resilient, too attractive for too many of its members, but also, and this is more interesting, because these rebels do not really wish it to. (They have no experience, and little imagination, of a genuinely revolutionary situation, when a social order is really losing all moral credibility for its members.) In a variety of ways, they refrain from cutting their lifelines to the established order, and thus belie the violence of their verbal, sartorial and pharmaceutical rhetoric.[5] This ambivalence is a greater compliment, just because it goes against the grain, than the subsidized, *voulu* conservative celebrations of consensus. The inability to choose between quietist withdrawal and revolutionary activism, and the fact that the quietism is anything but quiet, are further indices of this give-away ambivalence.

It used to be a point of pride of the modern age that it had revolutionaries rather than rebels: that those who rose up against order did not merely (or at all) wish to substitute themselves for the power-holders, but wished to change the order itself—to abolish injustice, rather than just to reverse its distribution. We are now back in a curious situation in which, once again, we are without revolutionaries. And the rebels are not mere rebels in the old sense either: they would be ashamed merely to be using rebellion to improve their position (though this will happen to some, whether they wish it or not). They have failed to be revolutionaries, though their rhetoric aspires to it, because they have been unable either to conceptualize an alternative to the present order, or even to criticize it in any systematic fashion. There is no unity in their angers. (And the justified ones, such as the concern with racialism, are only sullied by running parallel with causes as frivolous, questionable and unimportant as the legalization of pot.)

But they have unwittingly held up a mirror to literally thoughtless conservatism. The end of ideology has come home to roost. It is, I suppose, too much to hope that either side will recognize its image in the mirror. But if unreasoning consensus, if rejection of general ideas as such, is legitimate for one side, then so is *l'art pour l'art* dissent. This will perhaps turn out to be their greatest achievement: by showing that the rejection of orderly thought and real distinctions can be used in both directions, they will remove one inducement to intellectual emptiness.

1969

Notes

1 Cf. Melvin Richter, *The Politics of Conscience*, London 1964.
2 Cf. H. Marcuse, *One-Dimensional Man*, Boston 1964.
3 Cf. T. Bottomore, *Critics of Society*, London 1967.
4 It is amusing to note that even the communist regimes have learnt this lingo. During the recent Czechoslovak thaw, the official line of the moderate liberalizers, who wished to move ahead without too radical a break with the recent past, ran as follows: We have now achieved consensus concerning the socialist basis of our society. *Hence* we may move towards pluralism . . . the implication being that the previous harshness, if not its excesses, were justified by the same principle as now requires more liberty. Consensus makes freedom possible; its absence makes it difficult or impossible. Did the communists who told me this learn it from the Voice of America, or did they work it out for themselves?
5 One rebel set out to subvert what he considered a neo-colonialist African regime. When they put him in jail—he had left his schemes lying about in writing—he was outraged at failing to receive total and immediately effective help from the British diplomatic representatives (though these, presumably, must have been the puppet-masters behind that neo-colonial regime!). When in trouble, far from being a revolutionary, he had the instincts of an English spinster of the Palmerstonian era: if you do not do as I say at once, I shall inform the British Consul!

Chapter 7   How to live in anarchy

There is one particular primitive system which seems to me to throw some light on contemporary international politics, namely, the system of trial by collective oath. This system operated until very recently amongst the Berber tribes of the Atlas mountains, but similar systems have existed elsewhere.

This system originally functioned against a background of anarchy: there was no law-enforcing agency. But whilst there was nothing resembling a state, there was a society, for everyone recognized more or less the same code, and recognized, more or less, the universal desirability of pacific settlement of disputes. There was a recognized manner of settling them; namely, trial by collective oath. Suppose a man is accused of an offence by another: the man can clear himself of the charge by bringing a set of men, co-jurors so to speak, to testify solemnly with a ritual formula at a holy place that he is innocent or in the right. The number of co-jurors required will depend on the gravity of the offence. The co-jurors must appear and testify in a fixed order, according to family proximity in the male line to the man on trial. The order is the same as the order of claimants to the man's inheritance. Those who have a common stake in property are also those who are jointly responsible and called to trial.

The rule, the decision procedure, so to speak, is that if some of the co-jurors fail to turn up, or fail to testify, or make a slip while testifying, the whole oath is invalid and the case is lost. The losing party is then obliged to pay the appropriate fine, determined by custom. In some regions, the rule is even stranger: those co-jurors who failed to turn up or failed when testifying are liable for the fine, rather than the testifying group as a whole.

How strange it is that this system should work at all: strange not only by contrast with our own legal decision procedures, but strange in the light of the possible motivation of the participants. A genuine legal decision procedure, or for that matter a decision procedure in any other field, must not be predetermined: a penny that always comes down heads is not much use for a toss. Yet it looks as if this decision procedure were always bound to come down on the side of the defendant. Even a sophisticated social anthropologist to whom I described the system was puzzled, remarking that from all one knew of such clans the interest of the clan came above everything else, so that one should expect the co-jurors in all cases to testify by their clansman: my clan, right or wrong.

Incentive to perjury

Here there is an additional incentive to perjury in the system: a man who lets down a kinsman at the collective oath, refusing to testify, say, that his kinsman had not stolen a sheep when he knows full well that indeed he *has*—such an honest and truthful kinsman suffers the penalty of paying the fine whilst the perjured kinsmen do not. Yet the system did work, and if the system had been predetermined in all its verdicts, no one would have bothered to take recourse to it and it would not have survived.

What is the explanation? The participants themselves see the collective oath as supernaturally sanctioned: the temptation of clan loyalty and hence perjury is balanced by the threat of punishment by the offended supernatural forces. We might say that the tribesmen *believe* that punishment will descend upon the group of perjurors, and this prevents perjury despite the inducements to it. This kind of explanation, in terms of the transcendental beliefs of the participants, is inadequate. Although the tribesmen do or did believe in the supernatural sanctions and their effectiveness, their belief was either not so firm, or if firm not so compelling, as to prevent perjury occurring none the less. Secondly, I doubt whether any practice can survive which is propped up by nothing but transcendental belief. There are always more beliefs of this kind than are systematically acted upon: other, social, factors must operate before a belief really is compelling in practice.

What made the system work?

What then made the system work, if not the transcendental belief alone? We must remember that each of the two groups is just as anarchic internally as the two are in their external relations with each other: neither internally nor externally is there a law-and-order-enforcing machinery, though there is a recognized law, and a recognized obligation to respect order. In fact, the distinction between internal and external politics does not apply. We tend to see it as a sharp distinction in view of the effective internal power of national states, and the ineffectiveness of the international order. But internal and external are, in the context of such tribes, entirely relative.

Disputes can occur at any level: between two elementary families, or between two tribal confederacies numbered in tens of thousands, and at any of the levels in between, and the nature and context of the dispute will be similar.

Given this anarchy, this lack of enforcement within as well as without the group, one way short of violence or expulsion which a clan or family have of disciplining one of their own number is by letting him down at the collective oath. Far from never having a motive for letting down a clansman, or only a transcendental one, they may in fact frequently have such a motive: a habitual offender within their own number may be a positive danger to the group. If he repeats his offences he may well provoke surrounding groups into forming a coalition against it—if, that is, his own group habitually stands by him at the collective oath. They may do so the first time: the second time, they may, or some of them may, decide to teach him a lesson, even though it is to their own immediate material disadvantage.

In other words, members of a clan are sometimes prepared to impose legal defeat on themselves, and suffer the consequences. Thus trial by collective oath can be a genuine and sensitive decision procedure, a decision procedure whose verdict is a function of a number of things, amongst which justice is one but not the only one: it is a function of the cohesion of the clan of the accused, of their assessment of the rights of the case and of the general character of the accused, of their willingness to fight on the issue. This decision procedure does indeed automatically lead to a verdict of 'not guilty' when the clan is united and feels strongly and unanimously about the issue, and to that extent the procedure may seem unsatisfactory from the viewpoint of abstract justice. But in those very conditions—cohesion, unanimity and determination of the clan—a contrary verdict could not be enforced anyway: or, rather, it could only be enforced by war, and that recourse remains open to the plaintiffs anyway. So nothing is lost, while something may be gained, in those cases when cohesion, conviction and determination are lacking, for then the trial gives the accused party the opportunity of giving way gracefully.

Settlement out of court

Many issues are settled out of court, that is before an actual collective oath is taken but with the threat that it will be invoked if a settlement is not reached. The accused's party may bluff in offering to testify, the accusers may bluff in insisting on so grave a step. Inside the clan, there may equally be bluff in declarations both of willingness or reluctance to testify. The situation is particularly delicate for the alleged culprit; he may proclaim his innocence and his willingness to involve his clansmen in what he maintains is a truthful oath, but he is taking a risk even if in the event his kinsmen stick by him. The divine punishment of perjury is the kind of event which in fact sooner or later happens anyway: a flood, a drought, a plague. The accused is providing any enemies or rivals within his own group with a powerful handle against himself, when disaster comes. Thus every group polices its own members owing to the collective responsibility implicit both in the oath and in the feud. But more than this: not merely is there this kind of informal internal policing, each group enlisted to survey and warrant the good behaviour of its own members but also and equally there is what one might call 'cross-policing': the danger from the hostile group, the fear of being thrown to the wolves, is what enables groups to restrain their own members.

Thus the profoundly paradoxical trial by collective oath can work. It does indeed give any determined, cohesive clan the veto on any decision that would, in virtue of that cohesion, be unenforceable anyway; on the other hand, however, it gives groups the possibility of half-throwing culprits to the wolves, of giving in gracefully, of disciplining the unruly member without actually having to expel him or kill him, as sometimes they had to.

Thus one of the roles of the collective oath, the veto on unen-forceable decision, is analogous to the right of veto given to the Great Powers in the United Nations. But note that the tribal device is much subtler than the United Nations veto rule, which is ex-tremely crude. The tribal rule is *as if* certain countries did indeed have the power of veto, but only provided the head of state could muster forty MPs, selected cross-party-wise in a traditionally-fixed manner, and have them solemnly support his veto. When capable of doing that—and, for instance, neither France nor Britain would have been able to do this during the Suez crisis—this would unambiguously indicate determined support inside the country for the policy in question; and in this case such a reinforced veto would indeed fulfil a most useful purpose—the purpose for which the veto rule was devised—namely the prevention of the passing of a resolution which is then totally unenforceable.

But while there is merely an incomplete analogy between the tech-nical rules in either case, it seems to me that a far closer, though still of course incomplete, analogy does hold between the reality of tribal order and that of international politics. The principles elicited in trying to account for how the superficially absurd legal procedures of the Berbers could work are also in some measure applicable to the international scene. In both cases there is an anarchic situation with hostile groups or blocs facing each other and no effective authority to regulate or arbitrate their strife. In both cases, enforcement is as difficult inside blocs as between them. In both cases, one might easily be tempted to conclude that the setting up of arbitration and decision procedures, with participants being jurors in their own cases, is pointless, for would not loyalty to clan or bloc inevitably overrule other considerations? I think not. The seeing of United Nations voting alignments as analogous to collective oaths amongst Berbers, and working similarly, strongly suggests itself by the events of the Suez crisis.

Without undue cynicism one may say that it was not moral indignation alone which led the allies of Britain and France to take a stand against them and condemn the landings. In part it was also a matter of punishing, disciplining fellow-members. Britain and France were being taught a lesson by their own clan. They had taken a chance on external fears keeping their reluctant clansmen loyal at the oath—and for once they did not. Where fundamental divergences exist within a clan or bloc, such a letting-down at the collective oath may be the only way of enforcing discipline within the camp. There is an internal as well as an external trial of strength, a counting of allies and co-jurors; the internal and external strife are complementary, and each mitigates the other.

Compensations, tribal and international

In both cases, while groups may need to discipline their own members by letting them down at the oath, they also want to keep up their strength, not losing any member if possible, and hence will make amends after the disciplining has taken place: in the tribal case the reluctant co-jurors will pay the compensation. On the international scene, less formalized but equally substantial compensations may be forthcoming to restore harmony within the alliance. Also, any good bloc or clan needs some device for discouraging co-jurors from being too easily reluctant, too frequently high-minded and objective.

There are other analogies between the two situations: in both cases total war would be disastrous to each side in view of the superiority of attack over defence, and hence it is generally desired to avoid it. It has been suggested of late that the disastrousness of all-out conflict is a consequence of nuclear weapons, but something similar may hold of tribesmen in view of the precariousness of their economy. So-called warfare amongst tribes tends to be a matter of raiding, which respects women and property when it cannot be carried away as booty: fields are not ravaged. If they were, warring tribes could mutually reduce each other to starvation, and such methods are characteristically not employed.

Further analogies are the emergence of, so to speak, professional institutionalized neutrals, drawn from groups that are weak in physical strength; neutrals who become less than judges, and act rather as mediators or masters of ceremonies at peace-making occasions. Again, in both cases the opposing groups each cement their internal solidarity by dubiously valid myths or ideologies. Again, in both cases, there are beliefs sincerely held which nevertheless would not by themselves assure order. Tribesmen believe that the shrine will punish perjurors, and analogously Foreign Ministers believe it their duty to work for peace, but these convictions by themselves are a slender guarantee. These ideas, often ignored, can however conveniently be invoked by those who wish to break clan loyalty at the oath. In both cases it is known that if punishment comes it will be collective: the bomb or the famine will descend upon the innocent and the guilty alike.

It is often supposed that tribal society is characterized by a moral code which differentiates sharply between members and non-members of the group: the limit of the tribe is the limit of obligation, and only inside it is one required to take recourse to pacific settlements of disputes. Sometimes this may be so, but not necessarily: the tribal situation I have described is characterized by a more or less common and universal morality for all men, in and out of the tribe. Tribalism, partiality, enters not with regard to the content of the code but in connection with its enforcement, which has, as I have tried to show, a subtle machinery for adjusting verdicts to the reality of power.

There is similarly something like a common morality concerning fundamental issues in *our* case, disagreements on values being less than basic. Conflicts concern interest and security more than moral principle. But there *is* a sliding scale in the application of that morality, a sliding scale built into the actual operation of voting and the system of blocs, a sliding scale which ensures that the diplomatically isolated and weak plaintiff comes out worse than a strong and well-connected one: and this incentive to cultivate international friends provides some inducement to orderly behaviour. During the Suez crisis, Mr Ben Gurion complained that a different code was being applied to the weak and to the strong, and suggested this iniquity would undermine respect for international order. On the contrary such iniquity is absolutely essential for this kind of order. One cannot have small and isolated countries taking powerful or well-aligned ones to court, and even winning, for no better reason than that they happen to be right. That *would* undermine the order by leading to a series of totally unenforceable verdicts.

Might and right

The adjustable sliding scale of application, made workable by the presence of disunity within as well as without groups, must not be seen merely as might masquerading as right. This is not so either in tribal or in international society. It is, on the contrary, a compromise between brazen might and the rule of impartial and enforced justice. It also gives way to might where, in any case, there is no alternative, and it enforces justice against offenders who are also weak or undiplomatic. It gives justice a chance in the shadowy but extensive borderland between the two. Might is often an unpredictable matter. When both contestants stand to lose from open violence or when it is unpredictable which one would, it makes the verdict partly a function of justice. Only partly, but also at least partly: half a loaf is perhaps better than no bread.

I am trying to bring out the conditions and mechanics of obtaining that half loaf of justice. One common misconception is that the situation in anarchic contexts would be improved if only the participants could overcome their clan or bloc loyalty, if only, instead of 'my clan or bloc, right or wrong' they would think and act as individuals. This common assumption seems to underlie, for instance, Mr Hugh Gaitskell's regret of the existence of blocs, in his Harvard lectures of 1957. It seems to me, on the contrary, that unless and until there is genuine enforcement, only blocs or clans can make an anarchic system work. The Rousseau-esque ideal of individual judgments, unbiased by faction, contributing to a common pool, is undesirable. The vagaries of individual judgment are too unpredictable. The effective result would be chaos and insecurity. Admittedly even ordinary internal elections, just like the collective oath or the United Nations assembly vote, become a genuine decision procedure thanks only to the existence of *some* independent floating voters: but equally these systems require for their stability and survival a sizeable proportion of voters who are simply loyal to their party rather than swayed by what they think of the merits of the current issue.

So far, I have concentrated on the positive analogies between our international order and a kind of tribal law. That there is such an analogy is an old, platitudinous idea; I have tried to show that the analogies are different from what is often imagined. There are also points where the analogy fails.

In both cases, total war would be disastrous to both parties if they are anything like equally matched, and hence partial wars are the rule. But there is a difference: what militates against total war between tribes is not merely the unreasonableness of such a proceeding, but also that to initiate it greater co-ordination and cohesion amongst individuals would be necessary than generally obtains. In our case, it appears that total war could be initiated by even a small group of favourably placed people, and hence the danger is greater.

A part of the answer to the question of how the tribal system works is that it does not altogether work. I had to explain why it works at all, and partly it does, but not fully. Indeed, in order to work at all it is paradoxically essential that it should not work perfectly: for the ultimate sanction of its legal procedures is violence, and if violence never occurred the sanction would lose its force. Indeed, the system may seem to work more than it actually does by a kind of optical illusion: after a breakdown into total anarchy the surviving groups behave to each other as of old, so that one has the impression of continuity. Those who disappeared in the meantime might not agree. The system, however, survives.

We can hardly be expected to consider ourselves so expendable. Even if we were so detached, it is not likely that our system would survive the destruction of its parts. We cannot afford to tolerate the partial failures of the kind of system which we now share with tribal society. So I am not saying that such a system works well enough: only that it works in a different way from what is often supposed. Until there is effective central enforcement it would be worse, not better, to do without groupings. But this is not to say that the system will do: for, notoriously, we cannot afford those occasional failures which are inherent in it.

1958

Chapter 8   The concept of a story[1]

This is a book for which a review can perhaps perform a useful service: to offer some advice concerning how the book should be read. The title and the actual ordering of chapters—in effect, the book as actually produced by the printer—suggest one reading: the present reviewer wishes to recommend another. I hope the impertinence of this presumption is mitigated by the fact that the advice is offered tentatively, and with admiration for the book.

The actual arrangement of the book, and its title, encourage the impression that the book is *primarily* a contribution to the logic of historiography, and consequently, that it is the earlier chapters of the book which are the most important. This, in fact, would seem to me to be an error. The really crucial chapter is, in my view, chapter 8, on 'Essentially contested concepts'. It is the logical peak, the culminating point of a fine ridge, from which the subsidiary ridges and buttresses, valleys and foothills of the argument fall away and can be seen to their best advantage.

I may be predjudiced on this point. I remember hearing an earlier version of this chapter when it was read to the Aristotelian Society some years ago. I admired it greatly: it was one of those papers which permanently enter one's thought. Quite possibly someone who has not had this experience, who had not already earlier internalized this crucial step in Professor Gallie's argument, might not wish to see the book as a whole in the manner I recommended.

What are 'essentially contested concepts'? A formal definition might read something as follows: an essentially contested concept is one such that the criteria for an object falling under it are multiple; they are evaluative (i.e. to satisfy them is to satisfy a norm of excellence, as well as a mere precondition of a classification); the relative importance of the various criteria is itself unsettled and open to dispute, and this itself is recognized by the users of the concept, and is held by them to be compatible with the admission that what is at stake is *one* concept, variously interpreted, rather than simply a multiplicity of overlapping concepts. Above all, these characteristics, the on-going debate, are of the very essence of the concept: the debate is its life, and not a contingent attribute of it.

The definition is not quite identical with the one offered and discussed by Gallie himself (pp. 161 f.), partly because certain features indicated by him, notably those added on p. 163, seem to me objectionable. Whilst accepting intuitively the notion of an 'essentially contested concept' as conveyed by his own discussion, it also seems to me that some of the formal criteria offered by him do an injustice to that very notion. Most objectionable, in this way, seems to me criterion VI (on Gallie's count; p. 168), which is 'the derivation of any such concept from an original exemplar whose authority is acknowledged by all the contestant users of the concept'.

One can see the kind of thing Gallie has in mind here. For instance, 'Christian conduct' is an example of an essentially contested concept, and the relationship of rival churches, denominations and sects to each other is precisely that of rival users of such a concept. All of them claim to look back to an 'original exemplar whose authority is acknowledged'.

My objection here is an application of the 'genetic fallacy' argument: the present functioning of a concept (as of an institution) is logically independent of its history. Hence a recognition of an 'essentially contested concept' must be possible on the basis of the present working of a concept, irrespective of its real history. Some notions (e.g. Christian conduct), do indeed incorporate the *belief* in the existence of a unique 'original exemplar'. Yet the functioning of the concept is quite independent of whether this belief is correct. Would the relationship of Christian churches and sects turn out to have been quite different, should historical research disprove the historicity of Christ? If what is important for Gallie's argument is the real existence of the 'original exemplar', then its incorporation in the definition, intolerably, makes the status of being 'essentially contested' into a hostage of the past. It would also seem to give encouragement to the illusion, built into certain faiths, that they do indeed have a *single* origin, an illusion of course encouraged by the supposed supernatural status of that origin. If, on the other hand, what matters for Gallie is the *belief* in the existence and authoritativeness of the original exemplar, the definition again becomes too restrictive in another way. The relationship, for instance, of rival conceptions of Marxism, are reasonably analogous to the relationship of Christian sects. Yet in their case, presumably, not all of the contestants would, at least openly, subscribe to a kind of apotheosis of the historic Marx. Must these contestants be classed as non-Marxists? Is there no justice in their claim that their irreverence makes them *better* Marxists? (The same point holds, incidentally, of those modernist Christian theologians who would detach the essence of Christianity from the contingent facts ascertainable by historical research.)

Gallie does, it is only fair to stress, substantially modify this requirement of the existence of an exemplar, and himself speaks of the condition being satisfied even in the case of '*a number* of historically *independent* but sufficiently similar traditions' (p. 180, italics mine), when discussing another interesting example, namely, 'democracy'. Here, indeed, there is little temptation to believe in the existence of a single original exemplar, in any literal sense.[2]

Gallie here modifies the requirement so that it is also satisfied by 'a long tradition . . . of demands, aspirations, revolts and reforms of a common *anti*-inegalitarian character . . .' (p. 180, italics Gallie's). What is now left of the notion of 'the derivation of any such concept from an *original exemplar* whose authority is acknowledged by all users . . .' (p. 168)? The shared tradition, or multiplicity of 'sufficiently similar' traditions, are recognized as somehow forming a unity because they follow something which, however loosely, is one ideal: the ideal is not supplied by the exemplar, but on the contrary the traditions are endowed with such exemplars as they may possess *by* that ideal. The 'exemplar' is redundant.

My criticism at this point is, as indicated, a simple application of the 'genetic fallacy' argument. It is only fair to say that Gallie earlier (pp. 128 f.) disavows or seriously qualifies that very argument. He comments on the reaction which set in, 'especially in Anglo-Saxon philosophical circles', against the genetic approach (whether historicist or psychologistic), calling it the 'anti-genetic' attitude, and makes some interesting critical observations about it.

I entirely share Gallie's rejection of the 'anti-genetic' attitude, without, for all that, approving of the 'genetic' one either. The real trouble with the anti-genetic attitude was that it tore its objects— be they concepts or institutions—from the changing social contexts in which they exist: it saw them in a timeless and static way, 'Platonic' in the worst possible sense, even or especially when their idiom was nominalistic. It is possible to reject this kind of static and timeless interpretation, without at the same time going back to the 'genetic' mistake either. This mistake is the supposition that the antecedent members of a 'developmental series', e.g. earlier uses of (say) the same word or the same institution, have some kind of privileged position when it comes to explaining and understanding this concept, institution, etc. Of course, *causes* do, by definition, have a privileged place in explanation: but earlier members of a continuous series are not necessarily causes of later members of the same series. What do we mean by 'one' concept, or 'one' institution, with a life stretching over time? The continuity, continued identity, of a concept or institution, resides in the fact that roughly similar (but slowly changing) activities are *repeated*, over and over. This activity is 'caused' anew on each occurrence but not necessarily, or generally, by the previous cycle. Each turn of the wheel has similar causes which, however, are *not* the previous rotation of the wheel. *This* is the first and most important level at which causation enters. There also is a second and more abstract level, at which changes in the secular trend of the repeated activity also have causes—which means, roughly, that something is changing the various factors operative at the first, more concrete level of repeated activities.

For this reason the past does throw light on the present, but not more so than do distant objects in the present: analogies or comparative material drawn from the past, vertically as it were, are no more weighty than those drawn horizontally, from other places in the present. The occurrence of a similar institution or concept somewhere else (in time *or* space), illuminates the causal connections which are operative in reproducing the phenomenon, by presenting different combinations of factors, circumstances, etc., and highlighting their relevance or irrelevance by differences or similarities in the results.

I do not believe Gallie would accept this. His discussion of the practical uses of history (pp. 130 f.) asks 'what sorts of insight . . . can an historical or genetic approach, and *only* such an approach, provide?' (italics mine). His answer is (pp. 132 and 133) that it can help us 'to see what we can and what we cannot do with our institutions in view of the ways they have come to be what they are . . .'. In other words, the past *is* privileged as indicating the sociological limits within which given institutions can operate.

I also have doubts concerning Gallie's criterion VII (p. 168)— 'the probability or plausibility . . . of the claim that the continuous competition . . . enables the original exemplar's achievement to be sustained or developed in an optimum fashion'. Again, this either claims far too much, or will need to be watered down to the point of triviality. Not all those who share a loose ideal will admit or believe that the 'continuous competition' is for the best. Many may consider both the competition and the rival competitors to be an unmitigated nuisance. In this they may well be illiberal and intolerant: but is it not better to keep these intolerant and illiberal participants within the classification, rather than to rule them out by definition?

Perhaps, however, Gallie means not that the *participants* must concede the claim, but that the claim must in some objective independent sense be valid. But if Gallie does mean this, another difficulty arises. What meaning can be attached to the requirement that the use of the concept 'enables the original exemplar's achievement to be sustained or developed in optimum fashion'? What superhuman mind, what superhuman cognitive penetration, is to discern this norm, so as to be able to say that the 'essentially contested' use of this or that concept does indeed serve the end of approximating it?

The trouble here is that Gallie is, implicitly, betraying his own idea: he talks as if, behind each 'essentially contested concept', there was, hidden away in some Platonic heaven, a non-contested, unambiguously defined and fully determinate concept or exemplar. In *The Caves of the Vatican*, André Gide makes one of the characters, addressing another who is perturbed about finding the 'true God', express the following doubt: when you die and come face to face with God, how will you know that *that* will be the 'true one'? One feels like addressing the same question to Gallie: when the clouds of unknowing disperse, and you are allowed to gaze directly at the Exemplar, will *that* Exemplar be *un*contestable, and terminate all further discussion?

Gallie's motive incidentally, for introducing these two additional and in my view misguided characterizations of 'essentially contested concepts', is to distinguish them from concepts which are just 'radically confused'. I suspect that no such general differential is available. Some clusters of characteristics are accidental and as it were sterile: others have a real affinity and are stimulating and fertile just because of their internal conflicts, and it is these meritorious ones that concern us and Gallie. But I doubt whether we can sort out the sheep from the goats in advance by some abstract criterion.

The difficulties Gallie gets into when trying to do so illustrate something else: he tries here, like so many philosophers, to be all at once both inside and outside the human situation. From the inside, what characterizes essentially contested concepts is indeed that they are *essentially* contested, in other words that in principle no final, knock-down argument is available for settling the contests to which they give rise. But trying to describe the general situation, and tacitly adopting a kind of divine, external viewpoint, Gallie speaks as if such a criterion for terminating disagreements did exist.

This is not just an ordinary contradiction, but a rather special form of it which I like to call the Pirandello effect, which consists of talking all at once both inside and outside the play. In producing the Pirandello effect, and in other ways, what Gallie says about essentially contested concepts rather reminds one of the 'dialectic'. Like the myth of the dialectic, Gallie's account highlights interesting features —though not quite the same ones—concerning what happens in historically long-drawn-out disputes. Like the dialectic, his idea stresses an affinity between the movement of thought and of life. The defect of the metaphysical parable of the dialectic is that it exaggerates the cumulativeness and finality of historical developments: the picture somehow suggests that earlier participants or positions are definitively *aufgehoben*, finally eliminated and incorporated in later solutions. It really isn't as neat as all that, or only very seldom. More often, an earlier viewpoint remains latent, and bobs up again at an opportune moment. In some tribal societies, in which writing is known and used though literacy is far from universal, land deeds and genealogies and even royal patents of authority are stored up by families, waiting for the opportune moment, should it ever come, for reasserting them. Law suits are never really closed, for parties (which, being lineages, not individuals, are in principle immortal) are always ready to reopen them, when a new situation provides the opportunity. Many of the ongoing intellectual disagreements of European history—particularly those of social thought—are, in this respect, more like the literally interminable tribal law suits, than they are like the ever progressive and cumulative, never step-retracing 'dialectic'. This inherent and endemic litigation-proneness of concepts, as it were, is admirably brought out by Gallie's new notion

One more observation about the Pirandello effect: temperamentally I sympathize more with philosophers who do not go in too much for crediting themselves with a divine standpoint, and who try to content themselves with giving an account of the human situation from within. But it should not be assumed that it is possible simply to avoid the Pirandello effect altogether, by resolutely sticking to an 'inside', human viewpoint only. It isn't that simple. The paradox is that it is inherent in our human viewpoint, that we also credit ourselves, rightly or wrongly, with the capacity to transcend it. (A resolute resignation to immanence is also a kind of treason, internally betraying itself, for it also tacitly claims an independent and general validity.) As Kant stressed, we implicitly claim for our cognitive powers—and, according to him, for our moral discriminations also—an exemption, a kind of extraterritorial status or diplomatic immunity, excluding them from what, on other grounds, we know to be true about ourselves as human beings caught in this world. This problem of philosophic dual citizenship arises for Gallie and his thesis in a special form. What happens to the mechanics or dynamics of an 'essentially contested concept', when the principle of those mechanics has been laid bare by Gallie? Gallie's central point is that a kind of inner turbulence, a permanent disequilibrium between various elements within a complex concept, is an essential and inherent part of the very life of certain important concepts—and *not* something which could be eliminated by a resolute effort at logical tidiness, by a bit of clarification and definition: and, for the kind of concepts he principally has in mind, this seems to me a valid and important observation. But what happens when we have seen through this? Was not a kind of 'essentialist illusion', the mistaken supposition that one unambiguous fully determinate notion or norm is 'there' if only we could locate it, nevertheless necessary to keep going that ever-open and fruitful debate which Gallie clearly considers valuable?

Gallie offers an answer to this question (pp. 187 f.), but I do not find it entirely satisfactory. For one thing, he fears (p. 189) that a lucid appreciation of the situation will lead to greater *in*tolerance: 'But once let the truth . . . out of the bag, then . . . [there may follow] a ruthless decision to . . . damn the heretics and to exterminate the unwanted.'

This is not what has characteristically happened in the development of some at least of those 'essentially contested concepts', which Gallie himself takes as his exemplars. An awareness of the manner in which 'church, denomination and sect' are complementary to each other is fairly well diffused, for instance, amongst North American Christians. It leads to tolerance (or indifference), and not, in Gallie's words, to 'a ruthless decision to cut the cackle, to damn the heretics . . .'. As long as people believe that an unambiguous, univocal reason is on their side, they are often also willing to persecute: they are less often inclined to persecute in the name of doubt. The real danger attendant on letting the truth out of the bag is not intolerance but atrophy of the debate—and this must worry someone like Gallie, who clearly values the debate most highly. In fact, the feeble condition of academic political theory since the war has often been credited to the nominalistic temper of philosophers: if concepts are arbitrary conventions, why should one trouble to contest any of them?

Apart from what seems to me a misplaced fear, one may have one's doubts about Gallie's solution of the problem. It consists, essentially, of the description of moderate debate as it is happily practised in a country such as Britain: both sides have a sense of the value of the opponent, both distrust their own extremists. Nothing is more aggreeable than such a blessed condition (and recent debates concerning the 'essentially contested concept' of democracy have highlighted the importance of this facet of it, usually referred to as *consensus*): but Gallie lays himself open to the charge of parochialism through his failure to consider the question of how this consensus is brought about, or concerning the nature of its sociological preconditions, its price, or concerning what is to be done in those regrettable circumstances (do they not exist?) in which the extremists happen to be right. Moderates facing other moderates are a marvellous thing: but can moderates overcome a tyranny, or prevent its establishment, or pull a society or a group out of degradation and poverty? Sometimes they can, perhaps. But one should have liked a fuller discussion of this, if only in token recognition of the condition of that large part of mankind which is in a condition in which the extremists may have reason on their side.

The notion of an 'essentially contested concept' is the high point of the book, from which one can look towards and descend to two separate areas: Gallie's discussion of its application to philosophy, and his discussion of its application to historiography. The value of the notion seems to me to become particularly striking in the first of these two areas, in its application to philosophy.

Its value becomes particularly striking if one compares it with certain other notions, distantly related to it, which have recently had great currency. The idea of an 'essentially contested concept' throws a great deal of light on the slightly puzzling (but in my view indisputable) untenability of the distinction between ethics and meta-ethics. One can see why recent philosophers were drawn to this distinction, and why they tried to think in terms of it: surely, the argument ran, before we debate whether something is or is not an instance of X, we must have a prior notion of what X *means*? Does not connotation logically precede denotation? The concept must have a meaning independently of the range of objects to which it is subsequently found to apply. This argument was applied to ethics, and led to the distinction between finding out 'what ethical terms *mean*' on the one hand, and the 'substantive' passing of moral judgments on the other.

In practice this distinction never rang true. Leaving aside theorizing so abstract that it really seemed to lack substance (of the form 'approval is approval is approval'), actual 'analyses' of moral concepts always seemed heavily loaded with specific values. It was not the case, as the moralists in question like to think, that the passing of moral judgments became easier after their work of 'clarification' was accomplished: for disagreement remained as rampant after the alleged clarification as it was before. It was rather that the very 'analysis', far from being a neutral account of the meaning of a concept, was saturated with particular values. Moore's analysis, for instance, was soaked with a certain aestheticism which, in the minds of men like Keynes, who were influenced by it, was quite central to it. Or: the interesting thing about Professor R. Hare's work is the ethics (in the *substantive* sense) which is in fact incorporated in a supposedly neutral account of what moral terms 'mean'.

Gallie's notion does, I believe, help us to understand this. As Gallie emphatically insists (throughout chapter 9), moral concepts are complex, not simple. Moral philosophies generally or frequently consist of the reasoned claim that this or that aspect should be paramount, or be given greater prominence, and so forth. 'Analyses' are in fact moves in the ongoing and essential contest.

Gallie gives us a far better account of what actually happens in moral debate. Consider the picture associated with the idea of 'persuasive definition', with emotivism, etc.: what it amounts to, in the end, is the view that some words are charged with a kind of positive or negative load, and that rival propagandists try to steal the positive load for their own favoured descriptive content, and push the negative ones into association with the descriptive content favoured by their rivals. Has anyone ever really played quite such a simple and silly game? Perhaps.

But not often. More often and more characteristically, what happens is precisely what Gallie describes as happening. A complex notion is re-ordered, schematized, in rival ways with rival supporting reasons, by two or more opposing sides which do, however, share some ground, recognize the concept as ideally unique, and persist in the hope of converting each other.

Another recently fashionable notion to which Gallie's central idea bears a distant resemblance, but to which it is greatly superior, is that of 'family resemblance', the claim that general words may or often do cover a variety of things, which share only a series of overlapping traits, without all of them at the same time sharing any one trait and without it being possible, consequently, to give any simple, unambiguous criterion of the applicability of the word in question. The programmatic theory associated with this idea (which was, however, presented as an established truth) was that philosophic error is characteristically the by-product of wrongly supposing that a single simple criterion does exist: and that a problem could be dissolved by appreciating the rich variety of application of various crucial terms. I do not know of any problem that was ever dissolved in this manner. But the weakness of this static picture was that it gave no hint of the fact that the disparate criteria and elements in one concept often form an organic yet conflicting and interacting unity, that the conflict is of the essence of the concept, and that the life and history of a concept is best seen in this way. Gallie's formulation will not 'dissolve' anything either, and is not meant to, but it does provide us with a suggestive and realistic way of looking at intellectual change.

There is one point in Gallie's discussion of the complexity of moral notions where I find myself in partial disagreement with him. As indicated, he devotes a chapter on the complexity of moral concepts to the emphatic denial of any one single essence of morality. The assumption that such an essence does exist or may be found he considers 'one ghostly manifestation of the long-dead Aristotelian doctrine of real essences in minds otherwise thoroughly imbued with the pluralist spirit of scientific inquiry: in Kant, in Moore, in Bentham, in Mill, and indeed in C. L. Stevenson and A. J. Ayer'.

In addition to the enslavement to the ghost of Aristotle, Gallie suggests another explanation of why some thinkers are attracted by the (for him, mistaken) moral unitarianism: the (also in his view mistaken) supposition that unitarianism is required for the autonomy of ethics, that pluralism must lead to the assimilation of moral notions to non-moral ones. But one may be driven into ethical, epistemological or cosmological theorizing of an unitarian kind by a breakdown of the previous set of beliefs or principles, accompanied by the fear that the use of any existing, inherited principles is bound to be abortive, for they are bound to be infected with that error which had led to the breakdown of the earlier system. Fear of pervasive error made Descartes eschew (at least in intention) premises other than his own supposedly secure and new one; fear of contingent motivation and merely conditional goods made Kant avoid 'heteronomous' principles of morality. Unitarians are often, perhaps characteristically, those who wish to make a 'fresh start' (not necessarily in a temporal sense), to establish a radical break, a discontinuity, with some manifold which seems to them hopelessly contaminated, cognitively or morally. It is difficult to say whether Gallie has any sympathy for this kind of enterprise, for the desire to start radically anew, as he does not seem to give it much or any attention. Here, once again, one feels that he lays himself open to the charge of a kind of parochialism: he lives in a world of reasonably smooth continuous traditions. He lives in an admirable world which has a continuous tradition yet is open to change, which values its own diversification and pluralism. He is right to praise such a world, but wrong to offer it, implicitly, as a general account of history.

Perhaps this criticism does indeed hinge on the assumption, which Gallie considers mistaken, that *if* a discontinuity between value and fact is to be maintained, then value must have some unique underlying principle. Gallie suggests that whilst morality can be 'unique and irreducible', nevertheless it is 'an organic whole within which a number of facets may be distinguished and towards which a number of originally independent tendencies may have contributed' (p. 195). Descriptively and sociologically, no doubt this is so. But the scarcely questionable assumption that the actual phenomena classed as moral judgments and standards are complex in structure and in origin has not bothered determined unitarians: J. S. Mill, for instance, is quite willing to admit diverse psychological or social roots of (say) the notion of justice as actually operative, *de facto*, but to go on ruthlessly to separate that which *de jure* 'is moral', from mere accretions, and to use an unitarian principle for doing so. Is this practice not justifiable by the need to reassess and sort out a complex, messy, and in large part unacceptable conceptual or moral inheritance? Could a complex norm be disinfected from the past? And do we never need to be so disinfected?

In his final chapter, on 'Metaphysics as history', Gallie attempts a reformulation of Collingwood's views on the relationship between history and philosophy. If I understand him rightly, he is once again applying his central insight concerning 'essentially contested concepts'. One might say—though he himself does not put it quite that way—that the nature of the world or of science is itself an essentially contested concept, and that philosophies, 'regulative principles', are the participants, the dramatis personae, of this ongoing, salutary and never-ending process. Indeed, as we move along, the great philosophers are apparently those who have strayed furthest along either flank, heroically marking the extremities of possible aberrations. '. . . metaphysical statements stand up like monuments, marking certain extreme positions. . . .'

This differs from the notion of the 'dialectic', as indicated, in that there is no claim of reliable cumulativeness. As he observes (p. 218), '. . . these conflicts between absolute presuppositions, far from being invariably absorbed or "uplifted" in some more developed and reconciling unity seem rather to be repeated again and again . . .'. This has the very considerable advantage of being closer to what really happens. It has on the other hand the disadvantage of offering no solution to the problem of relativism which it itself raises, no answer to the question of what happens when this generalization about the role of philosophies is reapplied to his own position. (The dialectic did offer an answer which, however complacent and mistaken, was at least internally coherent.) The book ends with a plea for 'generous-mindedness', for a 'kind of self-transcendence', for a sense of how 'human thought and aspiration should have been pulled now this way and now that, . . . should have been whipped forward by so conflicting intellectual demands and tendencies . . .'. But at least one value or idea—the merit of this kind of pluralism— is prejudged by this attitude itself: at least one idea—that of a literal-minded and uncompromising monism—is by the same token excluded, though this very idea or attitude may have been an essential motive force behind the process which Gallie contemplates with such affection.

The point which is central to the book, the account of 'essentially contested concepts', illuminates both the late arguments, discussed above, and the ones which occur earlier in the book, concerning the nature of historical understanding. I feel much less happy with this part than with the latter sections, and my discontents fall into two classes, which, however, are not unrelated: one concerns presentation, the other, substance.

The anxiety concerning presentation is this: in the succeeding and related accounts of the nature of a story, the nature of history, and of historical explanation one seems far more frequently to be told what these things are *not*, rather than what they are. A certain measure of characterization by contrast or negation may be tolerable: but here the amount of it is such that one tends nervously to scan the page, seeking for a positive characterization which would tell one, firmly, what *is* being said and not merely what is being denied. We do get a kind of positive characterization of a story (and hence, for Gallie, of history), but it seems, somehow, elusive and intangible. If I understood it well, it runs something as follows: a story may and must contain surprises, but the succeeding stages of a story must yet fit each other, be acceptable members of one sequence —without for all that necessitating each other. It is a series of events connected in a contingent way such that the successive members of it do not necessitate each other, and yet are somehow plausibly connected and do not stray beyond the limits of what makes one coherent story. (An account of this kind is found in chapter 2: chapter 3 on page 67 tells us, amongst other things, 'that history is essentially story'.) This kind of characterization seems to me metaphorical or circular or negative: negative in that it tells us that a story is not a deduction; circular, in that it tells us that the relationships of events in a story are such as is characteristic of—a story; and metaphorical, in that it tacitly or overtly employs metaphors such as not straying beyond certain limits of recognizable continuity, etc., where we do not really know how to retranslate this ultimately spatial metaphor into non-metaphorical terms. But whilst I saw what he had in mind, I did not feel I was being given a philosophical or other *account* of it, something that would exhibit its inner structure, something which would *specify* that strange relation between events which is so much less than entailment, so much more than randomness. I was being given the *feel* of it, but not an explanaton of it. Is this asking too much?

It was only later, when reading this account of 'essentially contested concepts', that I had the feeling of curtains being drawn apart and something being positively revealed: when Gallie speaks of a story, he means, I think, the kind of interplay and growth which he describes for concepts, in chapter 8.

This is the objection to the presentation. Somehow a real account of what a *story* is slips through one's fingers—yet this notion is crucial to Gallie's argument—though for many pages it seems tantalizingly close: but it slips out each time one's hand attempts to grasp it. It is only later, when one is no longer trying, that one suddenly finds oneself gripping something firm: it is for this reason that I commend an order of reading of the book in defiance of the binder.

At the same time, the presentation has other and compensating merits. Gallie is not merely a philosopher concerned with contingency: he has something like a passion for it. Most philosophers have a passion for necessity, and this made them into philosophers: contingency made them nervous. Gallie, on the contrary, has a passion for contingency, and his prose communicates it. Approvingly, he quotes Charles de Gaulle on war: 'Ce caractère de contingence, propre à l'action de guerre, fait la difficulté et la grandeur de la conception.' And not only, for Gallie, of war, but also of thought, of history, of philosophy. . . .

So much for the presentation. But one may also have doubts about the substance of what he says.

Now there are senses in which the claim that history is, above all, a *story* (allowing for certain qualifications, which Gallie makes, such as that the story is based on evidence and fits into one wider world, and is not in a disconnected realm of its own) is fairly uncontroversial. A historian has to give an account of a sequence, whether the sequence be defined territorially or 'ethnically', or in other ways—one can have the history of an idea or an institution or a tool or a domesticated plant. Moreover, the historian is accountable for the plausibility of the sequence: any change or discontinuity, and indeed any stability as well, must be explained—though when the explanation is obvious, or is held to be such because the historian's audience is logically undemanding, the historian may concentrate on the sequence and leave the explanation implicit. Gallie's theory of historical explanation, if I understand it correctly, is that it does not logically differ from other (e.g. scientific) explanation, but that it differs from it pragmatically: its purpose is to enable the story to go on, in the face of something mystifying. The course of a true story never did run smooth, perhaps, but the job of historical explanation is, apparently, to smooth its path. But he goes on to stress (on p. 123, for instance) that this pragmatic difference is profound and essential, and that if we ignore it we are liable to 'gross misunderstanding' in 'assessments of the strength of historical explanations from the logical viewpoint'.

As far as this goes, Gallie might be interpreted as saying something not very different from those who insist that historical explanations show that an event was *possible*—not that it was necessary—or those who insist that the logic of historiography and of sociology is the same, the difference lying merely in the focus of interest—in whether one is concerned with the links in the account, or in the generalizations which bind them.

But I think Gallie means more than this (though I believe he does mean this as well). When Gallie says 'story', he means something additional—and questionable. That something more comes out most strikingly in a passage on page 59, concerning the preconditions of history (italics mine):

> All history presupposes, and ultimately rests upon, an amalgam of *memories*—personal, family or folk memories—and commonly accepted legends and myths . . . backed up by evidence.

This seems to me conspicuously and significantly untrue: it also illuminates Gallie's thesis. Earlier in this chapter, I pointed out that Gallie rejects in turn the customary rejection of the 'genetic fallacy': for him, the *past* of an entity which possesses a history, is specifically significant in explaining that entity, and it is more significant than comparative material from the life stories of similar objects. On page 130, he talks in a manner suggestive of some Burkean functionalist urging us not to be too readily critical of the seemingly absurd, by looking to the continuity with the past (p. 131):

> the historical approach often helps us to see the importance of features of an institution which at first sight seem unjustifiable or arbitrary. . . .
> . . . it is difficult to see how such understanding is to be had, except by an historical appreciation of how the movement has developed . . .

Thus the continuous past of an institution or a movement appears to have a privileged position with respect to understanding it. But more than this: memory, in some extended historical sense which includes shared legends, etc., not merely offers privileged access to the inner workings of an institution, etc.: it is, as the quotation from page 59 shows, a precondition of existence itself, of being an object of history at all, of having any story to tell, of having an identity.

For anyone who wishes, like Gallie, to reject the anti-genetic attitude, *memory* is indeed a good starting point. We are inclined to feel, in the case of concrete beings endowed with memory, such as ourselves, that knowledge of events in our own past is more significant for understanding than is knowledge concerning the development of similar but distinct 'individuals'—that 'historical' evidence is more valuable than 'comparative' evidence. (This may be a muddle: the relevance of the two types of information may be quite distinct, but let that pass for the moment.)

But irrespective of whether the genetic approach can be justified with respect to concrete human individuals, in virtue of their possession of identity-through-memory, it seems to me wrong to make such inner identity, the possession of a story-from-inside, of being a historical *pour-soi*, into a condition of historical existence itself.

History as it is practised today seems to me (rightly) to embrace both sequences possessing an inner story as their initial starting point, *and* sequences lacking it. For instance: from time to time, wishing to broaden and improve my mind, I try to read some history of India, and so as to remember something of what I read, I try to find some pattern, some *story*, in what I read, if only as a mnemonic device. In this attempt I have repeatedly failed, and I am left with the impression, which perhaps others have shared, that Indian history has no story, or at least no inner story. The fixed dates, the events with a clear outline and succession, seem to be provided only by the intruders—by Alexander, by the Moguls, by the British. Indian history proper has a kind of story, misty in outline, at the very beginning: the Aryan invasion. Thereafter, such events as occur appear like ghosts in a mist, only to fade out without manifest connection with the next ghost to appear. Does this mean that India has no history? For Gallie, it seems to me to follow that indeed India, having no story in his sense, also has no history. But in fact, history as it now interests us, seems to me to embrace both 'history-minded' peoples such as biblical Jewry,[3] whose conception of the supernatural leads them to record temporal succession and hence to have a 'story', *and* Hindus, whose conception of the supernatural leads them to disregard temporal succession.

It is the duty of a thinker to test his thesis not against the most favourable examples from the realm it is meant to cover, but from the least favourable ones. Gallie chooses his example from the Western, historically-minded tradition.

Another area which Gallie might have considered as a possible source of counter-examples to his own thesis is that of small, tribal communities, which, even when locating themselves in time, have legends which can only doubtfully qualify for the application of 'story', in Gallie's sense.

My criticism that Gallie is guilty of a kind of 'Western' parochialism culminates here. As stated, Gallie's account is reminiscent of the 'dialectic', notably in that it endeavours to offer a picture *in movement* both of the life of concepts and of history, and that it relates the two (even though the picture differs from that of the dialectic). The formal resemblance is close enough to make Gallie open to the same criticism as a contemporary 'dialectical' thinker, Sartre. It is instructive to look at the assault on Sartre's praise of the *raison dialectique*, in Claude Lévi-Strauss's *La Pensée Sauvage* (Paris 1962, pp. 328 f., pp. 248–9 of translation):

Que peut-on faire des peuples 'sans histoire', quand on a défini l'homme par la dialectique et la dialectique par l'histoire? Parfois Sartre semble tenté de distinguer deux dialectiques: La 'vraie' qui serait celle des sociétés historiques et une dialectique répétitive et à courte terme, qu'il concède aux sociétés dites primitives tout en la mettant très près de la biologie. . . .

Ou bien Sartre se résigne à ranger du côté de l'homme un humanité 'rabougrie et difforme' . . . mais non sans insinuer que son être à l'humanité ne lui appartient pas en propre et qu'il est fonction de sa prise en charge par l'humanité historique: soit que, dans la situation coloniale, la première ait commencé à intérioriser l'histoire de la seconde; soit que, grâce à l'ethnologie elle-même, la seconde dispense la bénédiction d'un sens à une première humanité, qui en manquait.

Sartre defines history, and hence humanity, in terms of a revolutionary dialectic; Gallie does the same in terms of a continuous, liberal discussion. My sympathies are all with Gallie, but that is not the point. The point is that both Sartre and Gallie circumscribe humanity too narrowly. What Gallie makes, implicitly, into a criterion of history and hence of humanity, one might gladly accept as a criterion of desirable, democratic liberal regimes, but not of history as such.[4]

Would Gallie also devise, like Sartre, a kind of second-class (short-term repetitive) version of 'essentially contested concepts', for the benefit of static societies, as Lévi-Strauss credits Sartre with devising an extra cheap dialectic for export? Would he allow them participation in history only through their incorporation in the Western world through the colonial situation, or through internalizing Western history, or by grace of the ethnographer?

I am also not clear how far Gallie is committed, through his insistence on starting with an inner story, to the view that the historian story must always remain intelligible to the participants, and not too far removed from the story as it was actually lived. If explanation only removes obstacles to the flow of narrative, which appears to be Gallie's view, then this would seem to follow. For Gallie, explanations are a bit like the liberal state, they remove obstacles, to allow something else—in this case the narrative—to fulfil itself. But it seems to me that the relationship between (say) sociological explanation and previously accepted narrative may be more dramatic than that. The explanation does not necessarily expand or modify the narrative or free it from obstacles in its path: it may cause it to be replaced altogether. The question of whether the concepts involved in historical or sociological explanation must remain close to those employed by the participants, and thus allow them a 'story', or whether it may declare those concepts, and hence the story, to be quite illusory is too big to be discussed here: but Gallie's attitude seems to me to prejudge the question in favour of the 'inner story', and to do this too easily.

Once again: is the vertical past of a society, institution, etc., really *specially* relevant to understanding it? Suppose a man is worried by authoritarian tendencies in contemporary Britain. Well, he could, if he wished to explore its authoritarian potentialities, look back to George III, to Cromwell, to the Stuarts. But surely the more realistic, and also the more common, approach would be to study the social roots of Hitler and Stalin, or even, despite the level of abstraction involved, to ponder on Wittfogel's account of oriental despotisms. The question 'Are the social consequences of a developed industrial system similar to those of an elaborate irrigation system?' seems to me more relevant than the question 'What are the factors in the local tradition, factors which may still be present, which led to authoritarian tendencies in [say] the seventeenth century?' Gallie, if I understand him rightly, would lead us primarily to the second type of question, and only invoke the former, if at all, as a shot-in-the-arm when the story flagged.

My criticisms boil down to the view that all humanity does have history, but human life is *not* everywhere a story. (Some stories are deformed, short-run, repetitive, and lack the characteristics valued by Gallie.) Historical understanding proceeds not by smoothing the flow of a story, but by exhibiting the structures which underlie sequences, whether they are experienced as stories or not, and it discovers these through comparisons which are, at least as often, and at least as legitimately, lateral or horizontal rather than vertical and in 'temporal depth'.

But I am moved and infected by Gallie's evident and joyful sense of the flow and uncertainty and openness of life, and even if this does not provide us with a clue to the nature of explanation, it does seem suggestive of the *feel* of events. The picture he mistakenly (in my view) offers as a *general* account, one can at least salute as a picture of something *specific* and desirable. Not all history is a story, in Gallie's sense, though one may wish it were. A philosopher whose passion is contingency, not necessity, and who communicates it so well, is rare. This review has in no way exhausted the topics which Gallie discusses, and it has naturally concentrated on those areas in which I feel doubt, rather than those where I am in agreement. I only hope I have conveyed something of the freshness, sincerity, independence and outstanding quality of the book.

1967

Notes

1 A review of W. B. Gallie, *Philosophy and the Historical Understanding*, London 1964.
2 The supposition that social forms have, in any important sense, points of origin, that they are 'invented' at some point of time, goes against the grain of any 'structurally' oriented sociologist. Social forms have preconditions, they are not invented. Philosophers on the

other hand still seem attracted by institutional or conceptual 'founding ancestors'. Thus, Professor Richard Wollheim (*Philosophy, Politics and Society* (second series), ed P. Laslett and W. G. Runciman, Oxford 1962, 71), is tempted by the supposition that democracy was indeed invented at some definite time and place, though he does make a passing bow to some of the objections which may be raised against this. Professor Bernard Crick (*In Defence of Politics*, rev. Pelican ed. 1964, 17) makes such claims for politics itself: 'politics . . . is unknown in any but advanced and complex societies; and it has specific origins only found in European experience'. It 'still appears to be a unique invention or discovery of the Greek world'. Having first spoken of it thus as something that can be invented or discovered, he does later (32) speak somewhat differently: '[its] social basis is to be found only in quite complicated societies'.

3   A curious question for Gallie: does the Jewry of the Dispersion also have a history? I remember once reading a fairly standard elementary work on this subject, and being infuriated precisely by the lack of a continuity in the book. Jewish communities bobbed up like pimples on the face of Christendom and Islam, but the author attempted no account of the intervening gaps. He didn't even ask the question. This was due in part to the attitude of the author, who had a headmasterish-cum-nationalist concern with high marks, achievements, recording them with pride but without having any sociological interest in the intervening continuities or gaps; but partly it was due to the fact that little evidence is available concerning the gaps. Communities of the diaspora do have—by definition—an 'inner memory' of *biblical* history, but not very much concerning the subsequent dispersion.

4   It is interesting to find another brilliant social thinker, Raymond Aron, independently of Gallie using his criterion of on-going debate, in precisely this manner: 'Les régimes que nous avons appelés démocratiques-libéraux sont ceux qui se définissent par l'acceptation de cette dialectique, c'est à dire par la reconnaissance *qu'il n'y a pas une formule, et une seule, de la liberté par excellence*.' (Emphasis Aron's.) *Essai sur les libertés*, Paris 1965, 229. Had Aron used Gallie's terminology, he might have said: liberal democracies are defined by their treatment of liberty as an essentially contested concept.

Chapter 9   Our current sense of history

1 Types of horizon

The horizon is generally conspicuous, whereas the surrounding land-scape, close to us, is taken for granted. Yet, in the social and historical world (and perhaps in some measure in the physical world also), the horizon we perceive depends on our more immediate environment and its general features. A forest or a savannah, a local hillock or a hollow, make a great difference to the kind of skyline that is seen. But it is in the nature of things that what is close and familiar should also be treated with familiarity and contempt, and that its importance should normally be ignored. It is its ordinariness, obviousness, which causes us to take it for granted: but the hold it has over us is immeasurably strengthened precisely by the fact that we do take it for granted. What is noticed can be queried, but that which seems utterly obvious eludes questioning. The horizon, by contrast, errs in the opposite direction. It is often quite spuriously dramatic. If you walk to the point on the distant skyline, you may well find, when you reach it, that it is just as ordinary a place as your starting point. But as long as it remains on the skyline, it occupies the dramatic point at which the sky meets land or water, the point where the sun sets or rises. It has a striking suggestiveness, and symbolizes our deeper or more ecstatic aspirations—quite unlike the close and dusty immediate locality, which tends instead to remind us of our compromises, shabbiness and mediocrity.

The horizons of a society, or at any rate of many societies, consist of a cosmogony and an eschatology, of an account of how things began and how they will end. As the horizon is dramatic, it is often easy to pick it out: the locals know how to talk about it, and ritual occasions abound which remind them to do so. Thus it is unlike some of those daily occurrences which may remain unnoticed or which may even be systematically obscured. But, of course, that which is high-lighted and that which is obscured may be all of one piece, or at least they may complement each other. It is a commonplace of anthropo-logical method that by skilfully interpreting that which is made conspicuous on the horizon, one may be led to a great deal of that which is hidden under one's very nose. To ask about the manner in which history enters our vision is, in a way, to ask about the manner in which our horizons are related to the style of our daily life. This being so, one might as well begin with a typology of the kinds of horizon a society can have. We can develop a typology by using the currently fashionable method of binary oppositions and seeing the types which are generated in this manner. The differences in attitude to history which one should expect to be relevant are these:

1. Naturalistic/discontinuous. A society is naturalistic if it assumes that the events on the horizon are, and must be, similar in kind to the ordinary events of daily life. Modern societies are naturalistic in this sense. They do not take seriously either an Age of the Gods or an Age of the Heroes, in Vico's terms. But most societies are not naturalistic in this way.

2. Within the class of societies which have non-naturalistic horizons, it is possible to distinguish between simple and ramified background stories. A ramified one will recognize two or more successive stages, basically dissimilar, within the general framework of the horizon story—such as, indeed, Vico's distinction between the Age of Gods and of Heroes. There is then a double skyline on the horizon—something that, after all, also happens in the physical world.

3. Cutting across these distinctions, there is the difference between historical and ahistorical societies. A rough criterion would be whether a society accumulates more and more generations with the passage of time, whether the ordinary world within the horizons *grows* in size with time, or whether on the contrary the size of the plain within the horizons remains constant, as happens when systematic omission ensures that the number of generations separating the present from the Founding Father remains constant. There will of course be borderline cases between historical and ahistorical societies.

4. The presence or absence of a sense of social structure. By this is meant whether or not a society recognizes a radical difference in type of event, or of sequence, of story, *within* the daily, ordinary, non-horizon part of the world—in other words, whether it has a sense of different epochs, of radically different patterns of social life, where the difference is natural rather than supernatural. A simple society which takes for granted the institutional and conceptual framework within which its members act, has of course no such sense of social structure. Its own structure is invisible to it, and others are barely conceivable. Naïvely, it absolutizes one particular set of conventions. But even quite sophisticated societies or historians are capable of this simplicity. It is arguable that Gibbon's vision was of

this kind, and I have heard this claim argued. So, clearly, holding such a view does not disqualify a man from the highest ranks of creative intelligence.

The four binary oppositions considered give us twelve possibilities (allowing for the fact that one of the four oppositions applies only to one half of the field, for it only arises if a particular answer is given to one of the other alternatives). It might be interesting to explore the resulting typology in relation to concrete historical and ethnographic material. Our present problem, however, is to isolate features of our own sense of history. For this end, we need only specify our own position within this range of alternatives and then seek to add further refinements to the resulting profile.

Our society is secularized/naturalistic, it sees the world as continuous rather than discontinuous, in as far as it does not take the supernatural cosmogonies and eschatologies, which it has inherited, with any degree of seriousness. It has not openly and generally disowned them, it merely surrounds them with a cloud of ambiguity, according them 'symbolic' status or whatnot, and it has been obliged to invent a special term, 'fundamentalist', for those who actually claim to take them seriously. This being so, the question whether the horizon is simple or ramified does not arise. In an important sense, we have no horizon. What is on the horizon is known to be similar in type to the ordinary stuff of daily life. We are also, clearly, an historical society. Generations are not spirited away by genealogical hocus-pocus, or by indifference, but, on the contrary, the slag heap of The Past is ever growing. Some have feared that the shadow it casts may tend to stifle us. Be that as it may: we clearly locate ourselves in a growing, cumulative, temporal sequence, which does not obscure change but records it. This, of course, is the first and most general reason why history is of interest to us. We are not alone in possessing this trait, but it is not an universal one either. Some simpler tribal societies quite independently possess it, and some complex, urban, literate societies do not. Finally, within the horizonless and cumulative temporal setting, we do have a sense of successive and radically differentiated social structures. We do not suppose that men throughout history have played the same game, that they were like us, only (at most) wearing different clothes and using different tools and weapons. On the contrary, we know that the games played have changed drastically.

This, then, is the profile of our historical sense. It is a very abstract outline, and a good deal more will need to be said before it becomes really informative. But the additional points which need to be made may be approached through questions arising about this outline. The various questions are cross-related, and they are:

What is a social structure, as opposed to mere historical narrative?

Be it noted that reputable thinkers exist who consider accurate narrative to be the only legitimate form of history, and who repudiate the abstract structures sought by sociologists and anthropologists.[1] To answer this question—concerning the nature and status of these 'structures'—is in effect to discuss the relation of history to anthropology and sociology.

Specifically, which particular structures, or classifications of structures, do we find relevant in categorizing our historical experience—and why?

Given that an important function was performed by the 'horizon' in societies which possessed it, and given that we are horizonless, at least in the old sense, what (if anything) performs that role for us?

If it should turn out that this role is now performed by the social sciences and/or 'futurology', just how do they perform it and what kind of sensitivity do they instil?

In the light of all this, how do we need to refine our initial classification of historical perspectiveness by a typology of horizons and horizon-surrogates?

2 Structure and story

Very roughly, a story is a sequence of events fused not merely by continuity (ideally, there ought to be no gaps), but above all by the fact that they happen to an individual (or a community) which experiences and conceives them as a unity, as its own fate or destiny or adventure. Perhaps it is of the essence of a story that the sequence should be more than contingent and less than necessary.[2] Such a definition is no doubt question-begging, or rather buck-passing, in that it shifts the burden to the question of just how the individual comes to attribute unity to a sequence of events, and indeed, to how he himself comes to credit himself with unity. One may well suspect that the unity of a self and of a story are correlative, mutually dependent notions. A very sketchy answer—which is all that we shall offer—to this question is one which invokes the notion of 'structure', which is both complementary and contrasted to the idea of a 'story'. What makes the sequence of moves in (say) a chess game into *one* game, which can (in the case of chess) be turned not merely into a narrative but into a precise and unambiguous one, is, over and above the fact that the moves happen consecutively in one place, the fact that they presuppose a shared set of rules which connect one move with the next. Naïve narrative history takes such rules for granted. Sociological history, at the very least, attempts to elicit and specify them. What is the status of these rules?

Some, but some only, are supplied by nature. Wheff the hero of a story undergoes an adventure in which bodily survival is at issue, when he must avoid physical destruction, starvation or exposure, we understand the 'logic of the situation' without needing to presuppose any information about his specifically social environment, about the cultural conventions within which he operates. But these natural constraints only account for a small proportion of the connections in a story sequence—for the need to swim to the shore when the boat capsizes, for the need to seek food and shelter on the island. The natural needs also enter as partial constituents into many cultural requirements, without dictating their specific form. Nature decrees you must eat, culture decrees when, how and what.

By far the greater proportion of connections in a story is made intelligible in a manner other than a simple invocation of a natural, physical law. The professional, ritual, familiar, political and other activities of man are constrained by conventions and guided by ends which are not simply or at all derivable from shared biological needs. Those needs certainly set limits to the kind of connections that a society can exhibit, but they most certainly do not determine their specific form. The nexus between an act and its consequences, or between the failure to perform it and another set of consequences, is dictated not by nature, but is somehow the consequence of a given social structure. A social 'structure' is, in a way, a system of such regular connections and the manner in which they are enforced. As stated, it somehow ensures that those consequences flow in a certain pattern (for a social environment is by no means wholly unpredictable). It somehow ensures it—but *how*? One facile, occasionally popular, but empirically and otherwise quite inadequate, answer is what might be called the 'Brave New World' solution—the view that concepts are so firmly internalized by members of given societies that they become, in practice, just as compulsive as natural necessity. The insulted man of honour 'must' fight a duel, the believer 'must' kneel, and so forth. But empirically, it simply is not true that men are quite so completely enslaved to the concepts and norms of their societies. Just as significantly, those concepts and norms are generally ambiguous and less than fully determinate in their requirements, leaving adequate loopholes for opportunism and variation in strategy. The socialization process is often less than homogeneous in what it indoctrinates, and its effectiveness in ensuring the internalization of what it preaches varies a good deal.

What, then, is the answer? We know, roughly, the elements which go into the answer. The manner in which these elements combine and contribute to the explanation of a given social situation can only be worked out by a specific investigation into that particular situation. The elements are the various forms of restraint and quasi-restraint which delimit human conduct. Physical, natural constraint, on its

own, accounts for a small part: in every society, much more is physi-
cally possible than is socially, 'morally' possible. A social system is
a system of un-thinkables and un-do-ables. A sociological account of
it explains how these limits come to be, but does not, like the society
under consideration, take these for granted. Over and above physical
restraints, it can invoke the range of available concepts, and, with
great caution, the hold these concepts have over the members of the
society. Pure unaided conceptual constraint may sometimes be
adequate, though this needs to be carefully demonstrated in each case.
But most generally, the constraint is situational: the institutions
surrounding an individual limit his options. Some options are
barred by a variety of social sanctions—punishments, ridicule, loss
of social credit and standing which the individual knows he will need
for many other ends, and which he must husband carefully. Such
options as *are* open, are generally open only by grace of the social
arrangement, so to speak: most actions involve effecting changes
which require the co-operation of others, which are beyond the
unaided physical powers of the agent. The enlistment of the required
co-operation requires, at the very least, that the act to be performed
is recognizable and sanctioned within the local institutional framework. Most 'actions' can only be performed if they have a recognized
local name and status. New 'actions' do indeed, from time to time,
emerge *prior* to their social recognition and christening: this is the
most interesting form of social change. But this process can also be
seized and explained by the kind of sociological explanation under
consideration.

A model of a social structure must sketch the situation in which
the individual pawn in the game finds himself, showing the 'rules'
which limit his possible moves—and above all, showing how those
rules are sanctioned. The pawn cannot do *this* because it would arouse
the wrath of his neighbours, he cannot do *that* because the idea of
it is simply absent and, even if *he* could conceive of it, he could not
enlist the required support because no one would know what he was
up to, and he cannot do *the other* because it would ruin him economically, and so forth. In as far as the situation leaves him some choice,
this must be taken into consideration in accounting for the constraints
placed on his neighbours: what would happen to their position in
turn if he, or he and too many others, took this option rather than
that?

The 'rules' under discussion are of course not the same thing as
the normative rules recognized within the society itself, though such
normative rules, if well sanctioned, can figure amongst the constraints
on conduct. What is at issue are 'rules' in the sense of *effective*
limitations on conduct. As it is not generally possible to work out
an adequate power-and-constraint balance sheet for every individual,

in practice it must be sufficient to do this for typical individuals in standard situations, plus some reasons for believing that not too many individuals deviate from this, and that such deviations as do inevitably occur do not disrupt the system, but are somehow absorbed by it. It then follows that for similar 'ideal types', i.e. social situations defined by similar premises, similar consequences follow. This is a matter of simple logic: from similar premises, other things equal, similar consequences must follow. And as a matter of fact, there is some justification for such a strategy: patterns of constraint do not appear to be endlessly various, there seems to be some justification for the hope that similar premises are crucial for defining more than one society. There do seem to be 'structural similarities'. Models exist which do illuminate large classes of societies.

Thus generalization enters indirectly, as a consequence of the applicability of 'ideal types'. Generalizations of a different kind also enter in as far as they are invoked to explain the connections between items within various models or ideal types. These kind of generalizations, borrowed rather promiscuously from anywhere, are admittedly invoked *ad hoc* and in a rough and ready manner.

Thus, generalization enters somewhat indirectly. On the other hand, the ideal types themselves are an essential, integral part of the method, and indispensable. There is no alternative to using them. The alternative is not some brave, tough-minded history, a pure unadorned narrative of 'what really happened', but only a childish narrative which takes the nexus between events for granted.

The account here offered of the nature of sociological method and of 'structure', its key concept, is a moderately materialist one. It is materialist in its insistence on starting from the physical constraints given by nature, and also, in its insistence that conceptual constraints are never self-explanatory, that they can only be accepted as elements in an explanation if it is shown how they in turn are sanctioned, how a situation arises in which men cannot easily evade them. The account is moderate in its materialism through its clear recognition of the fact that the pattern of physical constraints given by the environment, by ecology and available technology, seldom if ever uniquely determines the rest of the system: in other words, there most certainly is no one-one correlation between 'base' and 'super-structure'. It does not exclude the possibility that on some occasions the socialization process inculcates some concepts so firmly that their internalization and compulsiveness may be sufficient to explain some particular human conduct: but it is very suspicious of such explanations, on the grounds that, in most cases, concepts need to be sanctioned externally as well as internally, if they are to be truly compelling. The protestant who follows his faith without external ritual, the revolutionary who defies the external political symbolism of legitimacy and recognizes only his own inner political light, may exist, but they are rare in their pure inner-directedn ess. Moreover it is doubtful whether, sociologically speaking, they are often quite so pure: apparently pure inner-directedness often has some covert external reinforcement.

3 Structuralism

The structuralism here outlined and commended is meant to be an account of old-fashioned, square, not-with-it structuralism, which is not very close to currently fashionable *structuralisme*. The latter movement, if I understand it rightly, is a crypto-epistemological doctrine, starting from a point which was once a commonplace in the idealist polemic against empiricism: namely, that signs are not just echoes of things, trace-marks of experience, but that, on the contrary, they can only function as parts of a system, that to understand them one must see the system of alternatives of which they form a part. The essence of 'John' is not its relation to John, but its relation to 'Peter', 'Paul' and so forth. The system of terms faces the system of things, and *each* is to be understood more through its internal structure and its generation, than through some simple echo-relation between them both. Modern *structuralisme* differs from idealism primarily by not contenting itself with formulating this, in the abstract, as a criticism of empiricism, but by endeavouring to be specific, concrete, operational, and showing just how these cognitive systems are constructed and how they work. Chomsky starts from the fact that the boundary between what is and what is not an acceptable sentence in a given language can be indicated, and an abstract model can then be constructed which will show how the sentences within the range of acceptable ones can be 'generated'. Lévi-Strauss, using material which is ethnographic and less clearly self-defining than is the material of linguistics, and procedures which are suggestive rather than rigorous and precise, attempts something which is meant to be analogous in the more difficult, elusive and fluid spheres such as those of mythology. It seems to me that the kind of old structuralism which I am sketching and commending is both narrower and broader than the currently fashionable *structuralisme*. It is narrower in that one of its central concerns is not with what a society can conceive or say, but what kind of thing it actually does. It is concerned with conceptual limits in those cases in which they are crucial in limiting conduct; in those numerous other cases where the limits of actual conduct remain well within the limits of the conceivable, it is concerned with those other, non-conceptual constraints that were actually operative. The sociologist and the anthropologist must be concerned with many non-conceptual constraints, and it is not clear that (or how) these could have a logic similar to the generation of possibilities by (say) the combination of polar opposites. Moreover, the sociologist must also be very concerned with that most fascinating form of social change which occurs when conduct breaks through the conceptual barrier of a society, when people do something for which as yet they have no name, no niche within their system of classifications.

At the same time, the concerns of the sociologist are also broader than those of the *structuraliste*. The range of what is thinkable and the way it arises is something which must itself be explained. The present *structuraliste* vogue in sociology, with its idea—or jargon—of treating society as a 'code', is open to a number of suspicions or cautions. For one thing, the units of social life are far less clearly defined than those of language and much less homogeneous in kind. Linguists are fortunate in possessing a domain whose units are at least relatively self-defining and isolable. But actions seldom have the comparatively clear outline of a word or a sentence. They are certainly not all transmitted or experienced in more or less the same medium, as language is. Moreover, a society, if it is a 'language' at all, is a much more loosely defined one than is language in the literal sense. Its sanctions are for ever breaking down. A 'transformational linguist' can separate, relatively easily, acceptable from unacceptable sentences in a given language, and proceed to seek the rules which generate the former and exclude the latter. The sociologist has no such initial advantage. There is not much sense in describing any social event as 'unacceptable' (sociologically speaking that is, of course, not morally), and there is no clear equivalent in social behaviour to the incompetent user of a language.

Indeed, the whole *Problemstellung* is radically different. Though the sanctions are ever breaking down in social life, giving us but a hazy boundary between that which is acceptable and that which is not (sociologically, of course, not morally), at the same time the concrete nature of those sanctions, despite or because of their frequent failure, is of central interest to the investigation. This is not so in linguistics. The linguist is quite content with an abstract model of the generative procedure and its enforcement, leaving its concrete identification to some distant future advances in neuro-physiology. For the sociologist, the concrete identification of the sanctions is central and cannot be postponed.

The nature of the questions also differs in other ways. The sociologist, though interested in what could happen, is quite particularly concerned with what does happen. In other words, if society were a language, he could be said to be more concerned with *parole* than with *langue*. Moreover, he is quite particularly interested in the actual sequence of 'messages' and the way in which earlier items constrain later ones. This is hardly so in linguistics, which cannot have very much to say about the way in which earlier members of long sequences constrain later ones. (Long soliloquies are seldom uniquely determined.) For the linguist, what is of interest is the so to speak vertical nexus between the rules and the individual utterance. (These rules, admittedly, may sometimes exclude certain sequences.) For the sociologist, this kind of interest (which can only very partially be satisfied, owing to the looseness of these vertical rules in sociology), is at least rivalled by the concern with the horizontal nexus between successive events.

Thus, although social actions are presumably generated from some kind of matrix, and are selected from a bounded range of alternatives whose possibilities are limited by the elements used by a social system and by the rules for combining them, the relationships between social actions, and the relationships between messages, nevertheless are in many profound ways very different. In the end, a society is a more complex thing than a language. The problems which need to be answered are different in kind. The tempting analogies which seem to inspire *structuralisme* are suspect. The sociologist must beware of two dangers: those supposedly hard-headed historians or realists who deny the need of any account more powerful and abstract than mere narrative, and those over-optimistic and eager souls who think they can easily borrow and fruitfully adapt a formal model from simpler and perhaps more fortunate fields such as linguistics or even phonetics.

4 Self-generating games

Our present concern is with the relation of history to anthropology and sociology. It may be useful to go back to the chess analogy. A game of chess is, most emphatically, a story, a sequence of events meaningfully connected. Moreover, a precise notation exists for telling the story, without ambiguity. A sociological account, however, is analogous to explaining the story to someone, say a child, who is unfamiliar with the rules of chess: the rules must be specified, and it must be explained why and how they constrain certain moves, why some moves are mandatory, others preferable, some forbidden, some allowed but disastrous. To begin with, a sociologist is like a man among a population of chess experts who are so familiar with the game that its rules are nowhere written down. He must elicit the rules from the games in progress and relate them to the development of each game. But his task is harder still. The rules of chess are very stable, and they are imposed on each game by a convention external to that game, a convention which is a kind of absolute and extraneous datum as far as any one game is concerned. The account of the origin of that convention, and the processes by which it is sustained, is in no way part of the analysis of an individual game. Not so for the sociologist. The tacit rules or constraints limiting human behaviour are not stable, and the mechanisms which enforce them are not extraneous to the story in progress: on the contrary, from the sociologist's viewpoint, they are by far the most interesting aspect of that game. Many societies believe, of course, that the ground-rules *are* extraneously imposed: they shift onto the supernatural the responsibility for their own conventions. But this is an illusion from which the sociologist is professionally debarred. *The constraints, the 'rules' within which social life is played out, are themselves a consequence of the game.* (The only thing given extraneously are the rules imposed by nature, but they are minimal and in an important way unspecific: they leave quite open just *how* their imperatives are satisfied. They only require *that* they be satisfied.) A 'structural' account of a society is an account of how this comes to be: how the game itself generates and sustains the limits within which it is played. This is the really crucial fact about sociological method. This manner of formulating it shows why the task is so much harder than that of a chess analyst, who has no need to explain just why the players will not knock over the board, why the rook will not move diagonally, and so forth.

It would no doubt be unfair to imply that 'pure' historians are like chess journalists who give accounts of the development of given games without realizing that the rules themselves must be specified and cannot be taken for granted. In fact historians do frequently explain the nexus between successive events in an historical sequence, and indicate what background factors sanctioned, so to speak, the particular connection. But for better or worse, they do it *ad hoc* and unsystematically. I suppose that the most plausible case that could be made out for anti-sociological history would maintain that this can indeed best be done, or be done only, in an *ad hoc* manner. Sociology is based on the hope or conviction that it can be done systematically and not *ad hoc*. Social anthropology is interestingly contrasted with narrative history, in that everything is the other way around, as it were: narratives do occur within anthropology, but it is precisely the narrative which is *ad hoc*, illustrative, unsystematic, not bound by any obligation to be complete and rounded off. It is the structural account which is central—the specification of the constraining limits and their sanctions. The ideal sought is a kind of stalemate situation, the demonstration that whatever move is attempted by any participant, the resulting situation must needs remain the same. (This does not mean that the method is committed to some absurd postulate of universal social stability. Non-circular as well as circular situations can be constrained. Circular ones are only the simplest and most manageable ones.) The structure is the thing, the stories are incidental.

It is of course natural that anthropology should have developed these traits. It was initially concerned with milieux that were highly exotic, with games whose rules were far from familiar. At the same time, lack of historical records in the societies in question made long story-sequences hard to come by, and such records as happened to be available were highly suspect. Hence a concentration on eliciting the tacit structures was imposed both by the inherent nature of the material, and by the lack of opportunity for other concerns. But why should a similar attitude be mandatory closer to home, where fascinating and well-documented 'stories' are available, and where at the same time the rules of the game are not so exotic and unfamiliar?

For one thing, it seems to me that the familiarity, or at any rate the intelligibility, of the local rules of the game is an illusion. Though a society is not nearly as similar to a language or a code as current fashion would have it, nevertheless I am sure that what Chomsky says in the abstract and negatively about grammar is also true about the rules of social life: 'Clearly, the rules and principles of . . . grammar are *not accessible to consciousness in general*, though some undoubtedly are . . . What we discover . . . is that those principles and rules that are accessible to consciousness are interspersed in some obscure and apparently chaotic way among others that are not, the whole complex . . . constituting a system of a very tight and intricate design . . .'.[3] No doubt we are in thrall to a kind of social Unconscious, to a set of partly obscured conventions or rules governing our own operations, though this Unconscious is not at all of a Freudian kind (which was merely a weird and wild caricature of the kind of connections we recognize consciously). Nothing is more false than the supposition that we have easy, direct and privileged access to the conventions governing our own conduct simply because it is our conduct, because we 'live' through the concepts which accompany it. We have nothing of the kind.

What follows is that the whole notion of restricting history to an account of 'how it really was' is an absurdity. It is common to criticize this idea on the grounds that 'what really happened' needs to be selected and interpreted. No doubt. But the really crucial objection is that the connections between events that 'really happened' are anything but self-evident, and that such self-evidence as they may seem to have to the participants is illusory. In some measure, the rapid and dramatic nature of social change has brought this point home. Contemporary history is seldom a long story within a stable and familiar game. It does not encourage the illusion of the self-evident status of the rules of the game. It does not any longer make social structure invisible through excessive familiarity. On the contrary, it makes it painfully problematical. Our social environment is like the controls of a very unfamiliar vehicle. We gingerly press the accelerator, and find it to be a brake. We slam the foot on the brake and find it to be an accelerator. In such conditions, the illusion that there are no hidden mechanisms, that the role of the social levers is self-evident and inscribed into the nature of things, and that their instinctive mastery is our birthright—these illusions are no longer so tempting. Profoundly alien and barely intelligible conventions and connections are not exotic and distant, but close to home—and sometimes they envelop us.

All this being so, the sociologizing of history, the acquisition of the kind of sensitivity possessed by the anthropologist, is natural and inevitable.

5 Collapse of horizons

Within its seriously held cognitive stock, our society possesses only naturalistic and tentative cosmogonies, whose role in chartering current social arrangements is negligible; and, in the literal sense, it possesses no eschatologies at all. But given that cosmogonies and eschatologies, or what we have called the social horizons, did in the past constitute an important part of the vision of societies, one may well ask—what performs this role today?

The answer is obvious. The horizons have, so to speak, collapsed into the present. The crucial events which are the charters of moralities, which mould the decisive features of our life, which limit, articulate, and help evaluate our options, are not on the skyline, but, on the contrary, very close to home. The distant horizons, though not necessarily shabby or dull, are not very relevant. Contemporary history is not merely very dramatic, but, more significantly, it is crucial for the formulation, selection, validation of such alternatives as humanity may face. I used to think that we at any rate were a generation which could actually witness the drawing of the Social Contract, by observing the manner in which societies chose to 'develop' themselves. So we are, but it is really even deeper than that. We can witness a Creation story. Genesis is something that we read in the present tense. Let us recapitulate possible types of cosmogonies. The list may not be exhaustive, but it will include those species that make claims on our attention.

a Traditional Genesis-type stories
Usually located in the fairly distant past. Characterized by the fact that they are structure-blind—the rules of that distant game, the outcome of which was our world, are taken for granted. In this kind of story, the *dramatis personae* are introduced (or is introduced, in

the singular) and perform acts which bring about our world. Who or what decreed that they should have the options which they appear to have, and that the options should have the effects which, according to the story, they do have? Answer comes there none, for the question does not seem to have been asked. Take one example: there must, it seems, have been a kind of meta-world within which a deity chose, for ends which must make sense within that world and which would seem to be somewhat vainglorious, to create our world in order to augment its own prestige by receiving the adulation of its own creation. A curious story, and one which hardly lives up to the highest moral standards recognized inside our created world. Teachers, or manufacturers of artefacts, who openly avow the aim of having themselves praised by their own products, are somewhat comic figures. But what is relevant for our purpose is that this strange meta-story moves within a framework, the rules of which it takes for granted. Charles Lamb has some apt comments on this curious acceptance of mysterious rules:[4]

> That the intercourse was open at all between both worlds was perhaps the mistake—but that once assumed, I see no reason for disbelieving one attested story of this nature more than another on the score of absurdity. There is no law to judge of the lawless, or canon by which a dream may be criticized.
> . . . Our ancestors were bolder or more obtuse. Amidst the universal belief that [witches] were in league with the author of all evil, holding hell tributary to their muttering . . . no simple justice of the peace seems to have scrupled issuing . . . a warrant upon them—as if they should subpoena Satan! Prospero—in his boat, with his books and wand about him, suffers himself to be conveyed away at the mercy of his enemies to an unknown island. He might have raised a storm or two, we think, on the passage. . . . We do not know the laws of that country.

Lamb is tactfully commenting on those episodes in which the Other World impinges on our own, but his point is doubly valid for the Opening and Closing scenes of our drama, when the Other World initiates or terminates our play as a whole. 'We do not know the laws of that country.' Nor do we know those of our own, though when they are stable we may take them for granted. But just as in stable conditions our own are taken for granted, so the unsophisticated take for granted both ours and those of the other country. It takes a Robertson Smith to spell out the tacit rules which the simple believer knows only through their unquestioned effects, whose ground-rules he does not query. But, once queried, this kind of cosmogony collapses.

b The Enlightenment

In its typical form, this is a clear ancestor of our own vision, in that the crucial event is close to home and not somewhere in the sky-line. It takes the dualistic religious vision, and inverts and naturalizes it: where the Kingdom of God stood opposed to the world of the Fall from Grace, there now stood Reason and Nature as opposed to the illusion of the Kingdom of God. But, notoriously, the Enlightenment's understanding of the two crucial options was rather limited. It was the failure to implement its vision after 1789 that forced its votaries to develop a more serious sense of social structure.

c Evolutionist or Hegelian-type cosmogonies

The two-term vision of the Enlightenment was replaced by something far more ramified, and correspondingly less crowded into the historic present. Crucial things may indeed be happening now, but similarly crucial ones had been happening, it appears, for quite a time. *All* history and not just the elimination of infamy was the revelation of a Grand Design. The locus of crucial events remains the historic world, but the cruxes are, so to speak, far more dispersed. Romanticism is of course far less ethnocentric in time than was the Enlightenment. It naturally has a far better sense of social structure and a greater sensitivity to its variety. On the other hand, it tends to overrate historical continuity, the unilineality of development, and the identity of basic underlying plot. As a cosmogony, it is hardly acceptable to us, precisely because it overrates continuity, and uses this for facile and unacceptable solutions. 'More of the same', where what 'the same' was varies as between, say, Hegelians and Spencerians, is no longer a plausible formula when we come to choose our directions.

d The empiricist-atomistic picture

Officially of course this is not a cosmogony at all, but merely an epistemology. In fact, it does tell a kind of story of how the world came to be built up—*Der logische Aufbau der Welt*—as one of the authors in this tradition brazenly has it. Moreover—a fact not always noticed—this world-construction story does indeed perform the role of cosmogonies, and provides a premise and charter for a general world-outlook, for a view of human life. It says, in effect, that each man's world is built up anew, from homogeneous sensory constituents, which are the ultimate elements of all things. Its motto might well be: every man is his own cosmogony. The corollary of this, which in fact we frequently find exemplified amongst modern representatives of this school, is an almost total lack of a sense of history. Though they are sometimes called positivists, they differ markedly in this respect from Comte who bequeathed them the name. Given the importance they attribute to their own vision, one might expect them to be interested in the differences between societies Before and After Positivism. As Christians were sometimes worried whether Socrates ought not to have been amongst the saved, notwithstanding the unfortunate dating of his life, these positivists might wish to face the same problem in reverse and be puzzled by the occurrences of genuine cognition prior to their own Illumination. But it is not so. In many cases, their blindness to history and society is total.

e The Neo-Enlightenment view: our own

For a variety of reasons, since 1945 it has become difficult to begin a classification of societies with any dichotomy other than industrial/pre-industrial. This distinction, so platitudinous now, did of course require clear formulation before it became obvious, and Raymond Aron will remain associated with its brilliant articulation. A variety of factors made the categories which were still in use during the war —such as democracy, capitalism and socialism—visibly irrelevant. There is no need to rehearse once again the factors which contributed to this shift of vision. The consequence was a view which once again, like that of the Enlightenment and unlike the intervening Evolutionism, was a two-term one, and one which located the crucial transition somewhere near the present rather than at the beginning or the end of time. But it is a vision less starry-eyed than that of the Enlightenment, incorporating romantic regret as well as progressive hope, and above all, it is a vision taking over from the nineteenth century a far richer sense of the diversity and complexity of social forms.

I have endeavoured elsewhere to spell out the presuppositions and consequence of this vision.[5] Perhaps, like other and earlier (and hence more excusable) writers, I over-rated the homogeneity and simplicity of the transition. Formally, I doubt whether the text could be convicted of such an error, and the same is probably true of other writers of the time, and earlier. But what is at issue is not anyone's prophetic record, but rather the recognition of a shift of perception in recent years. Whether or not one formally excluded it, one did not sufficiently stress the manifold, complex, multi-stage nature of the 'development' process.

The work of the economist Arrow on voting procedures is well known. A famous point is that, given an electorate with a set of individual preference-rankings for a set of alternatives, if the alternatives are presented for voting in pairs, successively (with the loser eliminated in each case), the final option selected will depend on the *order* in which the choices have to be made. For reasons which cannot be so neatly formalized, the development process seems to possess a similar characteristic. A number of different decisions need to be taken, in the economic, political, social and other fields. The order in which the various choices are made have important, perhaps permanent consequences for the way in which 'development' is attained. To take the most obvious example, it makes an enormous difference whether a society embarks on the developmental process with well-established liberal pluralistic institutions, or whether the attempt to acquire them is only made in the course of it. The two traits, economic development and liberal institutions, are not just parts of a syndrome which may be expected to turn up in one order or another: the sequence of appearance or option may be quite crucial for the final pattern. It is hardly possible here to discuss specific theses in this area, but the kind of awareness described naturally leads to the formulation of questions such as Barrington Moore's[6] concerning the effect of the position of the peasantry on the subsequent pattern of development, or David Martin's[7] projected work on the quite diverse social patterns characterizable as 'secularization'.

Development is not a single path—unilinealism has by now died many, many deaths—it is a complex network of routes. Even Marx's 'Precapitalist social formations', if plotted on paper, would look not like a single great road, but more like the Southern Railway's commuter network. But the network is not endlessly permissive. Some early choices perhaps commit one, or damn one, for ever. So we are witnessing not merely the Social Contract and Genesis; we are also privileged to observe what normally is transcendental and hidden, that great existential moment when large portions of humanity commit, or hover on the brink of, Original Sin and Eternal Damnation. Admittedly, even when we see them take the leap, we cannot be quite sure that we can reliably distinguish the Saved from the Damned. We may be allowed to hope that in the end God's mercy will prevail and *all* will be saved. But nothing entitles us to reject with confidence quite the opposite hypothesis. This also is an essential part of our contemporary historical sensitivity.

6 The logic of creation

The price of the collapse of horizons, of the shift of cosmogony and eschatology into the present, is that one acquires only too intimate an experience of the logic of an absolute Creation situation. To be eye-witness of Genesis is not altogether enviable. Creation out of nothing—in other words Creation rather than mere creation—presents some rather special problems. I am not referring to the technical problem of how such a miracle can be wrought. This need not worry us: we know that it is happening, and the 'how' can be left aside. The problem which does concern us is how one chooses one's aims, one's course of action, in a Creation situation. Ordinary, non-Creation situations have a fairly straightforward logic. A stable identity is assumed for the agent, which implies reasonably stable basic aims. Likewise, a reasonably stable, determinate environment is assumed. These two things being given, it follows, for any given level of information, and assuming consistency, that one—possibly more if things are evenly balanced—optimal courses of conduct are indicated. But the point is that a real Creation situation is not at all like this. *Everything* and notably aims and environment, are themselves being created. What, then, can dictate, or even suggest, the course of action to be followed by the Creator?

Primitive cosmogonies evade this problem in their naïve way by covertly making the creation less than total, by tacitly or otherwise crediting the Creator with a given set of aims (such as a curious concern with his own glory, which apparently can be augmented when endorsed by his own, suitably programmed creation), and a constraining environment which must somehow limit his choice of means in the attainment of that rather peculiar aim. If such constraining circumstances were not present, he could presumably decree the end directly, without the cumbersome and troublesome intermediary use of an often recalcitrant creation. The story of religious creation mirrors the logic of action as we normally know it. It completely fails to give an account of the problem of what genuine Creation would be like. Perhaps this did not matter much, when a pure Creation situation was well outside the range of our own possible experience. My point is, however, that what is now known as 'development' has forced this unusual experience on us, and we must ponder its logic.

It may of course be objected that our situation is not a 'pure' creation situation at all, either because in fact we start not from a void but from a complex pre-industrial civilization, or because we are not bereft of all directives, of all given aims, but on the contrary possess, incapsulated in our nature, some 'basic human needs' or something of the kind: the need to cater for these saves us from the moral vacuum, from the normative *premiselessness* credited to a 'Creation' situation. These objections are invalid. Factually, it is of course true that our historic starting point was not some total void, but a complex social order. So it was. But the inheritance has no authority over us whatever. It is of the essence of the Development process, not that all of the past is abrogated, but that none of it is authoritative. It cannot be invoked; the fragments of it that survive do so either because they were validated by other, non-traditional considerations, or because they came into no conflict, were involved in no issue, and were perpetuated from a kind of indifference. As for those 'basic needs' (a favourite philosophical ploy under a variety of names), they are so basic, elementary, minimal and unspecific, that almost nothing can be inferred from the need to satisfy them. All important questions concerning the form of life that we are to mould are about *how*, not *whether*, they are to be satisfied—and on this, they can offer no guidance whatever. It could also be claimed that technology is not and will not be so powerful as to free us from all restraints. Certainly this is so. Nevertheless, the range of choice it now tends to offer is so wide that our problem is the choice within that range, and we are not much helped by the consideration that the range itself is not limitless.

The questions posed by a Creation situation have no determinate answer. The very terms of reference preclude it. Yet those terms of reference do, for reasons indicated, correspond pretty well to our general situation.

So? In practice, the problem is evaded. It is true that the old values are suspended. The famous 'transvaluation of all values' which pre-occupied most nineteenth-century moralists in addition to Nietzsche (such as the Utilitarians or Marx, though they used other terms) was really only a suspension of the old values: all those moralists are convincing when they suspend the old, and unconvincing, ambiguous and vacillating in their choice of new ones. But in practice, all the new options turn up, as we stressed in the discussion of the complexity of the development process, not all together, not on one agenda, not in one fell swoop, but in dribs and drabs, one by one. Moreover, so far at least, and by all appearances also for quite some time to come, the options arrive well before we are in full and un-trammelled possession of the new technological powers. They come when there are still strong pressures on very scarce resources, in circumstances which, by accident rather than from long-term and considered design, dictate this or that interim solution. So, by the time we do have full technological elbow-room, the options will have been prejudged by the more or less accidental pressures which oper-ated when the relevant crossroad was first reached. Interim solutions became parts of viable, habituation-hallowed cultures.

This, then, is another curious and ironic role history has within our general vision: it helps to prejudge questions for which, if we had to face them rationally, we could simply have no determinate answers. All the premises would be too slippery. One great interest of con-temporary history is just this: how does the sequence of alternatives, and the pressing circumstances in which they make their appearance in diverse societies, help prejudge the questions of value, which otherwise would be beyond the scope of rational decision? Tradi-tional societies credited their ultimate choices, over which they had no control and which they did not much understand, to the nature of things or the whim of gods. We have (we like to think) some under-standing of how the choices arise, and our history intrigues us by narrowing our range of choice, thus saving us from the embarrassment of excessive free will.

1971

Notes

1 For instance, Mrs Shirley Letwin writes (*Spectator*, 9 January 1971, 52 and 54): 'historians are not concerned with what might have happened, they try to explain what actually did happen. They do not explain an event in terms of its connection with universal laws; they trace its connection with other events. . . . as long as he remains a historian, he [does not use] events to illustrate laws.' Mrs Letwin, who clearly here speaks as the representative of a whole school, proceeds, rightly from her viewpoint, to repudiate Max Weber, ideal types, and the whole Kantian notion that rational explanation must mean subsumption under general law. The contrasted ideal appears to be accurate narrative, rational in some other, non-Kantian, sense.

2 Cf. W. B. Gallie, *Philosophy and Historical Understanding*, London 1964.

3 John Locke Lectures, given in Oxford in 1969. Italics mine.

4 Charles Lamb, *Essays of Elia: Witches and other night fears*, London.

5 Ernest Gellner, *Thought and Change*, London 1964.

6 Barrington Moore Jr, *Social Origins of Dictatorship and Democracy*, Boston 1966.

7 David Martin, 'Notes for a general theory of secularisation', *European Journal of Sociology*, 10, 1969, 192–201.

Chapter 10   Ernst Kolman: or, knowledge and communism

One can take a horse to water but one cannot make him drink. Similarly, you can thaw out intellectuals but you cannot make them think. Some will and some can't. The different degree to which various Soviet thinkers have liberalized their thought since Stalin's death illustrates this. This differentiation reflects or leads to an opposition between a liberal and a dogmatic wing.

A most characteristic, intelligent, and frank expression of the liberal view is a recent pamphlet published in Moscow by Professor Ernst Iaromirovich Kolman about the philosophic problems of contemporary physics.[1] This perceptive, closely argued essay shows how far things have moved: it could never be the object of the classical Russian joke of de-Stalinization that thought is the shortest line between two quotations.

The subject which, not surprisingly, appears to rouse very great interest in present Soviet thought is indeed the philosophical implications of physics. The effort is to show that the typically modern features of physics such as Heisenberg's discovery about sub-atomic particles, the transmutation of energy and mass, the co-presence of wave- and particle-models, Einsteinian relativity, are all to be interpreted in a 'materialistic' way. If one reflects on the extent to which modern physics has stimulated contemporary 'bourgeois philosophy' (e.g. Einstein's treatment of simultaneity preparing the ground for the positivist doctrine that a sign without a role is one without meaning, or the way the use of non-Euclidean geometries has helped revive positivist epistemologies), and on the eagerness of the official Marxists to turn the tables here, one is tempted to conclude that the prize is to gain the approval of physics: the truth of physics being agreed universally, the job of the philosopher is to prove that physics entails his world-view. We smile at medieval philosophers striving to prove what Revelation supplied anyway, but the job of their mid-twentieth-century descendants seems similar. What makes us all so sure that physics is our Revelation[2] is of course the atom bomb, Sputnik, and technology generally. Just this verification by human practice is naturally claimed by the Marxist as a confirmation of his thesis (though it is something the 'bourgeois' positivist or pragmatist would not dream of wishing to deny); whilst the apparent irrelevance of the rival older philosophic interpretations (materialism, idealism) is precisely what underlines the positivist, pragmatist, etc., re-interpretation. It is this alleged irrelevance that the Marxists are most concerned to deny: if it obtained, the significant and exclusive claim of 'dialectical materialism' to be a scientific philosophy, to be *the* world-outlook of scientific civilization and the sole repository of the authority and prestige conveyed by science, would lapse. The problem is however how to tie up Marxism and physical science closely enough to establish this claim, and yet not *so* closely as (*a*) to fall foul of the existence and excellence and historical importance of non-Marxist physicists, and (*b*) to hinder and irritate Soviet physicists. (The latter requirement is presumably more important: the former might, if it stood alone, be satisfied to some extent by censorship, rewriting of history, etc.) Light is thrown on the existence and particular form of this dilemma by Kolman's essay.

Two theories about physicists in a totalitarian society are I suppose now exploded. One is the theory that fundamental research is impossible without general intellectual freedom. The second theory is that whilst it *is* possible, it is achieved by a kind of internal iron curtain, by insulating scientific thinking from ideological thinking. This is more plausible, though it ignores two facts; the intelligence of the scientist and the stupidity of the ideologue: the latter cannot be trusted not to interfere even if the former could be trusted to keep his blinkers on. (Only a cynical ideologue might be good at surveying such an arrangement, and there is no evidence to suggest that the commissars are a species of Renaissance cardinal.) Anyway, plausible or not, it is clear on the internal evidence of recently published Soviet works, and particularly Kolman's pamphlet, that this did not occur either.

It is sometimes said of Soviet society and culture that it is at present passing through a Victorian stage. It does indeed display a characteristic nineteenth-century trait, the conflict between science and religion. We see earnest men facing the dilemma of how much freedom to allow to science, how much to concede to its discoveries, *without* undermining what they consider to be the essential ideological props of morals and society: or how much to insist on those ideological props without flying in the face of science or inhibiting it. Or perhaps one should look for an analogy earlier, in the Western Europe of the sixteenth and seventeenth centuries: quite obviously, on the internal evidence of these books, there must have been some anonymous Russian Galileo Galileievich Galileiskii of the Stalin period who went away from some Soviet Inquisition muttering, say, *à propos* of Heisenberg—'And yet it is undetermined!'

This analogy may be more apposite than the Victorian in as far as there appears to be little inclination on anyone's part to go the whole hog in the rejection of the social ideology, at any rate openly. The liberal wing try rather to make room for science as it now is and for liberalism *within* Marxism by reinterpretation and by making it more abstract and formal, reminiscent of the way once tried by some *philosophes* in the West. I doubt whether the failure of the liberal wing to go further can be attributed only to the fact that views that *did* go further would not reach print. No doubt this plays a part, but I imagine that national pride of achievement, the desire not to upset too violently a social fabric which on the whole is accepted, *and* the fact that Marxism *can* be made sufficiently formal (as many belief systems can) to allow all necessary elbow-room inside, are also factors in the minds of those who think inside Russia today. One does not get the impression that, in making Marxism formal, they have even potentially the desire to go as far as Polish intellectuals have gone (with some of whom one has the impression of purely nominal Marxism covering an appalling intellectual anomie, scepticism and readiness to turn to anything).

Logically, Kolman's essay might well have been included in the collection *Some Philosophical Problems of Natural Science* which appeared recently in Moscow: one wonders whether its isolation is significant and connected with its strikingly liberal tone. It may be worth specifying what little I know (not, I should stress, from any internal evidence of the pamphlet) about its author.

Ernst Kolman was originally a native of Prague, where he studied mathematics before the First World War, and at that time his orientation was Jewish rather than, or as well as, Leftish. He became involved with Russian Communism when, having been sent to the Russian front with the Austrian army, he found himself in Russia during the Revolution as a prisoner of war. Like some others in that situation, he joined the Bolsheviks and spent the inter-war period in the Soviet Union. (He does, however, remark in the pamphlet that he visited Cambridge and Rutherford's laboratory in 1931.) He returned to Prague only after the Second World War to become Professor of Philosophy at the Caroline University: presumably the Czech Communist leaders in Moscow during the war decided that it would be useful to take him back, given the dearth of Czech Marxist theoreticians of any calibre.

In Prague he made a considerable impression as a speaker and was said to be close to and influential with Gottwald. Even during the Stalinist period he published a book on logic which I have read but no longer possess, of which however I remember that it gave clear signs of acquaintance with and recognition of Western philosophical logic, including as it did a description of Russell's paradox and the specification of Russell's solution of it, without however naming Russell. (It also contained a surprisingly naïve discussion of probability and the status of empirical knowledge, equating the probability of beliefs with the number of instances supporting it.) An interesting story about him was brought back by one of the delegation of British Communist students to one of the many youth jamborees in Prague: namely, that he declined to speak on behalf of the Communist candidate in some student election, on the ground that his professional status required impartiality in such matters, and that the Communist students' organization succeeded in forcing him to reconsider this and speak on their behalf by appealing over his head to the Party. At the same time, in the comparatively liberal atmosphere of Prague prior to 1948, he appears to have depressed non-Marxists by his dogmatic but well-delivered and influential lectures, directed at presenting Marxism as 'the only scientific philosophy'. In 1949 he was sent back to Russia because, it is believed, he criticized the Party leaders and their way of life. (Presumably he was in fact lucky not to be in Prague during the period of Stalin's last years.) He then became a Professor in Tiflis. Apart from the fact that he is given the title of 'Professor', it is not possible to tell his present status from the pamphlet, which reproduces a public lecture delivered in Moscow.

Kolman's essay does admittedly very soon (in the fourth paragraph) bring in Lenin and *Materialism and Empiriocriticism,* thus legitimating his argument in the approved theological manner (though the first proper name mentioned is Roentgen). He does, however, soon go on to point out the fundamental transformation that physics has undergone in the half-century since Lenin wrote, and whilst the development of physics is asserted to have fully confirmed the basic views of Lenin's work of genius, none the less 'it would be a mockery of the creative revolutionary spirit of Lenin's work' if we were to insist on every letter of his text or apply uncritically every part of his position, stated in 1908 and true then, to the physics of 1957.

Kolman goes on to indicate the two main features of modern physics: (1) Its dependence on a new and massive experimental technology, qualitatively different from the experimental technology of the nineteenth century, and illustrating the ultimate dependence of science on the productive forces of society, and (2) the extreme abstractness and mathematicization of its theory. He makes use of the first point to attack the idealist philosophy of physics of the capitalist countries, which interprets physics as primarily or only theoretical. (It is in connection with this point that he mentions his visit to Rutherford's laboratory, where, as he mentions, Kapitsa was working at the time: he comments that Rutherford's equipment was still extremely simple and manufactured in an artisan-like way—with the exception of one powerful and essential dynamo—but that all this was the last survival of an out-of-date technology of research, only preserved so long 'thanks to the conservative English tradition'.) I do not know whether there are indeed 'idealist' philosophers of physics who would deny such a connection—one would not expect the instrumentalists for instance to do so—though there may well be some who fail to stress it. Anyway, this is a fair and significant point, and it is unlikely that difficulties in squaring physics and Marxism will arise on this score. Such difficulties as there are arise in connection with the second point, the abstract, i.e. counter-intuitive and hence prima facie non-materialist concepts employed in physics.

Kolman is clearly a man of very considerable philosophic sophistication, and in his Marxist apologetics he in fact employs philosophic weapons drawn from other systems and which look odd in the Marxist armoury. For instance, when face-saving materialism against the relativization of mass and energy and of matter and field in modern physics, he ultimately falls back on treating this as a striking *confirmation* of dialectical materialism, as follows: these oppositions merely show that both aspects are characteristics of one ultimate objective reality—active matter. This is of course a logical grammatical point very familiar in recent bourgeois philosophy, i.e. the notion underlying the Aristotelian–Leibnizian view of the ultimateness of substance, and which really boils down to no more than that, with some ingenuity, any theory can be verbally reformulated in a subject-predicate form, as the attribution of some characteristics to some subject. One wonders whether Kolman himself really treats this argument seriously: one has the impression that he does not, for having stated it, he brusquely says, 'But let us return to elementary particles', and without further ado does so.

Elsewhere, criticizing bourgeois cosmologies, he curiously employs the Kantian argument to the effect that the conception of the 'world as a whole' is contradictory (hence *bourgeois* cosmologies cannot be true: but does not this argument lend itself to a dangerous generalization?), and also an argument about different types of truth, curiously reminiscent of contemporary Western philosophy, to the effect that assertions such as that the universe is infinite are of a different kind from, and cannot be confirmed similarly and with equal force as, propositions such as two plus two makes four or that we are all mortal.

I have not commented on his exposition of straight physics, which I am unqualified to assess but which seems to me excellent as exposition and akin in content to similar semi-popular expositions available here, with the exception of those points where he throws doubt on interpretations of physical theories, maintaining, for example, that whilst relativity lends itself to the inference of the finitude of the universe, it is nevertheless insufficient to establish it. It appears that it is insufficient not because of something specific to it, but *qua* physical theory, the concepts of finitude and infinitude being essential components of our world outlook (i.e. more fundamental than any physical theory); at this point we are taken back to 'dialectical materialism', which is conveniently alleged to teach the incompleteness of our knowledge of the world at any given time—which presumably allows us to reject any interpretation not compatible with it (as illustrating that incompleteness). . . . We are once again reminded of those attempts in the West to 'square' science and religion by stressing all convenient aspects of the former, but promptly invoking 'levels of truth' or whatnot when they conflict. Elsewhere he more than throws doubt, he appears to reject outright the doctrine of a cosmological commencement, on the grounds that such theories inevitably lead to the invocation of non-material causes and hence to religion. Do they? How pleased some of our theologians would be if this were so, if interpretations of science with us really were in general so systematically distorted as to support religion!

One of the points at which Marxist theology is indeed liable to conflict with the freedom of physics is cosmology: the supposed need to combat religious theories of the Creation and of the Last Judgment drive the 'dialectical materialist' into an attempt to make eternity of the world, its unboundedness in space, and the conservation of matter, into dogmas. Kolman tries to undermine some recent 'Western' cosmologies by suggesting that the 'expansion of the universe' may be a 'local' phenomenon restricted to our meta-galaxy, and also by suggesting that entropy cannot be predicated of the universe as a whole. Kolman does allow himself some derisive remarks about the 'astrophysicists Hoyle, Gold and Bondi', rather unfairly giving the Russian reader the impression that theistic conceptions play a constitutive part in the theory of the permanent creation of matter. The present reviewer would at this point like to offer some aid to any Marxist who wishes to expose the full motives, the ideological roots of the views of Hoyle & Co. These roots do not really have anything to do with attempts to revive the Book of Genesis in modern dress. The real basis has always been obvious to me. The correct diagnosis is analogous to the classical one made by Marx and Engels of German Idealism, as offering the German bourgeoisie a transcendental consolation prize for the power it then so sadly lacked, and it runs as follows: in the nineteenth century, colonial empires were expanding, and the Western bourgeoisie was quite content with permanently conserved matter in physics. But *today*!—

we are losing one colony after another! The terrified bourgeoisie is only too delighted to let Hoyle, etc., console it with the doctrine that, whilst we are losing one *colony* after another, the amount of matter at least is increasing all the time. . . . (This is my own idea, but any Marxist writer on bourgeois ideology is welcome to borrow it, even without acknowledgment.)

However, Kolman's apologetics are less interesting than the liberal parts of his argument. He remarks towards the end that after the Twentieth Congress 'conditions in the Soviet Union favour the abandonment of dogmatism; they could bridge the gap between philosophy and the progress of science, and put an end to the notorious [*sic*] alienation of a part of our natural scientists from philosophy' (i.e. Marxism). In a preceding passage he gives us information about how this alienation came about: 'It cannot be denied that some of our philosophers have in recent years committed crude errors, attacking certain scientific theories, such as Relativity, for no better reason than that its authors appear to be idealists and add idealistic interpretations to them, and have characterized these scientists as politically reactionary. Such a nihilistic [*sic*] attitude to the achievements of world science has done harm to our science and technology. It has also led to the alienation of [our] scientists from philosophy.' Kolman goes on to qualify this by saying that some scientists, previously attached to Mach-ian positions, utilizing these errors of the (Marxist) philosophers, have rejected not only unfounded, but also justified criticisms. (Kolman does not pause to ask what tests can distinguish between the two kinds. . . .) Much dogmatism, *routineerism* (excellent word!—we must borrow that from the Russian), unwillingness to give way to new ideas and forces have used this for cover, it appears.

Kolman's problem clearly is the relation of philosophy (i.e. Marxism) and science: it is plain that he wishes to free physics from dogmatic control (and thereby incidentally mitigate the hostility of some Soviet physicists to Marxism), and yet he also wishes—or is obliged to pretend—to *deny* the neutrality, formality of philosophy, the possibility of, as he puts it, a 'non-interventionist' attitude on the part of philosophy. His official doctrine, embodying this compromise, comes out appearing somewhat strained. Philosophy is described as possessing more general laws than physics, but the 'concreteness of reality' is invoked to explain that, and how, these more general laws do not entail laws of the determined, specific sciences, so that the scientist remains autonomous. And yet one must not fall into the 'positivist' error of making it altogether formal. . . . He comes very close to this: at one point he declares that the question of which of two physical theories is true will never be determined by 'methodological sympathies' but by practice, and although the use of the word 'practice' gives this a Marxist ring, he also implies that the possession of, say, Marxist methodological sympathies is no key to truth in the understanding of nature. . . .

Essentially, what Kolman is attempting to do is to provide free thought within science (which occurred anyway) with a charter, thus both assisting it and saving Marxism from the muted hostility of the scientists. He strives to do this by making Marxism more formal, by diminishing its cosmological commitments and making it rather into a doctrine about the general rule and fate of human knowledge and, in connection with its status as a methodology, stressing the neutrality of method *vis-à-vis* content. He does of course have to face the opposition of those who maintain that to reduce Marxism to a methodology, and a neutral one at that, is to play into the hands of Western 'neopositivists' and hence of 'idealism'. The successes and prospects of formalistic revisionism, so to speak, in raising the standards of discussion, as observable in recent Soviet publications, are far greater in the abstract and natural sciences than in the human and applied ones. Heresy would be more apparent, inevitable and dangerous in the human studies: at the same time, the potential heretics in the physical sciences are a more indispensable and hence tolerated group.

1958

Notes

1 E. Kolman, *Filosofskie Problemy Sovremennoi Fisiki*, Moscow 1957.
2 Bertrand Russell has remarked somewhere that when physics and philosophy are in conflict, it is better to place one's confidence in physics. . . .

Chapter 11 Scale and nation

1 Nationalism

One of the obvious features of the modern world is the increase in the *scale* of social and political units. In the past, large, sometimes enormous empires existed, but these were relatively eccentric and above all, they were sociologically contingent. Their existence was not necessary. On the whole, the units which composed them could survive as well, or nearly as well, or better, if the totality remained fragmented. (*If* the Wittfogel thesis is correct, then some of the major river valleys, dependent on irrigation systems, may be an exception to this.) By and large, it is the empires which require explanation, whilst their break-up, or the persistence of fragmentation, do not. Self-sufficiency, local autonomy and fragmentation appear more natural and inherent in the available social equipment than their contrary.

The situation is now changed. It is the large and effective units which seem natural, and it is their breakdown and fragmentation which is eccentric and requires special explanation. Small units do indeed survive, but one may well suspect that they are parasitic on the larger ones in various ways.

All social units that manage to survive rely on a variety of mechanisms for their self-perpetuation. A sense of loyalty and identification on the part of the population is one of the factors which contribute to such cohesion as happens to be achieved. It is a factor which, quite plainly, is not always present in the same measure or proportion. It appears to be stronger in the modern world, in the attachment to the large units which are so characteristic of it, than it was in the past. What is even more striking, this strength of the sentiment seems to be quite independent of deliberate manipulation or stimulation by those political units which are the happy objects of this feeling of loyalty. Of course they do often foment and encourage it, but it can be and often is powerful quite independently of such encouragement. The striking demonstration of this is the force of such sentiments on behalf of large units which do not yet exist at all—in other words of irredentist feelings on behalf of units which as yet exist in the aspirations of their adherents only, and which consequently do not for the time being possess the resources or means for encouraging the sentiment. It is the sentiment which brings them into being, rather than vice versa.

All this is of course an oblique way of referring to the force and importance of modern 'nationalism'. In this name, we possess a term for designating the quite distinctive type of sentiment and feeling of loyalty and identification which is elicited by modern political units. Two traits which make up this distinctiveness have already been singled out: one, that the objects of these sentiments are generally larger than the traditional objects of social and political loyalty and identification, and two, that the sentiment can precede, and thus be manifestly independent of, the objective existence of the political unit which it singles out for its favours. In other words, nationalism is not an *ex post facto* ratifier of actual political might, but possesses a kind of independent criterion of legitimacy of its own.

There is a further distinctive characteristic of these modern and large political units, and one which is intimately connected, I believe, with the other two: this is the nature of the division of labour within them.

2 The division of labour

There are two well-known theories concerning the direction of the general and overall development of human societies. One of them asserts that the general direction of development is towards greater complexity, greater differentiation, and hence also greater inter-dependence and functional complementarity. The other theory, which tends to be slightly less global and all-embracing, and more specifically concerned with a trend highly conspicuous in the modern world, asserts that on the contrary our world tends towards greater standardization, conformity, uniformity, towards, in brief, a mass society. It is not difficult to think of great names in sociological theory as supporters of either of these two theories. Each of them is plausible, suggestive and illuminating, and at the same time, when articulated in their stark simplicity, they would seem to be in headlong collision with each other. How can two theories, which assert such diametrically opposed propositions, *both* appear so plausible and so illuminating?

In my view they are indeed both valuable and largely true, notwithstanding the fact that when articulated without qualification in their most basic and simple terms, they are indeed in conflict with each other. What follows is not the need to abandon one or the other, but to refine them both in such a manner that their compatibility, indeed their complementarity, become evident.

Take first of all the famous thesis of increasing differentiation and complementarity, the doctrine of the replacement of mechanical by organic solidarity. Initially, in the nineteenth century, the appeal of this theory was of course enhanced for many of its adherents by the fact that it fed and encouraged the hope of some kind of fusion of biological and social theory: the increase in the differentiation of social organisms seemed somehow to continue the story of the increased differentiation of living beings in general. Thus nature could be envoked to ratify a social trend, and social developments would confirm the wisdom of nature. This consideration is no longer so influential. But the pervasive theme of increasing differentiation has been rediscovered and revived and, in a new terminology, plays as great a part in contemporary theories of 'social development' (in the new sense of a specific theory of industrial transformation), as it did in the more far-reaching, history-embracing sociological theory of the past century.

Apart from the encouragement it offers for the hope of a unified general philosophy, the plausibility of the idea is also sustained by other considerations. It receives support above all from a very visible and manifest contrast between the past and the present, between the poor and the rich, between the small and the large society (and here the argument is visibly connected with our general theme). Small societies are also poor societies and mostly unspecialized ones. (Leave aside for the moment the fact that some poor ones are also large.) Rich societies tend to be large and to practise a high degree of division of labour, in other words to display great internal differentiation. Durkheim as it were stole this idea from the economists and showed that it had effects other than wealth: it pervaded the very texture of society, and profoundly modified the manner in which it had a hold over its members, its style of cohesion. There is indeed a great contrast between a clan society, which is segmentary in Durkheim's sense, and a society such as ours. One of the striking and I think profoundly significant features of many clan societies is the distrust, contempt, fear and ambivalence felt for the *specialist*. The moral norm is the unspecialized clan citizen, whilst the specialist, whether technical, ritual, political or any other, stands above or below, but not within society. If he is below, he is openly despised, but if he stands above, he still inspires feelings of hostile ambivalence, even when his power does not threaten the ordinary clansmen. The extent to which specialization is held to be *dishonourable* might well sadden any follower of Adam Smith: never mind whether it helps us to produce more, better and cheaper pins, the tribesmen seem to feel—specialization is nevertheless ignoble.

By contrast, more complex societies loose this revulsion against the specialist, and come to think of themselves as an assembly of specialists. The resulting functionalist theory of social cohesion antedates Durkheim and can be found popping up in many places and times. For instance (Shakespeare, *Coriolanus*):

> There was a time, when all the body's members
> Rebell'd against the belly; thus accus'd it:
> That only like a gulf it did remain
> I' the midst o' the body, idle and unactive,
> Still cupboarding the viand, never bearing
> Like labour with the rest, where the other instruments
> Did see and hear, devise, instruct, walk, feel,
> And, mutally participate, did minister
> Unto the appetite and affection common
> Of the whole body. The belly answered,—
> ...—it tauntingly replied
> To the discontented members, the mutinous parts
> That envied his receipt; ...
> 'True is it, my incorporate friends,' quoth he,
> 'That I receive the general food at first,
> Which you do live upon; and fit it is,
> Because I am the store-house and the shop
> Of the whole body: but, if you do remember,
> I send it through the rivers of your blood,
> Even to the court, the heart, to the seat o' the brain;
> And, through the cranks and offices of man,
> The strongest nerves, and small inferior veins
> From me receive that natural competency
> Whereby they live. ...
> 'Though all at once cannot
> See what I do deliver out to each,
> Yet I can make my audit up, that all
> From me do back receive the flour of all,
> And leave me but the bran.' What say you to 't?

The enormous increase in the division of labour and the pervasiveness of its social, political and economic consequences are scarcely in doubt. If the attainment of coherence in sociological theory required us to abandon this doctrine, which, if it does not exactly have the status of the Second Law of Thermodynamics, must at any rate come as close to it as the social sciences are capable, then the ideal of coherence would clearly have to be abandoned.

3 Standardization

And yet, the law, or statement of trend, which appears to stand in diametrical opposition to the first one, seems virtually as well documented. In part, the plausibility of either generalization hinges on the selection of the kind of society we invoke by way of contrast to our own. In the former case, the obvious contrast is the segmentary tribe, with its clans all resembling each other and differentiated numerically rather than qualitatively (this being Durkheim's contribution to the notion of segmentation). The clans also resemble the larger tribe as a whole, of which they are a part, *and* also their own sub-clans, in organization, so that similarity is preserved vertically as well as horizontally (this being, in essence, Evans-Pritchard's contribution to the notion of segmentation). If such a society is selected and juxtaposed with ours, there can be no doubt concerning what stands out as the salient difference: similarity amongst units and individuals in the one case, and differentiation in the other.

But we are not obliged to contrast modern society with the clans of segmentary tribes. We can also contrast it with something like traditional Hindu India, or the traditional Ottoman empire and its millet organization. These two, more even than traditional Europe with its proliferation of guilds, corporations, estates and so forth, bring out quite a different contrast. When placed alongside social forms such as these, modern society seems, and indisputably is, atomized, and drearily homogeneous. Regional and group differentiations are ruthlessly eroded by a standardized style of life and of production. The theme is familiar not merely from the work of sociologists but equally from the countless and not unjustified cries of anguish of those who cannot bear to watch character, individuality, uniqueness disappear from our world.

Here once again we possess a generalization which surely cannot be in serious doubt, and which nevertheless, as indicated, is in manifest conflict with the other and equally convincing observation. A simple solution, and a superficial one, would be to say that the actual curve of development is more complex than we had supposed: that the path from simpler tribal societies to complex civilizations, such as the Hindu or the Moslem ones, is one from smaller to greater differentiation, but that subsequently the direction of this particular tendency is reversed. This would fit in with, for instance, a similar thesis put forward concerning the general trend of human inequality.[1] But it would, I fear, be a superficial solution. The truth of the matter is that what is involved is more complex than a mere reversal of the direction of the trend at a certain historic point.

The economic complexity, diversity, the richness of the division of labour in modern industrial society is greater than that of a caste or millet society, great though it is within those types. It would be sufficient to enumerate the number of separately produced components, each produced by men who possess a distinct specialism, which go into some complex modern product such as, say, an aeroplane. Of course, against this evidence it could be argued that the *distance* which separates the various kinds of technician or their skills is not as great as that which separates a different kind of craftsman in a traditional society. Here we are getting closer to the heart of the matter.

It is not merely the case that diversification has increased further, as by some criteria it indisputably has, but also that it is different in *kind*. This qualitative difference is crucial and would be missed by an explanation which contented itself simply with noting a reversal in direction.

The central feature of a modern industrial society is that, in addition to a very elaborate division of labour, it is also one which changes rapidly and is hence doomed to occupational mobility. This distinguishes it from any traditional society, however complex its division of labour. In short, it is diversified not only over space but over time: it is not merely that people do different things, but the same people do different things at different times, or at least successive generations of the same family do different things. It is not merely that there are many diverse kinds of jobs, but the same people or members of the same family do different jobs in succession. The jobs that are available themselves change.

Change characterizes not merely the process of industrialization, but remains a permanent feature of industrial society. Change subsequent to the industrialization may be less profound and fundamental, but it nevertheless remains fairly radical. In the future, *perhaps*, the time may come when an industrial society is also a stable one, and relinquishes further change. So far, there is little evidence of this happening. For a variety of reasons—ranging from the alleged economic mechanics of a market society, to the psychological expectation of continuous improvement and the raising of standards, or the political requirement of ever-increasing Danegeld in various directions, or international rivalry—industrial society has not been able, or indeed has not been inclined, to rest on what, for any other society, would have been indescribably comfortable and relaxing laurels. For this kind of society it has always been a bed of thorns. It must continue to change.

The consequences of the pervasiveness of this kind of division of labour over time as well as over space, as it were, are enormous. Division of labour *plus* mobility, or division of labour over time as well as space, is quite different in its social implications from mere division of labour over space, accompanied by a good measure of stability. It requires that the personnel involved in this process be willing and able, in terms of skills, mental equipment and general readiness, to change jobs and to change their productive social milieu.

This readiness has two aspects: it requires a readiness of individuals to change their job or craft specification in their own lifetime, but it also requires the same to be feasible, and to constitute the reasonably normal expectation, over generations. This in turn implies that the main agency of professional training should be not the family but a specialized educational institution. This is of course one of the most conspicuous features of modern societies: they either possess universal elementary education, or aspire to achieve this with a seriousness which is far more convincing than that which characterizes their efforts in pursuit of other aims that are officially proclaimed.

The requirements of mobility over time are of course reinforced by another feature which is in any case connected with them, namely the very high level of minimal educational and technical competence which is presupposed by modern productive efforts. Not only is it not feasible to hand over professional training to the family in view of the professional rigidity which this would engender—it also is not feasible in as far as the level of technical competence required is higher than can effectively be inculcated by the family unit. The educational process itself grows, becomes complex and is diversified, and cannot be incorporated in the skills and competences of a father or a family group.

The basic shift of the process of education from the family to a specialized educational institution is one aspect of the situation. But it is not the whole of it. The educational system itself, though it possesses incomparably greater resources than the family ever possessed, has to cope with the fact that the future professional allocation of the pupils passing through it is unpredictable and unstable, and cannot even be assumed to remain stable for any one individual. It must train them, but it cannot train them specifically. It can only give them a kind of generic training, leaving the specific job training to a much later stage.

We can now see the way in which contemporary society differs both from the undifferentiated 'segmentary' tribes and from the very highly differentiated complex societies such as those based on the institution of the caste or the millet. Modern societies possess a very homogeneous educational system which provides a basically common generic training for the whole population, or for as much of it as possible, and on the basis of which a very much more specialized and extraordinary diversified system of occupations is erected, as a kind of second stage. But it is an essential attribute of the modern diversification, of this extraordinary division of labour, that it is as it were a second story, erected on that base of a shared basic education. This above all differentiates it from any past division of labour, however ramified, and it is this of course which enables it to cope with the division of labour over time as well as over space. A modern society in some measure resembles a modern army with its shared 'basic training' and its specialized jobs superimposed on it, and its hope that the basic training is sufficient to enable any one of the specialists to be re-schooled for another specialism without much loss of time.

Something further should be said about this universal generic training. One should not be too misled by its nominal content, or by the manifest rationale or question-begging self-characterizations of that content. Educational systems claim to prepare those who pass through them for the full life, to make them into good citizens, to develop their human potentialities, etc., etc., etc. These are pious phrases. In no field is there a greater gap between real and manifest function than in education—if only because educationists naturally have the gift of the gab. In terms of actual specifications of content, the types of skills of literacy, general information and orientation, and numeracy, which are at the heart of the basic educational system, are indeed continuous with traditional educational institutions, or with some of them. Nevertheless this continuity of content, and of accompanying justificatory verbiage, should not be allowed to establish the idea that there is any important continuity between the educational institutions of traditional and of modern society. This view is of course part of a favoured self-image of the educational system. There are many who like to present the modern system as an extension to all men of privileges and values previously reserved for some only.

But sociologically, this is largely an irrelevancy. The continuity is largely illusory. Even in traditional societies, at any rate in complex ones, the family did not, of course, monopolize the process of education. More complex skills and types of information had to be inculcated by schools, guilds, apprenticeships and whatnot. Good *clercs*, literate men in whose keeping the holy and secular writings of society could be kept, and who could perform such services as judges, administrators or tutors, could seldom be produced by an unaided family tradition, and could generally only be produced by specialized educational centres. Nevertheless, these only produced one kind of specialist amongst others. This is where the important difference lies. Modern elementary education, which has no doubt inherited much of its curriculum and ideology from those specialized centres, nevertheless fulfils a totally different role. Even if content overlaps, its use and significance is quite other: there is a world of difference between the use of certain skills to define a *special* social role, one amongst others, and on the other hand their use as *a universal condition of citizenship.* Elementary schooling now provides a kind of universal minimum, which is the necessary precondition for almost *any* job in the society, though perhaps not a sufficient one. It produces not a privileged élite, but merely satisfies the minimal conditions for full citizenship. (The fact that it no longer produces a privileged élite or guild, whilst retaining many ideas, slogans, rationalizations and trappings dating from the days when it did, may be the main factor explaining why it has such trouble maintaining discipline, and why it cannot control its students. They enter institutions which have the promise of privilege pretty visibly inscribed over their portals, but once inside they discover that this is merely a survival from the past. No wonder that some of them are furious and, having been deceived with a false promise of privilege, take it out on the institution in the name of egalitarian principle.)

Thus, in brief, the complex nature of modern technology and the high-powered training it presupposes, in conjunction with rapid mobility and the requirement of job-switches within one lifetime and between generations, ensure that modern society is *both* more homogeneous *and* more diversified than those which preceded it. It is more homogeneous in that it presupposes a shared universal basic training of a very serious nature, and at the same time, on the basis of this shared foundation, a rapidly changing superstructure is erected, which contains far more and more profoundly diversified elements than were found even in the more complex traditional societies. It is of course difficult to see how 'distance' between kinds of jobs or performances would be measured. In terms of a kind of manifest physical similarity, or even the type of principle involved, the distances between jobs in a modern industrial society are probably greater than those which exist in a traditional setting. At the same time, it is true that a kind of felt social and psychological distance is much less, simply in virtue of the importance of the deep internalization of that basic training which *is* shared and presupposed by all the jobs.

Thus we can see that both the generalizations with which we started are in a sense true. Their harmonization is not a matter of some mechanical splitting of the difference, or of saying that a trend went in one direction up to a certain point and was then reversed. It was a matter of a more subtle analysis, which highlights the way in which *each* of them is true, and yet compatible with the other.

4 Loyalty to large units

It is possible, on the basis of these very simple but pregnant premises, to construct a theory of nationalism. Nationalism is notoriously one of the most powerful forces of the modern world, but oddly enough one which has received relatively little systematic treatment by sociologists. I have expounded this theory elsewhere,[2] but shall allow myself to restate it here with some comments on criticisms that have been levelled at it.[3]

It is widely agreed that the extraordinary force of nationalism in the nineteenth century and since has contradicted many widespread expectations concerning the comportment of men—both high-minded ones, and others not so high-minded. It has contradicted high-minded expectations of universal brotherhood and love. It has equally contradicted much less high-minded expectations of universal rational self-interest and materialist self-seeking. Men have violated humanitarian ideals and rational self-interest alike in the cause of various nationalisms. The most popular theory which purports to explain it all runs as follows: the old Adam will out. The call of blood or group loyalty or territoriality, awakened by who knows what—modern disruption or perhaps the loss of a faith in God— overcomes the flimsy barriers set up by fragile rationality or universal affection. And once these slender barriers are down, the powerful current of atavistic feeling carries all before it.

This picture is dramatic rather than illuminating. That men are vicious, violent and irrational is not in doubt. They are also lazy, lethargic, slaves of custom, frightened and fond of their pleasures. It is by no means clear why the first group of characteristics should suddenly begin to win so handsomely over the second set. Furthermore, the theory does not explain why those deep and turbulent passions should suddenly begin to exercise themselves on behalf of rather abstract and distant allegiances, encompassing large populations, and to refrain from differentiating significantly within them. Men have in the past found it possible to assuage their need for loyalty, and their need for hate, by struggles between small and intimate communities: for very obvious reasons, such local and concrete allegiances and animosities can be much more satisfying emotionally than distant and abstract ones. What remains puzzling, on the theory which bases itself on the resurgence of atavistic feelings, is why curiously abstract loyalties should have emerged just at the very time they did, rather than at any other time, and why they should prevail over other, more customary forms of group feeling and antagonism. To explain this we must look at the social structures within which men act, rather than attempting to argue directly from some alleged inherent tendencies of the human heart.

The central features of a modern division of labour which we have selected are the following: maximum diversity over time as well as space, in other words *mobile* diversification. All this on the base of a *shared* common minimal culture, including a reasonable measure of literacy and numeracy, which alone makes possible the switches from occupation to occupation over the span of a single life or 'career'. The level of this shared minimum is such that it cannot be inculcated by a family unit, but only by an elaborate educational system.

Thus every man is a clerc. Max Weber stressed the significance of the way in which Protestantism made every man his own priest; but the extension of clercly literate status to every man, inherent in the economic transformation under discussion, is perhaps even more significant.

What follows? The mobility tends to destroy—in as far as they are not already destroyed—the various intermediate kin and social units. They do not disappear altogether, but their importance either in production or in the maintenance of social order, in other words in the economy and in politics, becomes very small. Life becomes a matter of specialized, partial contacts and contracts. Contract replaces status, partly because status is hard to maintain in very fluid contexts. An unspecialized, diffuse, multi-purpose relationship is then largely restricted to the nuclear family, which thereby acquires extraordinary importance and emotional significance. All this, of course, is only a simplified schema of the situation.

But with every man a mobile clerc, who gains his entrance to full social, economic and political citizenship only through that minimal shared training, the really important boundary becomes the one which delimits the range within which this mobility is practicable. That range, of course, is the range of the language and/or the culture, which happen to be the media of the educational system which formed the man in question. In the medium in which the educational system operates, the man can also function, and its limits are then in general the limits of his effectiveness and acceptability. His investment in the language, not of his mother as the mythology would have it, but of his *école maternelle* as the French put it, is enormous.

It is these culturally imposed limits of mobility which are decisive, and which thereby generate the limits of loyalty and the concepts in terms of which effective loyalty can be felt. Other kinds of units have no comparable hold over people. Even in societies such as Japan, where men stay with the same industrial enterprise for a lifetime, they do not necessarily stay with it over generations. But a culture is, in principle, for keeps.

Nationalism is basically a movement which conceives the natural object of human loyalty to be a fairly large anonymous unit defined by shared language or culture. It is 'anonymous' in the sense that its members do not generally have positive links with each other, and that the subdivisions within the nation are not of importance comparable with the larger unit. (This is quite different from many tribal social forms, where the clan may be just as important as a tribe, and the sub-clan just as important as a clan, and so forth.)

Traditional societies, however diversified in the social roles they possess, when stable over time, tend to be tolerant of deep, permanent human and moral chasms between their members, or rather classes of members. Above all, the sheer number, multiplicity of such chasms, prevents any one of them standing out and polarizing the whole society. In a complex stratified society, the sheer number of status distinctions weakens the moral impact of any one of them. Colour, for instance, matters less when people use many other grades and ascriptions. But if it remains as the only one of visible, shameless ascriptive sign of rank. . . .

To us, nurtured on egalitarianism and in a social milieu which makes it plausible, the moral gap between two castes, or between master and slave, may seem deeply repugnant and humanly unintelligible. Perhaps there is indeed a slight *inherent* human revulsion for such social forms, in as far as at least those who are the losers in such relationships tend to rebel against them once constraints are removed. Be that as it may, the inherent revulsion does not appear to be strong enough to prevent very effective widespread acceptance of such moral chasms, in milieux in which they are sanctioned and hallowed by custom. People seem willing to accept and internalize any degree of inequality, however extreme, provided it is *stable*, complex and habitual. The lack of symmetry and universalizability seems to be compensated by symmetry over time: however unequal we may be, if it was the same yesterday and the day before that, and will be the same tomorrow, it is acceptable. You may be discriminating against *me*, but you are not discriminating against me *at this moment*. Thus equality over time appears to make up for inequality over space. This is odd, but it is so.

But it is here that the modern world destroys the balance and makes acceptance impossible. It destroys equality, symmetry, universalizability over time, in other words stability, and, as if in compensation, homogeneity over space, and over the range of social roles, comes to be required. Anything which obstructs it—caste, estate and such— tends to be eroded. Fluid, loose classes, or classes that as least seem to be such, are tolerated instead.

The various past classifications, the moral chasms between classes of people, were of course accompanied by cultural differences, by differences in style of life and comportment. When the chasms themselves become unacceptable through widespread mobility, the cultural differences which accompanied them themselves tend to become blurred. Society once was like a box of children's plasticine, with each colour neatly separate, but as children play with the different colours and tend to make them up, in the end it becomes an indistinct grey mass. There are still cultural differences, of course, within national communities, but they are gradual and non-extreme, and it is generally possible to 'pass'. It may of course take a generation or, as folklore has it, three. But that is not an intolerably long time to wait.

The trouble arises, however, where one of the old chasms is accompanied by cultural differences which cannot easily be blurred: not all bits of plasticine will really mix with others. One example of this is of course those cultural differences which are associated with differences in pigmentation. You can change the cultural differences but not pigmentation, and this prevents 'passing' and in turn pushes the cultural differences back into place and reinforces them. But genetic traits like these are not the only ones which can have this effect. Very deep and profound cultural differences, notably religious ones, can be virtually as irrevocable as physical ones.

It is at these boundaries that new nationalisms are born. A chasm which is accompanied by differences which, for one reason or another, cannot become blurred, becomes a septic sore in a modern society. Mobility across it is not possible and the blurring cannot be achieved. People on either side of it come to have an investment in the maintenance of the boundary—and not only those who are located on the favourable side of it, whether it be favourable economically, politically or in any other way. Of course, in any society the rich tend to fear and dislike the poor; what a horrid style of life they have! They smell, they do not wash, their children are nasty and so forth. This is no disaster when the nature of the differences is such that there is no way of stopping individuals, even of especially large numbers of individuals, from crossing the boundary. You may not like them but you cannot do much about it. It is a mild source of embarrassment, that is all. But if you can stop them, or rather, if those who cross the boundary continue to be conspicuous as ex-members of the despised group, trouble is inevitable. And of course, in the traditional set-up, a few may also have passed the chasms but, owing to occupational rigidity, there was no need for them to do so. Under modern conditions, it is precisely the economically imposed mobility which makes rigidly ascribed status, frozen by deeply ingrained cultural traits, unacceptable.

Thus the natural limit of the political unit, if not bedevilled by the chasms, is the limit of the validity of its educational certificates. But where their limits do not correspond to the deep chasms, the old inequalities that cannot be obscured, there is the basis for an irredentism, a nationalist movement on behalf of either a unit which does not exist yet, or at least on behalf of radical re-drawing of existing boundaries.

This, in substance, is the theory linking the new style of division of labour with a new pattern of political units—large and co-extensive with cultural homogeneity, where the relevant shared culture is that of the modern-type primary school, not of the old folk culture. I believe this to be the key to the central phenomenon of modern times, nationalism.

5 Some objections

The previous argument merely attempted to state, in the simplest and schematic terms, the nature of the basic connection. This general schema took little notice of local variations in the way in which the pattern comes to impose itself. Though tied inherently—if the argument is correct—to the new type of division of labour, which is often referred to as 'industrialization', nationalism can either precede or follow industrialization, in its more specific and narrow sense. Industrialization, in the sense of large-scale factory production, can be in full swing before the tension between culturally different groups really asserts itself, or, especially in our century, the disruption caused by the tidal wave of industrialization *elsewhere* can by itself activate these processes. The details vary a great deal: the principle remains the same.

For instance, Professor Elie Kedourie argues[4] against the view 'that nationalism is a movement which develops in the poorer part of the empire in reaction to the wealth of the imperial rulers'. But the contention that this does sometimes happen, and is indeed highly characteristic, is not the essence of my theory, and is not co-extensive with it. It is only what it implies for *some* kinds of circumstances, which are indeed common ones. It is true that whilst 'poverty in certain circumstances does breed discontent, just as in other no less important and numerous instances it breeds a passive and fatalist resignation'. But the argument never claimed that poverty alone breeds discontent. Notoriously, it does not, as Kedourie rightly stresses. It is mobility which disrupts the acceptance of an inequality, and mobility *in conjunction* with even relative poverty does breed discontent, where much greater poverty in stable conditions does not. Kedourie goes on to point out, correctly, 'that many well-known nationalist movements rose among populations which were not manifestly poorer than their rulers, whilst other nationalist movements appeared among populations which were clearly more well to do than their rulers'. As he says, Poles, Italians and Czechs were not manifestly poorer than their Russian, Prussian or Austrian masters. Greeks and Armenians were richer than their Ottoman Muslim overlords. This is indeed so. But poverty is not the only chasm which exists between people, and which in conjunction with cultural differences becomes intolerable under modern economic conditions. An economically privileged stratum may be politically under-privileged. This conjunction is indeed a very common pattern in many traditional states, which can only tolerate economic enrichment amongst segments of the population which are at the same time made politically powerless. Enrichment amongst those who are not debarred by religion or otherwise from political office would be dangerous and indeed disastrous for the power-holders. In stable conditions, communities of this kind continue to exist, relatively well off—the rulers tax the traders but cannot entirely impoverish them in most cases—whilst at the same time politically under-privileged, and, with the resignation which is so characteristic of stable societies, these communities accept their lot. But under modern conditions, both their economic privilege and their political disfranchisement become intolerable, in one way or another, to occupants of both sides of the chasm. If the frontier is not marked by anything insuperable, mobility in both directions results, and the erstwhile deep difference is obscured. If, on the other hand, the old frontier is marked by irremovable markers, then *two* new nationalisms are born.

Again, Kedourie invokes German and Japanese nationalism during the period between the two wars. Admittedly, neither of these countries had suffered from foreign occupation or colonization. This objection has a certain force, in as far as the theory probably cannot explain, on its own, why a relatively satisfied nationalism—that is to say one already possessing a national state more or less corresponding to its aspirations—should become particularly violent and explosive in certain conditions. The theory merely explains why these units should become natural at a certain stage of social development, and why it is difficult to go against the principle by which they are delimited. Once a system of nation states is established, and the states coexist in hostile rivalry and with military sovereignty, fluctuations in the degree of violence and passion which accompanies the conflict will no doubt occur, and the theory itself cannot explain these fluctuations. Having said this, one can point to the fact that the factors which led to the acuteness of these two nationalisms are not far to seek. In the case of the Germans, they included economic rivalry with a minority group which was economically and culturally prominent, and which had difficulty in obscuring the old chasm; and it also included recent loss of territory which by the normal nationalist criteria could very plausibly be claimed. And in the case of both German and Japanese nationalism, there were the disadvantages of late-comers in an international competition in which, illogically as it later turned out, prestige was still measured in terms of territorial empire. In the post-war world, the lack of correlation, or inverse relation, between size of territory on the one hand and wealth, power, influence and contentment on the other, became very manifest. Before the war, few people had the capacity to see this. Though normally loath to explain things in terms of survivals, this particular trait was indeed an atavism, dating back not perhaps to the sense of territory in the Stone Age, but at least to the prestige rankings in international politics established in the nineteenth century.

Kedourie also disputes the view that 'the need for economic growth . . . generates nationalism'. Here one could above all object to his conception of economic growth: 'If people have wants which they are eager to satisfy—and this surely is the mainspring of economic growth—it is only by applying their ingenuity, inventiveness and capacity for labour to precise and specific tasks that they may hope, with luck, to satisfy these wants.' But in fact, economic growth in developing societies has nothing to do with 'wants which [people] are eager to satisfy'. This may seem paradoxical, but it is true. The need for economic growth in a developing country has few if any *economic* springs. It arises from a desire to assume full human status by taking part in an industrial civilization, participation in which *alone* enables a nation or an individual to compel others to treat it as an equal. Inability to take part in it makes a nation militarily powerless against its neighbours, administratively unable to control its own citizens, and culturally incapable of speaking the international language. Pre-industrial man is human, in the modern world, only in a latent sense, by courtesy. There is no point in beating about the bush. This is how things are.

Individual motives are neither here or there. The rulers generally want to be powerful and above all, to *remain* rulers, and some of their subjects no doubt would like to be rich. There is nothing unusual about all this. But the reason why 'development' has become a valid international ideal and yardstick of political performance is that it is conceived, rightly, as the gateway to the kind of life style and organization which alone confers equality and full recognition in our world. This at least is almost universally agreed.

And what is the style of organization which is a precondition of the full international citizenship? In essence, it contains precisely those traits which we singled out as a precondition of the style of loyalty known as nationalism. But it is not only the case that the development drive in the Third World aims at producing the very circumstances which will make nationalism easy (though indeed, the rulers and educators in those countries constantly preach to their tribesmen about the need 'to become a nation'); it is also that the disruption which it had already produced, causes a movement towards the crystallization of new cultural units, which will be acceptable by the new nationalist criteria. So nationalism and development, properly understood, are intimately linked, after all.

Further on in his interesting work (p. 132) Kedourie cites further instances against the theory. 'Large industrial enterprises have taken root and flourished in multi-lingual societies: in Bohemia and the

United States in the 19th centuries; in Hong Kong, Israel, French Algeria, India, Ceylon, and Malaya in the 20th.' But Bohemia was in fact, notoriously, one of the fountains of nationalism, both for Germans as well as Czechs. The United States is notorious for the way in which its educational system acted as an agency for transforming ethnic groups into a culturally homogeneous mass, until it failed in our time to do the same for the coloured groups, thereby once again producing a nationalism.

The same is true for Israel. The educational system was successful in moulding a relatively heterogeneous immigration into a homogeneous nation, until the oriental Jews arrived *en masse*. Since then, it has not been entirely clear whether, with a greater effort, the educational system would repeat its initial success, or whether on the contrary a new nationalism would be born. Needless to say, the international situation has complicated matters, by providing strong inducements for this new emergent Sephardi nationalism to remain moderate. To invoke Malaya, Ceylon, and above all French Algeria, as instances against the emergence of nationalism is odd. India is indeed an interesting case. One can only suggest that the shared Hindu culture is more important than the diversity of languages, and that in certain cases 'language' (culture) is more important than language in the literal sense.

1973

Notes

1 Gerhard Lenski, *Power and Privilege. A theory of social stratification*, New York 1966.
2 *Thought and Change*, London 1965.
3 For instance, Elie Kedourie: *Nationalism in Asia and Africa*, London 1970; or, K. R. Minogue: *Nationalism*, London 1967. See also A. Smith, *Theories of Nationalism*, London 1971.
4 *Nationalism in Asia and Africa*, 19.

Chapter 12 **The pluralist anti-levellers of Prague**

> *Differences which can be summed up in a few words can mean, in historical reality, enormous, complex and difficult social transformations.*
>
> PAVEL MACHONIN

The destiny of the so-called socialist societies of eastern Europe is one of the great questions of our time. The communist counter-reformation may plunge eastern Europe into the same kind of somnolent torpor which the original Counter-Reformation imposed on southern Europe, and from which it has not yet really recovered. The abortive Prague Spring will remain a good source of evidence for what countervailing forces are available, which could possibly save eastern Europe from such a fate. It was a revolution of intellectuals, a fact which may perhaps have always augured ill for its final outcome, though it was a hopeful sign for the quality of its literary and scholarly accompaniment.

One of its most remarkable products—quite possibly *the* most remarkable one—is a tome of some 620 pages, *Czechoslovak Society*, which its authors still managed to bring out towards the end of 1969.[1] It is a collective work by diverse members of a team which had co-operated in a big study of social stratification in socialist Czechoslovakia, with its major survey carried out in 1967, and which had the very important support of the official statistical services. The various chapters are written in Czech and in Slovak, but at the end of the book there is a nineteen-page summary in English.

It is unfortunate that this work is likely to remain inaccessible to most of its potential readers for some time at least. The English summary at the end does not even remotely do justice to its richness of thought and documentation (nor, alas, is its English particularly attractive or wholly free from ambiguity).

For the main thing which needs to be stressed about this volume is that it constitutes a very remarkable achievement. Had it been produced in politically stable or uninteresting conditions, in a country whose contemporary condition makes no special claim on our interest, and were it available in an easily accessible language, it would *still* make its mark as a very major contribution to the literature on social stratification in industrial societies, and would become one of the most important texts in the field. It would still command the attention of general sociologists, specialists in stratification and methodologists of survey research.

As it is, it must still claim their attention, but of course its significance and relevance are far wider. It is a major study of stratification in a socialist society; it is an important pioneering (even if not wholly successful) attempt to include the dimension of *power* in stratification and to do so under 'socialist' conditions; it contains an interesting attempt at a social theory of socialist societies and a general typology of industrial societies, and it contains, in restrained and sober, but very substantial terms, the theory of the Czech liberalization movement, both in the sense of offering an explanation of it, and of specifying its rationale.

It is the intimate and organic link between the methodological seriousness and thoroughness of the work, and the richness and importance of its ideas, which gives the book its unique flavour and is perhaps its most fascinating feature. (Very little of this aspect of the book is, alas, conveyed by the brief terminal summary in English.) The fact that Czechoslovakia is atypical amongst the eastern European socialist states in many important ways, of which the authors are of course fully aware, does not diminish the interest of the book, though naturally it imposes severe restrictions on any facile extrapolations of its findings.

Before discussing the book further, it may be worth saying a little about what is publicly known of the subsequent fate of its author and the institutions connected with it. An important source on this is an article in the journal *tribuna* (sic),[2] by a man whom it may be more charitable not to name. The article in question, nominally a report on sociology and on the Seventh World Sociological Congress, tells us that Pavel Machonin, the principal author of the book under review, represented in sociology that which O. Šik represented in economics, Z. Mlynář in political science and K. Kosík in philosophy. (During the Prague Spring, Mlynář was responsible for an inquiry into the political structure of the Communist Party itself.) It tells us that Machonin is now a 'political corpse', that he has been expelled from the party, and that the political battle with revisionism has now been substantially decided, though elsewhere the article implies that not all its representatives have given up the struggle. It also tells us that the Sociological Institute of the Czechoslovak Academy of Sciences had been the 'ideological centre of revisionism' and, interestingly, that the party branch at this institution had been consequently dissolved, and also that a majority of the Czechoslovak Sociological Society had passed a resolution requesting the sociologists of the world to boycott the Seventh World Congress in Bulgaria, in protest against that country's participation in the military occupation of Czechoslovakia.

Information or reminders of this order can only warm the heart of the members of that Czech majority which does not welcome the present Stalinism with a human face, and consequently one must wonder whether the author of the article is an opportunist time-server *and* a fool, who unintentionally gives much comfort to his enemies, or whether on the contrary the article is a double-take, deliberately letting slip information under the guise of somewhat nauseating abuse and question-begging denunciation of 'petit bourgeois revisionism'. At this distance, it is impossible to tell. The hypothesis of irony is less likely than the straightforward inter-pretation, but it is by no means excluded, being as it is entirely in keeping with the present general situation in Czechoslovakia, the *Švejkovina*, the widespread complicity in a reluctant collaboration which does not defy, but endeavours to minimize the consequences of submission. The abuse does however highlight the relevant back-ground of the work under review.

In fact, sociology played a crucial role in the liberalization process in Czechoslovakia. (The term 'liberalization' was not used, inci-dentally; 'democratization' was preferred.) The full story has not yet been told and ought to be fascinating when it becomes available. It has both ideological and organizational aspects. Ideologically, the global fashion of sociology of the 1960s coincided and fused with the local liberalization impulse. But there was more to it than simple coincidence and conflation. The precondition of the successful liberalization had been an economic and social malaise and stag-nation (even actual economic decline), for which plainly no solutions or concepts were available within the official ideology. So it seemed both necessary and permissible to turn to sociology, though of course the permission was not granted at once, nor without a prolonged struggle. A major turning point in favour of the sociologists had come when the Party, at the highest level, not merely allowed sociology to exist, but after prolonged inquiry allowed it a legitimate existence *without defining it*. (Previously, rival definitions had ranged from 'bourgeois pseudoscience' to 'applied Marxism' or 'the study of socialist social forms'.) The importance of existence without definition, without essence one might say, was of course that any definition might well have been used to inhibit research. In the event, one of the invoked, though not sanctioned and enforced, inter-pretations was that the new work was *adding* sociology *to* Marxism, which itself was not a sociology at all, though evidently it could serve as the base of one. Whatever other merits this view may lack, it certainly had the signal advantage that if Marxism was not and did not already contain sociology, then naturally the new sociology could not come in conflict with it, and could pursue its own work unhampered.

The organizational aspect of sociology and its participation in the thaw is interesting and amusing. In common with non-socialist societies, the Czechoslovak Socialist Republic had to face the problem of what to teach young technologists, over and above technology itself. An objective need, or the conscience of the pedagogue or of the educational administrator, or who knows what, cannot quite tolerate a higher educational course containing nothing but technology: there must be a bit of humanity, civics or morality somewhere. Almost symbolically, this little bit extra, by way of literary or philosophical edification, tends to be called 'liberal studies' in Britain, and under socialism it is called 'Marxism–Leninism'.

Now this is all very well as names go, but *what is it*? If you are a Director of an institution training young (say) chemical engineers, or the man under him made responsible for giving that course of Something Extra, what, concretely speaking, do you talk about? They tried Marxist philosophy, but evidently no one could stomach for very long the drivel about Negation of a Negation and Interpenetration of Opposites. So they tried labour history instead. Now that is a very worthy and genuine subject, and scholarly, even interesting books are written about it. But, let us face it, the flesh is weak, and though perhaps it may not be the dullest of all subjects, it must at least be in the running for such a title, and it is hard to hold the attention of the young with it. Now sociology and political science (known in Czechoslovakia as 'politology') are—at least during the decade of the apotheosis of sociology, the 1960s—quite another matter. So, within the crucial period of the build-up to the Prague Spring, the very extensive and well-centralized network of teachers and centres of Marxism–Leninism was *überschult* to sociology, and sociology itself placed in the service of finding a way out of the desperate social malaise.

As the rather unsavoury article in *tribuna* observes, when the Spring came, those who wished to build, in theory and practice, 'an unbounded "pluralistic" political system' (as did Mlynář), did so on the basis of the sociological work of Machonin and his colleagues. In 1967, their institute was indeed still called a 'Marxist–Leninist' one, though at that time there was a tendency to apologize even for the name.

This much by way of background to the book, which does not itself indicate it, except at a rather high and theoretical level, in as far as it considers the general problems facing its own kind of society. It does not stoop to the tactics of down to earth political struggle, or its unhappy termination. Nevertheless it was worth while to indicate this background. But it is important to stress with the utmost emphasis that the outstanding merit of the book, as a piece of sociological thought and research, is quite independent of the crucial position which its authors and sociology occupied in the political struggle.

It is impossible to summarize all aspects and details of this massive and thorough study. The various individual chapters, concerning the relation of stratification to complexity of work, life style, education, income, prestige, self-image, family, generation, social contacts and so forth, clearly deserve thorough consideration, from the viewpoint of both substance and method, and above all from a comparativist angle. I shall content myself with a partial summary, and some comment concerning certain key chapters.

One of the most interesting aspects of the book is the attempt to formulate a typology of possible relevant types of social stratification (pp. 39 f.). The aim is to identify a characteristically *socialist* kind of stratification. As Machonin observes, one might approach such a model by a kind of inductivist procedure, seeking the shared traits of societies which consider themselves to be socialist, or are considered to be such. Such a procedure would need to include not merely communist states, but also reformist or nationalist socialist ones, without regard to their specific culture or level of social development. Machonin rejects such an approach, on the grounds that such a synthetic concept would have very little content, if any. Instead, he prefers the construction of an 'ideal type' of socialism, to use his own words, precisely analogous to Marx's construction of an ideal type of capitalism. The notional content of such a 'mature socialism' may be rich, and the author notes the danger of its detachment from reality, and of utopianism.

The author clearly believes that though this danger exists, his work has evaded or overcome it. He notes that the whole of Czechoslovak development from the 1950s to 1967, and in particular the developments 'after January 1968', justify the belief that this ideal type is such not merely in the sense of seeming desirable, but also in the more important sense of corresponding to the real developmental possibilities of industrial societies.

Here I wish to anticipate somewhat, in the interest of making clear to the reader the general direction of the argument. The connection between Machonin's enormously thorough empirical research into Czechoslovak socialist stratification, and the political morals drawn from them, is interesting. It is *not* the case, as the reader might suppose, of a shocked discovery of the form—despite official socialism, so much stratification! *Quite the reverse.* The general argument has the form: despite all the official deformation, so much *good* and desirable stratification, corresponding to the real functional needs of industrial society!—but not enough, alas; let us have more of it, and let us call it socialism. (Paraphrasing Huey Long, he might have said that of course one may have liberal pluralism and differentiation in Eastern Europe, but one must call it socialism and indeed, why not.)

It may be relevant at this point to note that Machonin not merely proclaims the Marxist foundations of his thought at the beginning of the book, but also that it is my strong impression that his declaration of faith is sincere. Naturally, one can never be sure about the *pensée intime* of people who have the misfortune to live under a dictatorship. The Marxism to which he declares his loyalty (p. 18) is formulated in extremely abstract terms and might in fact accommodate many of us: it is defined in terms of the

> complex and developmental, or structural–genetic character of social phenomena, a developmental dynamism which allows an objective evaluation of progress, inner tensions, and the capacity of human knowledge to advance to greater social understanding, notably by combining theory and empirical work.

He rejects economic reductionism, and the absolutization of class conflict. He rejects vulgar Marxism, though interestingly he admits that his own generation had made its first acquaintance with Marxism only in this form and was obliged to overcome its influence. Equally interesting is the proclaimed ambition to use the general Marxist foundations to build a modern sociological theory, and in particular one facilitating the empirical study of contemporary social forms, including those which emerged in the course of socialist reconstruction. The significant negative implication of this is that Marxism as yet does not contain a sociological theory—a contention which, as indicated, was important in avoiding the possibility of conflict between Marxism and the newly emergent sociology.

For purposes of comparison, the author suggests six currently relevant types of social stratification: capitalist, dictatorship of the proletariat, bureaucratic, egalitarian, technocratic-meritocratic, and socialist. Of these types, the second is apparently meant to have some relation to the conditions prevailing immediately after the Communist coup of 1948. One of the less interesting or surprising, but conclusive, results of the empirical research is that this type has no relevance to contemporary Czechoslovakia. The workers as a general class are neither beneficiaries, nor homogeneous in their position, nor in any significant sense associated with power. The other types, disregarding capitalism for a moment (which is admitted not to exist in pure form), are interesting in that they purport to name close alternatives, either in the recent past of the country, or still available as (in the main regrettable) options. Bureaucratic stratification ascribes status on the basis of a monopoly of power and operates distribution so as to favour bureaucrats—power-holders; egalitarian stratification operates an 'inverted' ascription in favour of the less qualified and the less productive, who benefit from its distributive principles; whereas the technocratic model ascribes status to technocrats or meritocrats, and also favours them distributively.

When, then, is *socialist* stratification? It may be best to offer an abbreviated version of the author's own words (pp. 44 f.):

> mature socialism is conceived as a formally and substantially democratic community of effort, based on collective ownership . . . doubtless a socially differentiated society (dominated, but not exclusively, by professional differentiation) and stratified, mainly on the basis of the effectiveness and hence complexity of labour. The span of the stratification of mature socialist society corresponds to the functional requirements of the development of industrial society . . . it is gradual, (without excluding altogether the influence of inheritance and ascription) . . . and consists of largely open strata. . . .
>
> To arise and function, mature socialism requires, apart from favourable international conditions, a certain technical, scientific and educational level. . . .
>
> . . . this mature socialism is not the only possible type of social organisation of industrial society, though in our view it comes close to an optimal arrangement of the relation between industrial culture and human personality (at least in our conditions). . . . No doubt there is a whole array of common traits and tendencies of all industrial societies. . . . Various kinds of such societies can be considered as variants of one structure, and the question of their relative merits must be left to the real development and the scientific investigation of reality. . . .
>
> Should our conception of socialism seem to some to consist simply of the shared characteristics of modern societies, then such an objection is valid to the extent that we really do not deem it fitting to invent our socialism—we prefer rather to deduce it from the real trends of development. But the criticism is invalid if it underrates the difference of socialism so defined from capitalist society, which has as yet never managed to reduce the span of stratification and to turn achievement into the veritable base of social status; or if it underrates its difference with bureaucratic–egalitarian society. Differences which can be summed up in a few words can mean, in historical reality, enormous, complex, and difficult social transformations.

We are now in a position in some measure to sum up the central thesis of the book, and to do it at least partly in terms of its own very interesting conceptual framework. The book does not polemicize with the 'capitalist' variant of industrial society; as we have seen, it leaves the relative merit of the two systems to further developments and future research, and even hints that optimality may hinge on local (presumably historical) circumstances. Its interest in American society, for instance, is largely comparative and methodological. The contrast with which it is genuinely concerned is the one with the conflated 'bureaucratic–egalitarian' type of society, which it finds conspicuous in the recent Czechoslovak past. Nevertheless, the general form of the connection between the empirical data and the political moral is more subtle: despite the bureaucratic and egalitarian deformations, a 'socialist' pattern in its own sense (i.e. a meritocracy, within the bounds of social justice and humanity) has been asserting itself, and constitutes the main feature of Czechoslovak stratification. But not sufficiently: further economic and social progress hinges on giving this principle free play, and on removing hindrances to its full development.

This argument, be it noted, gives a special nuance to the more conventional theories of pluralism, quite apart from using a new name for it. Other pluralists tend to concentrate on the multiplicity of autonomous groups and institutions, as a necessary means of producing the countervailing forces to the state and to possible other dangers to liberty; but inequality as such they tend to see as an inevitable price of this plurality, rather than as making a direct and valuable contribution to social health. In fairness to Machonin, it should be added (though this is not evident from the book) that he also looks forward to an ultimate *re*-levelling, presumably at a stage of real industrial maturity, following the de-levelling which he holds necessary at the present stage.

It is well worth following the author in the more detailed expositions of his ideas (pp. 156–70).

The central conclusion of the stratification research is that social status in Czechoslovakia is determined above all by what the author calls the bundle of social–cultural differentiations: type of work, style of life and leisure, and education. (Note: *not* income or participation in management.) The author goes on to add that although complexity of work plays a primary role within this bundle, he does not interpret the results of the research as a confirmation of its decisive role, precisely because, contrary to his expectations, it is so tightly fused with the other two 'social–cultural' components of status.

The author proceeds to comment on power (p. 158):

All this is not to say that the power–political–organizational system played no significant role in this period in forming stratification. For one thing, this macro-research could not catch the occupants of the summits of power, and their stratificational characteristics. But above all we could not capture the mechanism of the influence of power. . . . We could only infer its role . . . partly from the very reduced participation in political activity by the broader strata . . . and partly from the levelling effect on the standard of living, which by its lack of congruence with social–cultural components betrays the presence of non-economic pressures. . . .

At the same time we can assert positively that even the sharpest un-evenness of power and the greatest levelling of income were unable to prevent people from differentiating in work and above all in leisure according to the cultural parameters of modern socialist society. . . .

People developed their leisure activity in a manner roughly corresponding to their education and type of work, and managed to use their levelled and not always congruent incomes in diverse ways.

On page 160, the author makes some comparative remarks:

we consider the differentiation in complexity of work, education and the cultural use of leisure to be, all in all, close to the analogous differentiations in industrially developed lands, or rather in lands approaching this stage, except that we lack the luxury style of leisure and the luxury orientation of consumption, and that the lower levels of complexity of work, education and presumably of life style are relatively larger. . . . Income differentiation we reconsider to be levelled out, in contrast with capitalist countries with their high incomes of the upper strata, and also in comparison with European socialist countries. Political differentiation we consider to be somewhat steep.

He sums up his finding (pp. 161 f.) in relation to the previously postulated typology of relevant forms of stratification: . . . 'social differentiation in Czechoslovakia is explicitly non-capitalist . . . forms of ownership play no role, least of all private ownership.'

There can be little doubt about the correctness of these findings, if the influence of property is interpreted in a narrow, literal and strictly contemporary sense. The only people whose social position is determined by currently and legally owned property are small-holders on marginal (generally hilly) land, whose land was too poor or awkwardly situated to be worth collectivizing. These smallholders are socially and economically at a very low level, comparable to that of unskilled agricultural labourers, and hence it is not surprising that, judged by this literal criterion, there are few or no survivals of 'capitalist' stratification. In some other senses this is by no means so obvious, and the failure to deal adequately with those other possibilities is one of the lacunae of the book (which was to have been filled, perhaps, by the projected study of social change, the prospects of whose completion and publication must now alas be slim).

In saying this, I have no wish to challenge the author's expressed conviction that yearning for 'capitalism' is rare and a survival rather than 'a phenomenon connected with contemporary structure'. What I do have in mind is this: given stress on qualifications, complexity, of work and cultural level as determinants of stratification, one naturally wonders about the role of past wealth as a correlate of educational opportunity or aspiration. (There are reasons for suspecting that working class entry into higher education suffered from the egalitarianism, by diminishing financial incentives for undergoing it, and thus encouraging the self-recruitment of those oriented towards it as an end in itself.) One would also like to know the long-term consequences of the erstwhile favouring of working class candidates, and the discouragement of 'bourgeois' ones, unless they and their fathers enthusiastically overcompensated for their background. The regime had previously used educational opportunity as a means of social control, withdrawing access to education from the offspring of those failing to display conspicuous conformity. Even lukewarmness of the fathers was visited upon the children. My suspicion is that the effects of this policy were relatively small, in the long run —those who wanted education in the end obtained it. (This of course in no way excuses those repellent measures nor does it constitute much consolation for those who had to suffer from them, least of all for those who never recovered. All the same, it would be interesting to know just how effective, or possibly how counter-productive, such persecution was.)

In addition to excluding any significant survival of 'capitalist stratification', the author also and similarly excludes the applicability or survival of the 'dictatorship of the proletariat'. He observes that, on the contrary, the unfavourable traits of the political system affected above all the workers, as the most numerous segment of the population.

The author *does* attribute a good deal of relevance to the 'bureaucratic' type of stratification. The main evidence for (or meaning of) this contention is indeed the sharp differentiation in the distribution of power, in such marked contrast to the absence of great inequalities in other spheres. At the same time, he firmly asserts that his material

refutes the contention that power is the crucial principle of differentiation in all socialist societies—whether such an assertion is made by
way of hostile criticism, or in the spirit of a romanticized endorsement of 'revolutionary violence'.

> Without wishing, like the apologists of bureaucratism, to
> under-rate the importance of the sphere of political power, we
> must respect the facts which prove that in Czechoslovakia as
> of November 1967, power was not the axis or basic skeleton
> of social differentiation and social life altogether, but rather
> a kind of external form, in part adapting itself to, and in part
> obstructing, another type of social differentiation. It is hard to
> speak of the 'theory of the new class' as a power élite with all
> the other attributes of a top stratum . . . even though the
> research could not have seized its possible inner centre. But it
> showed that around this centre—if it existed at all—there was
> no *larger* group of power-potentates, with privileges but without
> the required education and expertise.

The author proceeds to tell us that the egalitarian type of stratification was also found to be important, notably in producing the
narrow span of income and some degree of incongruence between
the standard of life on the one hand and educational level, complexity of work and leisure styles on the other.

He also considers the 'technocratic' (or 'culturocratic') stratification to be relevant, notably as an imminent danger. By this he means
a replacement of the current bureaucracy by one that is selected for
technical competence, but a replacement *not* accompanied by democratization (which seems to mean greater genuine participation
through pluralism and liberalization).

But his final conclusion—an encouraging one from his viewpoint
—is that a 'socialist' (in his sense) type of stratification is asserting
itself, despite its inadequate influence on distribution (too egalitarian)
and the power-political realm (too *in*egalitarian). It was also in
conflict with *in*equality arising from economic backwardness (the
backwardness of rural areas, agriculture, Slovakia, and the under-
privileged position of the economically inactive and of women).

So, if the author is right, the liberalization movement of the 1960s
saw itself in a midwife role—assisting in the birth of a social form
which was *in any case* emerging:

> A realistic socialism is beginning to emerge with us as a socially
> just form (i.e. one which has removed capitalist inequality
> and displays no tendency to return to it) of an industrial
> achievement society, a richly differentiated and stratified one,
> though not too sharply—and hence differentiated in terms of

interests and viewpoints. A realistic conception of socialism, respecting this differentiation of interests (and hence the existence of tensions and possibly their accentuation) has begun to gain recognition with us and in other socialist countries in the '60s. . . .

All in all, what characterized the Czechoslovakia of 1967 was the tension between bureaucratic–egalitarian relations on the one hand, and socialist ones on the other. Technocratic relations represented a kind of middle point between the two extremes (approximating socialism by its stress on qualifications, and resembling bureaucratism by its lack of democracy). This tension was made possible by the existence of 'traditional' inequalities springing from the inadequate industrial development of the country.

Bureaucratic–egalitarian social relations were demonstrably the main brake on further development of industrial culture. . . . Czechoslovakia of the early '50s and early '60s was a proof of the futility of considering whether it is possible on the present social foundations to replace material incentives by others, such as moral ones. It also refutes the efforts . . . to prove that the socialist type of society can replace . . . the differentiation of rewards by the force of organizations, administration and power.

The application of the principle of achievement, which was implemented in its technocratic form . . . was incomplete and limited. Reforms imposed from above (e.g. de-levelling, general economic reform, application of criteria of competence in appointments) received an administrative form which hampered initiative . . . and any real achievement. Without democratism, technocratic reforms failed to achieve their ends and were sterile through the endless struggle with the ubiquitous bureaucracy.

The author proceeds to list those who were interested in either opposing or supporting those reforms, which would overcome these brakes on development and the whole 'bureaucratic–egalitarian' system. Those opposing the changes were the carriers of the 'past of the revolution', 'unable to understand the transition to the positive construction of socialism'. There was the relatively influential group of bureaucrats, based on power positions, and a more numerous and more dynamic group of technocrats. There was also the group of unqualified but well-paid workers, who might have an interest in maintaining the 'egalitarian' system.

For the other side of the conflict, the author claims the interests of the 'broadest masses'. He goes on to note that these conflicts of

interest, unable to articulate themselves fully in exchanges of view
and in political activity in 1967, were producing a latent tension of
critical dimensions. The 'bureaucratic–egalitarian social relations'
were thus opposed by a powerful coalition of social forces.

The final and equally fascinating section of Machonin's crucial
chapter in the volume is concerned with the origins of this situation.

> The Czechoslovak revolution of 1945–1948 [i.e. the Communist
> takeover] resulted from the confluence of two currents: a
> socialist one and an egalitarian one. The socialist reconstruction
> of society needed the political support of the masses: this it
> gained above all by concessions to the egalitarian sentiments,
> which in our socio-cultural community find support in
> centuries-old objective and subjective traditions. . . .
> Whereas national democracy was not thoroughly implemented
> after February 1948, and on the contrary the '50s saw . . . a
> good measure of bureaucratism, egalitarian ideas were for this
> very reason implemented further. Otherwise the régime, which
> did not continue to implement the democratic programme,
> could not have gained the minimal support for . . . the real or
> supposed class struggle. The extensive [i.e. a non-intensive]
> industrial development . . . corresponded to this social
> trend. . . .
> Almost simultaneously with the declared completion of
> socialisation, the protracted economic-cultural crisis of the '60s
> broke out, caused by the inability of the bureaucratic–egalitarian
> system to satisfy the elementary cultural needs of society (this
> was manifested by the stagnation and partial decline of
> production), and even less to stimulate further progress . . .
> after the inner resources of extensive industrialization came to
> be exhausted.

The author refers to the 'trial run' reforms of the 1956–8 period,
inspired by the Twentieth Congress of the CPSU, without however
either identifying them or explaining their lack of immediate impact.
But they were followed up in the 1960s (a later paragraph says 'from
the first half of the 1960s') by the reform movement. He lists its ideas:
economic reform, intensification of the economy (i.e. as opposed to
mere 'extensive' expansion of production, which had operated
simply by recruiting rural workers and women into industry),
speeding up of the move towards the so-called scientific-technical
revolution, the overcoming of the notion of the class war as the
main motive force of inner development, a critique of egalitarianism
and bureaucratism, the evolution of socialist democracy including
national equality, humanism.

The author attributes importance to the fact that the regime of the socialist Czechoslovak republic was born from a genuinely democratic and socialist revolution, that its bureaucratization was carried out as it were 'behind its back', and was contrary to the intentions of the major part of its creators; hence there were many who had not forgotten the 'original sense of socialism' and found the social crisis hard to bear, seeing it subjectively as the result of 'deformations'. Here the author's own explanation does not really go much beyond what he himself describes as the 'subjective' perception of the situation. Contemplating the horror of the 1950s, he says in effect—we were betrayed, we had not willed *this*.

It is interesting, however, that in as far as there is a diagnosis of the 'deformations', it is the inverse of the one conventionally current in the West, which sees Stalinist inequality as the price of a rapid and ruthless industrialization. Machonin (though he stresses the industrial backwardness of Czechoslovakia by the standards of today) in effect says: just because the country was *already* industrial, it could use egalitarianism to compensate for the *other* deformations and buy off popular discontent in some measure, and postpone through 'extensive' expansion that stagnation which, in the end, was the inescapable penalty of the 'egalitarian–bureaucratic' syndrome.

Even the power élite, he goes on to observe, did not remain untouched by the movement described—especially some of its segments. Others adjust to it, sometimes hesitantly. And the bureaucratic segment opposed it.

The 1960s did not achieve an intensification of production. But many other preconditions were laid then. These trends became stronger during the second half of the 1960s and reached their height by attaining the first steps of an income de-levelling, and by some manifestations of a 'changed consciousness' on the part of the 'active segments of society'. De-levelling and consciousness—an interesting pair drawn I suppose from functionalism and Marxism respectively —are the main themes. And he goes on to add, with great passion:

Those ordinary, despised, derided, yes hated '60s, in which we often see only the unsavoury banality of a criticized régime, the stagnation of the economy and the standard of life, in reality gradually assembled a mass of deep cultural changes, which could not but express themselves in a differentiation of men, work and life-styles . . . which partially weakened but did not overcome egalitarianism, and undermined the bureaucratic– autocratic aspects of direction. . . . Well—this is the social condition we seized by our research in November 1967. The empirically indicated direction of our evolution did not surprise us, for all in all we expected it. What did surprise us was how

far the evolution had already progressed. The findings can only
be understood from a dynamic viewpoint.

In other words, they reflect a powerful, and perhaps irresistible
trend, and one which, for this author, plainly is an object not only
of investigation but also of love.

In the West, many of us find it possible to be both pluralists and
egalitarians (though admittedly we do not give it much profound
thought, for the danger of the implementation of equality is so small
as to make its compatibility with liberty a less than pressing problem).
We assume that political plurality and opposition can arise on any
base, even sheer unaided competition for power or rivalry of ideas,
and that consequently we are not obliged to create or demonstrate
the existence of social diversity, in order to underpin plurality.
We have diversity anyway, but we do not feel we need it specifically
for the purpose of political pluralism. We assume that plurality is
self-generating, unless forcibly suppressed. Are we too complacent?
In any case, Machonin and his colleagues evidently live in a world
which does not encourage such complacency. They seem more sure
of their local stratification than they are of pluralism, its alleged
or desired political expression, and clearly wish to use their documentation of the former as an encouragement for the emergence of
the latter.

The nexus between the stratification they document and welcome,
and the pluralism they desire, is of the utmost importance, but the
details of this connection are left a little obscure. Is it that here, at
any rate, the authors are clear and unambiguous Marxists, in a
straightforward and specific sense, and believe that unless you have
classes and opposition, you cannot have political plurality? This
would admittedly be out of tune with their opposition to the old cult
of the class struggle, but it would also constitute an interesting back-
to-front use of the erstwhile Communist orthodoxy, which maintained that just because classes were in the process of abolition,
there was no further need for a multiplicity of political parties. Or
do we find signs here of a residue of political caution, concerning
the extent of political plurality which is to be encouraged (e.g. was
it to be only internal to the Party, rather than multiplying effective
parties?), in which case publicly acknowledged stratification, with
a recognized right of self-expression, would be a *substitute*, in some
measure, for complete political freedom? This would be an interesting version of neo-corporatism in a Marxist guise. Or were both
these arguments present? Most probably, the authors had not entirely
made up their minds. In any case, the book is not explicit enough
about the nature of that nexus between stratification and pluralism
which is so central for it.

In stressing the need of a stratificational base for political plurality
and hence freedom, the authors may be more realistic than the starry-
eyed Western progressive, who thinks he can without strain love
both liberty and equality. They can certainly cite Tocqueville as well
as Marx in support of their fears. Machonin invokes Marx's analysis
of Bonapartism, as basing its tyranny on the equality of smallholders,
in his characterization of the pre-1968 dictatorship-with-equality in
Czechoslovakia. One should also note L. Brokl's chapter, which
deals with stratification and power, and is incidentally one of the
most interesting ones in the book, not merely through the inherent
fascination of its topic, but also through its struggles with the
methodological problems of perceiving power, and through the
author's quite exceptionally frank use of 'Western' sociology and
disregard for Marxism.

Thus the book as a whole in fact contains both the philosophy
and the sociology of liberalization. Philosophy provides the major
premise, which is of a 'historicist' kind, i.e. an appeal to strong,
perhaps irreversible trends. It is in the light of this principle that the
author defines 'socialism', trying to capture the appeal of this word
both for his values and his interpretation of current social trends,
and observing that there is no point in 'inventing' one's socialism:
one must deduce it from real social tendencies. These real trends
reveal a diversified, achievement-oriented industrial society, and a
pluralistic one. And that is the minor premise. Unfortunately the
full emergence of these trends is hampered by the egalitarian–
bureaucratic political system—egalitarian in order to hide its lack
of political democracy, egalitarian economically but inegalitarian
politically—which is at the same time incapable of making the society
function, economically and otherwise. Thus we have, once again,
a midwifery kind of social philosophy.

This is quite unlike those reformers who seek inspiration or vindi-
cation in the young Marx. The philosophical premise drawn from
Marx in this scheme is of the *hard*, historical-necessity-recognizing
strand in his thought, and not from the recently popular soft and
mushy centre of his youth; but it is made revolutionary in its context
by the addition of the empirical minor premise, and this is indebted
to the western theory of 'industrial society' and to western research
techniques. Interestingly, the social research concentrated less on the
abuses of the old regime than on the force of the tendencies making
for the new birth, tendencies which, it claims, legitimate themselves
by their very strength and their deep social roots.

1971

Notes

1 Pavel Machonin (a kolektiv), *Československá Společnost*. 'Sociologická analýza socialní stratifikace', Bratislava, *Nakladatel'stvo Epocha*, 1969.
2 *tribuna*, ročník 2, 14 October 1970, číslo **41**, 3.

Chapter 13 The dangers of tolerance

> *... the tension between ... 'science' and the*
> *sphere of 'the holy' is unbridgeable. . . . But never*
> *as yet has a new prophecy emerged ... by way*
> *of needs of some modern intellectuals to furnish*
> *their souls with, so to speak, guaranteed genuine*
> *antiques. By way of substitute, they play at*
> *decorating a sort of domestic chapel with small*
> *sacred images from all over the world, and they*
> *produce surrogates ... which they peddle in the*
> *book market. This is plain humbug or self-decep-*
> *tion.*
>
> MAX WEBER, *Science as a Vocation*

Compared with the nineteenth century, ours is an age of intellectual dishonesty. The nineteenth century did not invent the modern vision of the world, nor did it work out its implications. All that was already done in the seventeenth and eighteenth centuries. But it was in the nineteenth century that the awareness of these implications became widespread, partly through the sheer lapse of time, and more significantly, through the emergence of a large literate middle class which possessed the means, in various senses, for contemplating the new vision. The consequences of this are well known. The nineteenth century satisfied the demand and produced the secular prophets who wrestled, heroically, with the problem of finding a new meaning for life, honestly acceptable in the light of new critical standards and of the new knowledge.

Nothing is more sadly characteristic of our time than that these men are now held in contempt. It is said of the English eighteenth century that the spirit of its time is best conveyed by its pejorative use of the term 'enthusiasm'. The spirit of our age is perhaps best seized by considering the current or recent contemptuous views of terms such as *Weltanschauung* or Grand Theory. I do not here wish to defend any specific feature or doctrine of any particular nineteenth-century Grand Theory. And equally, their modern denigrators are not only concerned with decrying specific doctrines. What they spurn is the very principle of the thing. And it is here, it seems to me, that they condemn themselves.

The nineteenth-century approach was based on some very simple assumptions: that you cannot live without having, or at any rate presupposing, views about the nature of man and his place in the world. Second, that the answers to these questions inherited from traditional faith are indefensible. Third, that this being so, we must find some new answers to those questions. This may be very difficult, but we have absolutely no choice but to do it. If the view in front of us is painful, the only alternative to taking it in nevertheless, is— to shut your eyes. Of course you may do that if you wish. If you wish to walk through dangerous and uncharted country with your eyes shut, that is your privilege. But do not claim intellectual distinction and depth for your position.

How old-fashioned this nineteenth-century vision seems! If there is one thing on which a very large segment of academic philosophers agrees, it is in indulging in a snide snigger at the expense of the alleged nineteenth-century intellectual hubris. They know that it was presumptuous, not to mention logically incompetent, of their nineteenth-century predecessors to reject and criticize the various traditional visions. This is not our task. Our task, it appears, is something else. The problem of a general stocktaking of our situation is not fit for our attention or for rational inquiry at all.

The characteristic twentieth-century philosopher, by contrast, takes a step back. He operates at a 'higher' logical level, at the 'meta-level', this thought is 'second order', and examines the nature of belief as such, or indeed the nature of knowledge, but does not stoop or sink to consider the content of it. He endorses the legitimacy of some vaguely specified or unspecified content, but he does not consider the content itself to be his own proper concern. (Do not be deceived by phenomena such as the recent revival of a so-called Marxism. It invokes the name, but neither the spirit nor the letter of the original thing. The characteristic feature of this Carnaby Street Marxism, of the pot-and-Marx syndrome, is that it seeks out in Marx a kind of Permissive Relativism, a charter for dismissing intellectual coherence as mere official ideology, for the suspension of any need to criticize rationally and concretely, and a *carte blanche* permit to reject without either analysis or norm or alternative. It is entirely in the contemporary spirit.)

It is easy to draw up the general formula for a real contemporary, twentieth-century philosophy. It starts with some second order or meta-theory concerning the nature of belief as such. One could take some familiar examples: belief is commitment, and can be nothing else. Or: belief is the distillation of a given social tradition, and can be nothing else. Or: belief is the way a given 'language' divides the real from the unreal, and can be nothing else. Or: belief is the function of one type of use of language, and it would be absurd to judge this type of employment of language by the standards of some other type.

In each case, the basic argument is breathtakingly simple. In each case, however, it is camouflaged by a complex terminology and specialized style and enveloped by a scaffolding which ensures that its simplicity is not evident. To understand the argument, or rather to discern it under the verbal foliage and supporting struts, a fair amount of training is required which at least militates against doubt, for the trainee has invested much time and energy in mastering the structure in question, and the untrained are scared off by the elaborate scaffolding which they dare not climb.

In each case—and this is by far the most significant point—we are not really given any evidence for the truth of a specific belief, but merely an argument concerning the status of belief as such. This abstract re-endorsement is then, however, treated as if it were a specific demonstration of a concrete belief. This step is also camouflaged. What has really happened, in terms of Max Weber's simile, is that exotic ritual objects are assembled in an antiquarian spirit, but then suddenly treated as if they were the real thing.

The crucial weakness, *logically*, of these re-endorsement philosophies is of course that they cannot be selective. They must re-endorse everything (or, in the negative versions, damn everything). They cannot select one way or the other, for they are inherently blind to specific content.

This inherent logical weakness in fact in a way manifests itself in the concrete specimens of the approach. It is this which is one of the striking continuities between what might be called the hysteria of complacency of the post-war period, and the hysteria of protest of more recent times. The style of reasoning is extraordinarily similar. Only, in the one case, one had a totally indiscriminate, unselective conservatism, and in the latter case, a similarly unselective and incoherent protest. The point about our world is of course that any conservatism or radicalism, if it is to be of any use, must be *selective*. One cannot blindly endorse everything: some regimes are indeed intolerable. *Carte blanche* conservatism is worthless, but so is its brother-under-the-skin, chaotic doctrineless protest.

The philosophers of re-endorsement like to assume a mantle of modesty, and indeed this modesty tends to be the most assiduously advertised aspect of their thought. The (alleged) neutrality with respect to content of belief is presented as humility and caution. In fact, of course, it is thinly disguised dogmatism. The modesty is above all a modest disavowal of the possibility of *criticism* of belief, and the immediate implication which the listener is meant to draw is that some belief set favoured by the author is thereby automatically endorsed. If 'modesty' rules out criticism, superstitions can live unmolested. *Logically*, of course, the weakness of a method is that the endorsement endorses too much. Everyone's superstition benefits from the same device. This does not bother the practitioner very much, for he only remembers this blessedly unselective endorsement when dealing with beliefs that he actually favours.

There is an admirable passage on this practice of handing over the content of belief to someone or something else, in R. G. Collingwood's *Autobiography* (Pelican ed., pp. 36 and 37): 'The pupils, whether or not they expected a philosophy that should give them . . . ideals . . . did not get it; and were told that no philosopher (except of course a bogus philosopher) would even try to give it. The inference which any pupil could draw for himself was that for guidance . . . since one must not seek it from thinkers or thinking, one must look to people who were not thinkers (but fools), to processes which were not thinking (but passion). . . .' This passage should not be taken as mere rhetoric. It makes a very serious logical point. The view it attacks has since become a complacently confident orthodoxy. When a thinker tells you eagerly that he is too modest to handle some question or other, that really this question cannot be handled at all by the kind of professional tools that are ever available to us, then it is important to look at what he *then* does, at the direction in which he passes the buck, at the identity of the person or agencies to whom he hands over that which he claims that we cannot handle—and at the tacit reasons, if any, which he can have for selecting that person or agency. This is the real brass tacks of his thought, not the attention-diverting conjuror's patter concerning what other activities he now plans to devote himself to, and which he commends to our attention. A great deal of contemporary fashionable philosophy is conjuror's patter; it hides the crucial moves, and distracts attention from them. *Trahison des clercs* is not new; what is new is the baroque elaboration of its variety and its mass-production.

As indicated, these philosophers live at two levels. The second-order level is the one at which they propound some argument which terminates in the recommendation of endorsement of any belief that happens to be dominant in the local tradition, or which pervades the language, or which expresses the individual's commitment, etc., according to variant. At a more specific level, they sometimes illustrate their main argument by descriptions of the kind of tradition, language, categorial system, commitment, which they think will aptly illustrate their point. This duality of level can sometimes perplex commentators. For instance, Bernard Crick notes the perplexity which can naturally arise concerning whether Oakeshott is conservative or anarchist:

we were not much impressed . . . by . . . [being told that] Oakeshott was a CONSERVATIVE . . . it was . . . [in] an attack on the possibility of any theoretical knowledge about politics and society . . . [that] there was something beyond the fringe of normal conservative experience. . . .

He is Tory not Conservative, and if Tory, 'a Tory
anarchist'. . . .

Well, which is he?

The answer is, of course, that he is *both*. There are two levels. He
is totally anarchist as between traditions. All traditions are equal,
or equally self-authenticating (though in practice of course some are
more so than others), and all have the blessed property that they
cannot be judged from outside. But within each tradition, the per-
missiveness lapses, and he can become conservative. This of course
happily allows support of liberalism within societies which are
already blessedly liberal. It equally allows the bland, not to say
brutal endorsement of illiberalism in traditions which are as yet
illiberal.

The continuities between these types of conservatism and the
equally unselective hysteria of protest are of course numerous and
extend far beyond this crucial character of inherent unselectivity. In
both cases, there is an epistemology of the heart as against the head.
In each case, there is a doctrine of knowledge as involvement-in-a-
situation, rather than as inquiry. One man's intimations are another
man's unity of theory and practice. In each case, under the rhetoric,
there is great logical simplicity and total circularity. In each case,
there is a kind of facile parasitism on the past achievements of our
society. As is well known, the protestor's impassioned denunciation
of the iniquities of the current system tacitly presupposes the fact
that the system tolerates such denunciation without any real sanctions, even economic or social ones, let alone penal ones. Similarly,
the blindly unselective conservative blithely takes for granted that
the tradition, within which he can indeed be so blessedly complacent,
is not of those many unspeakably repellent traditions which are
pervaded by oppression, superstition, brutality, arbitrariness and
inefficiency—for such is the stuff of most traditions. Traditional
societies generally *smell*. Many of the adherents of this kind of
conservatism were born into societies in which the basic decencies of
liberalism are so totally taken for granted—in this they are *just*
like the protestor—that they cannot really even imagine them absent,
and hence are attracted by the apparently 'tolerant' conservatism
as a kind of romanticism, all the more titillating for the rather *faisandé*
style in which it is presented. They embrace the most brutal nihilism,
as a premise for their conservatism, with the same nonchalance as
their opposite numbers claim to embrace 'revolution'. They accept
an odd cult of continuity with the same blindness as their mirror-
images flirt with a bowdlerized 'revolution'. In each case, the insou-
ciance springs from a complete emotional, and often intellectual,
inability to perceive that our orderly and liberal society could possibly

be threatened. Our thinkers really have come to resemble the precious antiquarians so well characterized by Max Weber. But they suppose that their spiritual pilgrimages are real. They are about as close to solid reality as a Hilton hotel with local ethnographic motifs in its dining-room décor is to peasant life.

Once the basic principles of the re-endorsement style of thought are grasped, belief, and equally movement between beliefs, becomes very very easy. One promising ideologist of our generation has moved, in the span of a relatively brief professional life, between almost countless varieties, species and sects of Christianity, Marxism, Existentialism, Freudianism, Wittgensteinism and heaven knows what else both in succession and simultaneously. His heart cannot say No to any faith that is luscious enough. He gives himself to all Truths. Such rapid, joyful and total abandon to all current faiths presupposes a complete underlying lack of seriousness. This lack may be temperamental, he may just be a cognitive psychopath, but the self-endorsement logic of the faiths makes its indulgence easy, the transitions well-oiled. What all the positions have in common is simply an endorsement meta-theory which accompanies them and which nowadays they tend to have built into them. For note, that although the nineteenth century was more serious and on the whole did not indulge this facility, by now its own secular faiths can also be revived in this spirit (as Marxism has been). The butterfly under discussion is even, at one level, aware of what he does. His first book, devoted to the exposition of one of the countless ideologies that he has embraced with such warmth and ease, contains a fascinating discussion of the idea of proof. What is proof?—he asks. There is no such thing as proof in general, he answers himself. There is only proof persuasive for this, that or the other *kind of man*. Cogency of proof is relative to what you *are*. He notices that this does not seem to apply to mathematics, and brazenly comments that just this has always made him suspicious of mathematics. That which has been the glory of mathematics for philosophers from Plato onwards—its unmeretriciousness, the fact that its proofs cannot be bought, but hold for all men alike—actually *scandalizes* this Belief Machine. . . .

In practice, these re-endorsement philosophies can be tolerant of anything, except serious critical thought. This they tend to proscribe, as breaches of professional etiquette or decorum. The meta-theory, the rules of the game by which they play and which they sometimes specify for our benefit, in fact exclude any moves which could harm them. But this they do not see as prejudgment, but merely as recognition of some inherent, supposedly given set of rules. Sometimes, these can be enchanting in the naïve thoroughness with which they pre-determine the game which they allow to be played. Returning to our philosophical conservatism, the really curious thing about

Oakeshottian philosophy is that virtually everything is built into the ground rules, with such thoroughness that in the end, only *one* move becomes permissible within political thought: namely, to teach students that all political theory that claims to be independent of practice, and sovereign to it, is mistaken, and that practice is always self-sufficient. Any other view is not just wrong within the subject, but violates the very rules of the subject as such and hence academic propriety. (For some reason, one may also teach past theories, always provided one does not treat them as their authors treated them, namely as something to be taken seriously, with commanding implications for conduct. This accretion is in fact inconsistent with the main position, but arises presumably as a concession to the established custom of treating some old doctrines with respect.) One can only wonder how a university subject which consists of only one proposition, and a negative one at that, can continue to be taught.

It is this kind of modern 'tolerance' that deserves scrutiny and scepticism. It is logically and absurdly unselective at the formal level, and as in practice it must be and is selective (if only to give its proponents what they want), its selectiveness becomes tacit, camouflaged and totally arbitrary. It is also obliquely intolerant. But to be suspicious of the antiquarian unselective collections of exotica, which cover up effective abandonment of serious thought, is not to advocate *social* intolerance. Let us, as Preston King observes, fight intellectual issues with intellectual weapons. Our rejection of spurious tolerance, of unselective mish-mash, gives us no warrant to use force, violence, social or any other pressure—anything other than argument, in fact—against those with whom we disagree. But we are *not* obliged to equate rationality or tolerance with the observance of rules of argument which are invented for their own convenience, sometimes with childish simplicity, naïvely generating a game which can only lead to one result. The rules of procedure, the meta-theory, must also be examined. When we examine it, we shall often find that it is pathetically feeble, and that what it professes to endorse is in fact logically indefensible. Not to say so merely debases intellectual currency. We shall of course still tolerate it socially. Absurd views must not be debarred from a forum, their holders ought not be hampered in their career or their comfort. But let us not confuse this kind of social toleration, which is morally obligatory, with logical toleration, which is nothing of the kind. But we have witnessed a sustained effort to confuse the two.

1971

Chapter 14   On democracy in France

Raymond Aron: *Essai sur les libertés*; Calmann-Lévy, Paris, 1965.
Jean-François Revel: *En France. La fin de l'opposition*, Juillard, Paris,
1965

Raymond Aron is probably the most brilliant sociologist alive. He
combines an effortless mastery of ideas with a most remarkable sense
of social reality. These complementary qualities, all too seldom
combined in one person, are most effectively displayed in his im-
pressive work, which does indeed deserve to stand beside J. S. Mill's
classic of very nearly the same name.

It is a treatment of the social problem of liberty, which combines
philosophical depth with an excellent summary of the social conditions and institutions, in the context of which the problem of
liberty must in our time be discussed. In some parts of the book, the
argument is particularly concerned with the French experience: this
gives it an additional interest, without diminishing the applicability
of its conclusions. The author is clearly and explicitly aware of the
specificity of the French situation, and indeed offers an interesting
discussion of the extent to which it is possible to generalize from that
situation.

The book concentrates more heavily on the problem of liberty in
developed (i.e. industrialized) societies, than it does on the way in
which the problem arises in the transition to industrialism. While it
seems to me entirely correct to place the problem of liberty in the
context of industrialism, the relative stress on the conditions of
achievement, as opposed to the conditions of transition (weighted
by Aron in favour of the former) seems to me misguided, and to be
one of the few weaknesses and near-contradictions of the volume.
There is not an outright, but an as it were pragmatic contradiction,
between on the one hand his priorities of concern, and on the other
certain positive and valid assertions. His priorities of attention are
justified as follows (p. 83):

Sur les chances de diffusion, en dehors de l'Occident, de la
liberté . . . je me bornerai à quelques brèves remarques. Le
sujet est pour ainsi dire marginal . . . après tout, en dehors de
l'Occident et parmi les nations . . . nouvelles, il en est peu qui
méritent d'être appelées industrielles.

But it does not follow from the contention that few nations outside
the West are industrial, that the fate of liberty in non-western nations
is irrelevant, or even anything less than crucially relevant, to the
question of the future of liberty in fully industrial society. On the
contrary, it may well be that the decisive choices concerning industrial society are taken not *in* industrial society itself, but on the way
to it. It is curious that Raymond Aron should seem to be denying
this, even if only by implication and in one part of his argument, for
he himself supplies and stresses the premises of the opposite
consideration (p. 105):

les institutions . . . caractéristiques de la liberté proprement
politique . . . me paraissent . . . compatibles avec la société
industrielle mais non impliquées par celle-ci, même au stade de
l'opulence.
     La particularité historique de ces institutions tient à des
causes multiples. Tout régime, tout pays conserve l'esprit de
ses origines et l'idéal de ses fondateurs.

But the effective founders of most societies are those who presided
over the society's modernization. If their spirit and ideals are
subsequently preserved—and this may well be generally true—it
follows that the place of liberty within those ideals, and the institutions engendered by them, is crucial not merely for the heroic age
of the founders, but also thereafter. Let us suppose, as might con-
ceivably be the case, that the existence of 'countervailing forces' in
advanced industrial societies depends on the previous presence of
capitalism. This gives rise to a problem. Capitalism differs from God
in one important respect: where it does not exist, no one will bother
to invent it. Hence the crucial question may well be the discovery
of alternative social bases for political pluralism.
     Much of the argument is conducted, with great effectiveness, in
the form of a confrontation between the ideas of Tocqueville and
Marx. Here again I feel a certain doubt, not unconnected with the
preceding one, this time concerning whether Tocqueville is indeed
a good guide to the formulation of the question. (Aron does not
claim that he provides the answer.) Once again, the doubt can be
supported by premises formulated by Aron himself (p. 31): 'Tocqueville . . . définit la société moderne non par l'industrie à la manière

d'Auguste Comte, non par le capitalisme à la manière de Marx, mais par l'égalité des conditions. . . .'

Let us grant Tocqueville that modern society is, for various reasons, incompatible with estates or castes (because, for instance, it requires occupational mobility, and because men are formed for their social roles not by their families but by an educational system, which has no reasons for restricting its principles of recruitment by respect for ancestry); nevertheless, it is by no means obvious that modern society is inherently egalitarian in any further sense, as Aron himself stresses (p. 202): 'Toutes les réformes . . . laisseront subsister l'antinomie entre l'idée démocratique et la structure hiérarchique de l'activité productive. . . .'

If this is so, should we start from a thinker whose concern is with the dangers in the implications *of* equality, rather than with the dangers *to* equality, and the implications of its absence? This qualm is connected with the preceding one, in as far as Tocqueville's weakness (if such it be) is connected with his assumptions that he was observing the characteristics of 'modern society', as a more or less stable condition, and not the characteristics of the transition towards modern society. The transition to modern society may tend to be egalitarian in that it erodes traditional stratification—through fundamental social disturbance, through undermining of the ideological props of the old stratification, and because in times of great turbulence, ideologies must cast their net wide, so as to appeal to as many potential converts as possible, and hence be, to that extent, egalitarian. But it is not clear whether modern society itself need be egalitarian, though it may well retain an aspiration towards equality in as far as it remains loyal to the ideals of the transition.

These are fairly minor doubts or queries. The mainstream of the argument I find both compelling and cogent. It is far too rich for a brief summary, and I shall merely outline its general structure. It opens with a prolonged account of the contrasted views of Tocqueville and Marx and their contemporary relevance. Here Aron continues his long dialogue with Marxism (p. 56):

> Je songe à la révolution hongroise de 1956. . . . Or cette révolution est celle . . . qui ressemble le plus à celle dont rêvait Marx, en 1843 . . . 'La philosophie, écrivait-il, est la tête de cette émancipation, le prolétariat en est le cœur.' En Hongrie, ce sont les intellectuels . . . qui mirent en branle la révolte populaire. . . .

One of the attractions of Tocqueville, for Aron, is what he calls his 'probabilism' (p. 31).

Il n'annonce pas un mouvement irrésistible vers un régime,
positiviste ou socialiste. Il pose, comme allant de soi, que
certains mouvements se prolongeront, que certaines institutions
sont mortes . . . d'autres fatales. . . . Mais il n'y a pas
détermination adéquate . . . de régime politique par l'état . . .
de la société. La superstructure politique peut être despotique
ou libérale. . . .

This indeed is the logic of his own position, and I find this entirely
convincing. The point of sociology is that not all possibilities are
open, that certain limits (though not perhaps those envisaged by
Tocqueville) are set and given, and that it is as well to explore these.
But the realm of possibility which remains cannot be narrowed
down to a single, uniquely determined path. It would be idle to try
to reject the drive towards industrial society and affluence, but it
neither excludes nor guarantees political liberty. At one point he
observes that the best contemporary defence of liberty is the demonstration that it is not incompatible with economic growth; at another
point, he castigates the illusion that economic growth will, in Marxist
societies, generate a striving for Western liberal political institutions.
Aron uses his probabilism not merely to criticize Marxism, but, at
least as much, to criticize a certain recently developed new conventional wisdom of the West which, as Aron points out, is a kind of
inverted Marxism, and which consists fundamentally of a new kind
of one-one correlation between economic base and political super-
structure. The modern conservative improves on de Maistre and knows
that it is not the executioner, but the washing machine, which stands
at the base of the social order. But the washing machine does not
uniquely determine a social order, any more than did the plough or
the steam-engine (p. 97): 'Que l'on dise "croissance économique"
au lieu de dire "développement des forces productives" importe
peu.'
This new unilinealism does of course have both its facile and optimistic aspect—it is enough to enrich ourselves or others in order to
liberalize—and its pessimistic, defeatist aspect, which despairs of
liberalism in transitional societies. Concerning this latter, crucial
question, Aron maintains his probabilism, but he is not exactly
encouraging (p. 95):

S'il n'est pas vrai que les phases initiales de l'industrialisation
déterminent . . . les despotismes . . . il est vrai que les tensions
inévitables . . . réduisent la probabilité d'un régime qui
comporterait à la fois rivalité des partis, participation des
masses, libertés personelles.

This latter discussion takes place in the context of the second chapter on formal and substantive liberties, which succeeds the first chapter on Marx and Tocqueville. It is impossible to summarize what Aron has to say about the dialectic of the two concepts of liberty, but one should note that the concreteness of his sociological illustrations makes his discussion greatly superior to mere 'conceptual analyses' of the two concepts, and that much of his argument is based on the observation that while in one sense Promethean ambitions have been abandoned—no ideology now engenders the faith which moves mountains—in another sense, all modern societies are firmly Promethean (p. 67): 'Aucune condition sociale ne doit plus être tenue pour indépendente de la volonté rationelle des hommes. La formule est presque textuellement marxiste, mais elle exprime la foi commune ou l'illusion universelle des sociétés modernes.'

While it is impossible to summarize Aron's arguments and illustrations, it is possible to indicate his conclusion, which is put forward not within the chapter itself, but in a separate concluding section. It amounts to a pluralistic conception of freedom, incorporating both liberal, democratic and technical-effectiveness components. He does not suggest that these elements can be fused into a stable harmony—on the contrary. He defines democratic–liberal regimes as those which accept the unstable dialectic between them.

The third chapter (the final one but for the conclusion) is devoted to 'Political liberty and technical society'. The concern with 'technical societies' in effect leads Aron back to what may be called the Tocqueville parish of the three great Atlantic nations, extended (but not much affected) to include the other English-speaking and minor-European nations, plus Western Germany and Italy and Japan.

This chapter contains some amazingly succinct comparative political sociology: there could hardly be a better guide to the political realities of the great stabilized democracies. I shall content myself with attempting to summarize only one crucial argument of this chapter, namely the one dealing with pessimism (concerning the prospects for liberal democracy) and with France, or rather, with pessimism inspired by the French experience. This is a line of argument which has so far made little impact, I think, outside France: for although non-Frenchmen may look at de Gaulle with irritation or admiration, they have not tried to read him as a portent of their own future. In France, on the other hand, attempts at such an extrapolation seem to be fashionable. Aron does not accept this pessimism (p. 152): 'Il demeure vrai que, en France aussi, les institutions démocratiques sont moins instables aujourd'hui qu'hier.

. . . La IVe République a été victime d'une mauvaise constitution et des circonstances.'

It is true that France, like Italy, has not yet overcome the vicious circle in which both the old ruling classes and the working class do not inwardly recognize the legitimacy of the regime, which contributes to its instability, which in turn keeps alive that very non-recognition. His manner of making this point—'La France et l'Italie ne sont pas encore sorties de ce cercle vicieux'—seems to imply that the circle *will* be overcome.

But the most significant passage in this context is perhaps Aron's summary, on page 154, of the reasoning which leads from the French situation to a generalized political pessimism with respect to developed societies. The arguments invoke the general tendencies towards personalized power and charismatic leadership, the strengthening of bureaucracy and administration, the decline of parliaments into merely symbolic possessors of sovereignty, the increase of the power of cabinets, officials and professional groups, the tendency to consider economico-social problems as crucial, with a consequent loss of interest either in ideas or in the distribution of power within the state, and finally, the manipulation of public opinion by mass media, providing a further reason for by-passing political representatives. At one point Aron observes that the present condition of the British House of Commons provides the pessimists with their most crucial argument. Aron's comments on the pessimistic arguments are too subtle, rich and complex for brief reproduction: suffice to say that he attempts to limit rather than refute outright these interpretations. In the end, consistently with the 'probabilism' which provides him with a starting point, he does not prejudge either the form of the future or of our values: but there can hardly be a better framework than his within which to attempt to understand the alternatives and choices which face us.

The same year as Aron's essay on liberties there appeared another essay concerning the destiny of liberty and opposition in France. Much of the thesis of M. Jean-François Revel's book *En France* is conveyed by its subtitle: *La fin de l'opposition*. As the main title implies, the book is concerned with the state of France, not with the destiny of industrial society in general. Nevertheless, a crucial, negative and in my view quite mistaken thesis is present, presupposed by the very structure of the book and occasionally asserted in so many words, and with some impatience: the thesis being, that the present state of France has nothing to do with industrial society, but simply flows from the French character. Politically, aesthetically and perhaps in every other way, the French are beyond salvation. All that has happened now is that their true nature has been revealed, that it has emerged unimpeded. If progressive ideas or democratic

or liberal strivings occasionally made their appearance in the course
of French history, this was an accidental and untypical aberration,
due to special and extraneous circumstances. But these fortuitous
and external circumstances are now absent—this is about as much
concession as Revel makes to the idea that the social conditions of
the second half of the twentieth century may be new and important—
and France stands bare, revealed in her true and horrible colours.

The silliness of its central idea does not mean that this is a worthless book. Though it is impossible to admire it, it is also impossible
not to enjoy it. For one thing, Revel is a witty and devastating writer,
as indeed one would expect from the author of the magnificent
Pourquoi des Philosophes? For another thing, though *En France* is
not of the same calibre as Aron's essay, it is illuminating to read it in
conjunction with it, if only as a document. The roots of Revel's book
are summed up firmly by Aron (p. 189):

> le caractère progressif de l'économie modifie les termes dans
> lesquels était . . . formulé le problème social . . . l'expansion
> ayant été admise comme un fait durable, . . . la plupart des
> intellectuels . . . se sont résignés ou résolus à se désintéresser
> d'une société qui se tirait d'affaire sans philosophie et sans
> violence. . . .

Monsieur Revel will indeed have nothing to do with a society which
can cope without either ideology or revolution, and the noises he
makes in the course of resolutely turning his back—or pretending to,
as the case may be—are witty, brilliantly formulated, entertaining
and revealing. He is both symptomatic of the class which would turn
its back on contemporary social reality and independent of that
class, for his perceptions and abuse spare no one and include the
left. But where Aron is sociological, comparative, balanced and mildly
optimistic, Revel is psychologistic, insular, irresponsible and, it
seems, totally and self-indulgently, masochistically pessimistic.

It is a fundamental frivolity, which is in no way required by
determined satire, but on the contrary undermines its effectiveness,
which is somewhat off-putting. Either/or: either this is a *normalien*'s
joke (characteristically he speaks of *l'esprit moutonnier qui règne
d'ordinaire à l'École*) which is fair enough, but in which case he ought
to keep off serious matters such as torture in Algeria; or, on the other
hand, he is seriously concerned, in which case he ought not to devote
so much of his fire to matters such as the allegedly low sartorial level
of the French. The real trouble is that the level at which the book is
to be taken does not remain consistent, but wobbles disconcertingly:
the weakness of the book is not that the satire is too vicious, but
that, despite appearances, it is not nearly vicious enough. My

indignation or my shame cannot really be aroused by a book which from time to time gives me the impression that all this verbal violence is but horse-play; that I am really witnessing a cosy family joke. In fact it is by no means all a joke, even in Revel's mind, but there is just enough of this cosy-childish prank quality to destroy the effectiveness of the whole. His indifference to his own contradictions, his lack of interest in exploring what can be saved from the alleged wreck, his manifest and self-indulgent pleasure in proclaiming that nothing, but nothing, escapes the all-pervading rottenness—it is these, and not the splendid and aphoristic abuse, which give one the feeling of assisting, as the French would say, at a joke.

The general structure of the book is something of a *tour de force*. If the book did not actually exist, I should not believe it possible. Imagine a literary competition which required you to do the following: write a brief book, in elegant and vigorous French, beginning somewhat in the style of English aestheticism of the early 1900s—nothing but taste and culture matter, and a plague-on-both-your-houses as far as the socio-political struggle between rival bands of philistines is concerned. I remember in Clive Bell's *Civilization*, a paean to the high standard of Toulon bookshops, which apparently showed that French naval officers required their mistresses to have exquisite literary taste (the implication being that the bookshops in Portsmouth show either that British naval officers have no mistresses, or that the said mistresses have no taste). The difference between Clive Bell and the opening passages of Revel is that this time it is France which is execrated, for Revel will not forgive the mistresses of naval officers, and the rest of the French nation, their present taste for Saint-Ex, Teilhard de Chardin *et al.* (Revel's literary judgment is sounder than his politics.)

But the complaints of the aesthete-mandarin are only the beginning. The end is not at all Clive Bell. The end is very nearly pure John Osborne (in the style of one of those passionate denunciations sent from the Riviera), with whom he shares the gift for truly eloquent abuse. Anyone who refuses to believe—as, *a priori*, I should certainly have refused—that a book can start as Bell and end as Osborne, and yet maintain a perfectly coherent style and spirit, can only be invited to inspect the volume.

The abuse (pp. 15, 21, 48, 85, 87):

Alors le Français retrouve en lui sa nature profonde: celle d'un microcéphale médaillé, à la gorge serrée, au foie congestionné, à l'œil menaçant, bien résolu à venger tout ce qu'on 'a fait' à la France et commémorer tout ce que la France a fait aux autres.

. . . la seconde guerre mondiale . . . est présentée en France

uniquement sous l'angle nationaliste . . . Du reste, quel que
fut le camp vainqueur, un militaire de carrière était là de deux
côtés pour, dans les deux hypothèses, avoir sauvé la France.

La prospérité permet de s'offrir ce qu'on désire: les Français
se sont offerts une dictature, qui leur coûte un peu cher, mais
c'est dans le même esprit qu'ils préfèrent une automobile à un
logement.

. . . le style assassin et barbare des Français affirmant leur
vocation virile, qui est de guerroyer, mais si possible jamais
contre une armée.

. . . pays qui n'a même pas la fantaisie de sa folie ni la sagesse
de sa mediocrité. . . .

And so on. Jimmy Porter has met his match.

But the Osborne conclusions from Bell premises do not exhaust
the intellectually acrobatic achievements of the argument. Mediating
between the major premise and the conclusion, there is a remarkable
minor premise concerning the nature of democracy. It is I suppose
refreshing nowadays to hear someone speak of the general will with
a straight face—this is, perhaps, one of those modern archaisms or
archaic modernisms which, according to Revel, abound in France.
One would charitably assume that Revel's theory of democracy is
just a perfunctory manner of speaking, were it not for the fact that it
fits in with too much of what he says. His theory of democracy is
both metaphysical and psychologistic (this latter trait pervades the
book). If there is anything to be learnt from either classical political
theory or modern sociology about the real social conditions of
representative, limited and responsible government, it has by-passed
Jean-François Revel (pp. 25, 43, 62):

le principe démocratique de l'obéissance volontaire à la Loi
conçue comme expression de la volonté générale.

. . . les gouvernements inspirés par le peuple . . . sont
exceptionnels: ceux-ci occupent, en tout et pour tout, quatre
ans à la fin du XVIIIe siècle, quelque mois en 1848, un total
d'environs quatre années disséminées çà et là au cours de la
troisième République et deux ou trois mois après la Libération.

Que la transmission de la volonté générale et le contrôle du
pouvoir exécutif prennent la forme qu'on voudra, pourvu
qu'ils existent.

Note the assumption that there is something called the general will,
which has an existence, and a direction, independently of the socio-
political forms which 'transmit' or express it.

The book abounds in internal contradictions. For instance, there is a blatant contradiction between his mystical notion of democracy and his aesthetic élitism. Revel, especially in matters of taste, has his own private version of the Maurrasian distinction between the 'pays légal' and the 'pays réel', which he calls 'le divorce entre la culture française et la réalité française', and which seems to him 'une constante essentielle de notre histoire' (p. 49); but either he has never bothered to think about his political populism and his aesthetic élitism at the same time, or, worse still, his general will and the will of all must not merely be distinct, but diametrically opposed. A believing and authoritarian rightist may consistently live with two distinct conceptions of France, ideal and real, but it is hard to see how Revel, empiricist and democrat, can do so.

Revel turns his back on attempts to explore the social causes of either the successes or the failures of liberal democracy: he is far too anxious to blame the failures on to French character, and to treat the successes, or what he considers to be successes, as accidental aberrations. His concern for liberty seems sincere, yet he never seems to wonder about its compatibility either with his conception of democracy, or with his cult of revolution, or with his demand for a *unified* left ideology. Similarly, he seems sincere in his rejection of all romanticism of violence, but nevertheless himself romanticizes a revolutionary tradition. He tells us (p. 100) that no war ever has been, will be or could be 'ideological', while we were told (p. 20) that the Second World War had 'un contenu idéologique assez marqué'.

On the very same page (54) he tells us that 'l'unité d'action n'est souhaitable . . . que pour l'action, non pour la pensée', yet a little later he regrets the absence of 'une pensée révolutionnaire complète, dans laquelle les positions philosophiques, scientifiques, morales, politiques, économiques, religieuses, eussent été unifiées'. On page 190 we are told that intellectuals have renounced opposition from opportunism and nothing but opportunism, notwithstanding the earlier demonstration that intellectuals are not doing well out of the regime, that (p. 179) 'la rapide progressivité de l'impôt . . . devient meurtrière pour les revenus issus du travail intellectuel . . .'. What strange opportunism! Moreover, as the whole book is devoted to showing that a military dictatorship corresponds to the deepest aspirations of the French, what need also to invoke opportunism, especially as it all doesn't pay? To read Revel, one would think that the average intellectual Frenchman lives in a kind of technocratic *Rouge et Noir*, wondering whether to make his career in the *force de frappe* and indulge his taste for military display, or to devote himself to conformist mystification on the mass media. Concerning these, I am quite prepared to believe Revel that French TV is bad, though on internal evidence Revel seems to be glued to his set.

Still, there are splendid things in the book. The remark that de

Gaulle does indeed incarnate France, but that this is not flattering for either party, has been much quoted. Personally I liked best the superb comment on Sartre, which incidentally occurs in the context of an excellent and illuminating summary, running over several pages, of left-wing French intellectual trends since the war (p. 53): 'Sartre . . . s'efforça . . . d'introduire un peu de déterminisme historique dans le *self-service* de sa conscience libre. . . .'

It would be interesting to list the number of premises shared by Aron and Revel, and to contrast the rival formulations of identical observations. Even the starting point is, in a way, the same: the impact of affluence on political and intellectual life came in the United States as the 'End of Ideology', in Britain as bi-partisan policies, and in France as de Gaulle. Aron and Revel agree in refusing to explain de Gaulle in terms of de Gaulle: both are concerned with deeper trends. But Revel is not interested in exploring the opportunities and dangers of industrial society, because the only deeper trend for him is the original sin of the French soul. In the course of denouncing this soul he is very entertaining, though for some reason he forgets to castigate one defect which he himself conspicuously exemplifies—insularity. But it is Aron who puts us in his debt by relating an account of the French situation to a serious and totally unparochial framework.

1966

Sources

The following are the original places and dates of publication of the chapters in this volume: chapter 1: *Listener*, **61**, 19 March 1959, 510–11, 514; chapter 2: *Political Quarterly*, **40**, 1969, 472–84; chapter 3: *European Journal of Sociology*, **8**, 1967, 47–70; chapter 4: *Philosophy*, **32**, 1957, 336–57; chapter 5: *The Times Educational Supplement*, 12 September 1969, 33; chapter 6: in David Martin, ed., *Anarchy and Culture*, London: Routledge & Kegan Paul 1969, 129–47; chapter 7: *Listener*, **59**, 1958, 579, 582–3; chapter 8: *Ratio*, **9**, 1967, 49–66; chapter 9: *European Journal of Sociology*, **12**, 1971, 159–79; chapter 10: *Soviet Survey*, **23**, 1958, 66–71; chapter 11: *Philosophy of the Social Sciences*, **3**, 1973, 1–17; chapter 12: *European Journal of Sociology*, **12**, 1971, 312–25; chapter 13: *Government and Opposition*, **6**, 1971, 211–18; chapter 14: *Government and Opposition*, **1**, 1966, 255–64. We wish to thank the respective editors and publishers for permission to reprint.

Index of names

Index of subjects

absurd, nonsense, 44, 47, 57–9
academics, 169–72; *see also* intellectuals
accident, historical, *see* contingency
action, 118, 122, 130, 191
activism, 71, 73, 81, 85; *see also* protest
ad hoc, *see* circularity
adjustment, 3, 6
aesthetics, aestheticism, 3, 102, 189–91
affluence, affluent society, 9*ff*, 26, 28, 33–4, 36–8, 77, 80–1, 84–5, 146, 153–5, 166, 185, 190
Africa, 38, 86
Age of Gods and Heroes, 114
Algeria, 78, 157, 188
Alice Through the Looking Glass, 62, 68
alienation, 11, 18, 28, 33, 73, 77, 79, 81, 85
allies, 22, 39
ambiguity, 21, 99–100, 115
ambivalence, 1, 7, 143
America, *see* United States of America
analogy, 98
anarchism, 178–9
anarchy, 87–94
anonymity, 151
anthropology, 88, 110, 113, 116, 120, 124
anti-intellectualism, 78
anti-utopia, 1*ff*
Ape and Essence, 2, 6
apotheosis, 96
Aparatchiks for Freedom, Inc., 75–6

arbitrariness, 4, 5
arguments, *see* criticism; on-going debate
Aristotelian Society, 95
aristotelianism, 103
arithmetic, 4, 5, 137
Armenia, 154
Arrival and Departure, 10
Aryan Invasion, 109
atavism, 150, 155
Atlas Mountains, 87
atom bomb, 133
atom spies, 7
Austria, 154
authoritarianism, authority, 37–8, 69, 72, 82–3, 96, 100, 101, 111
Autobiography, R. G. Collingwood's, 178
auto-functionalism, *see* function, functionalism
Axis, the, 22, 39

basic training, 147–9, 151
Beat Generation, 84
belief, faith, 7, 9, 12, 15–16, 18, 25, 30, 41, 48, 50, 52–3, 58–9, 66, 88, 176–7, 180
Belief Machine, 180
Berbers, 87, 90, 91
Berkeley, 81
blackmail, 13
bohemians, 80, 157; *see also* intellectuals
Bolsheviks, 135; *see also* Communism; Communist Party
Bounty, 72
Brave New World, 2–6, 117
bricoleur, 14